Hadoop Operations and Cluster Management Cookbook

Over 60 recipes showing you how to design, configure, manage, monitor, and tune a Hadoop cluster

Shumin Guo

BIRMINGHAM - MUMBAI

Hadoop Operations and Cluster Management Cookbook

First published: July 2013

Production Reference: 1170713

Published by Packt Publishing Ltd.
Livery Place
35 Livery Street
Birmingham B3 2PB, UK.

ISBN 978-1-78216-516-3

www.packtpub.com

Cover Image by Girish Suryavanshi (girish.suryawanshi@gmail.com)

Credits

Author
Shumin Guo

Reviewers
Hector Cuesta-Arvizu
Mark Kerzner
Harvinder Singh Saluja

Acquisition Editor
Kartikey Pandey

Lead Technical Editor
Madhuja Chaudhari

Technical Editors
Sharvari Baet
Jalasha D'costa
Veena Pagare
Amit Ramadas

Project Coordinator
Anurag Banerjee

Proofreader
Lauren Tobon

Indexer
Hemangini Bari

Graphics
Abhinash Sahu

Production Coordinator
Nitesh Thakur

Cover Work
Nitesh Thakur

About the Author

Shumin Guo is a PhD student of Computer Science at Wright State University in Dayton, OH. His research fields include Cloud Computing and Social Computing. He is enthusiastic about open source technologies and has been working as a System Administrator, Programmer, and Researcher at State Street Corp. and LexisNexis.

I would like to sincerely thank my wife, Min Han, for her support both technically and mentally. This book would not have been possible without encouragement from her.

About the Reviewers

Hector Cuesta-Arvizu provides consulting services for software engineering and data analysis with over eight years of experience in a variety of industries, including financial services, social networking, e-learning, and Human Resources.

Hector holds a BA in Informatics and an MSc in Computer Science. His main research interests lie in Machine Learning, High Performance Computing, Big Data, Computational Epidemiology, and Data Visualization. He has also helped in the technical review of the book *Raspberry Pi Networking Cookbook* by *Rick Golden, Packt Publishing*. He has published 12 scientific papers in International Conferences and Journals. He is an enthusiast of Lego Robotics and Raspberry Pi in his spare time.

You can follow him on Twitter at `https://twitter.com/hmCuesta`.

Mark Kerzner holds degrees in Law, Math, and Computer Science. He has been designing software for many years and Hadoop-based systems since 2008. He is the President of SHMsoft, a provider of Hadoop applications for various verticals, and a co-author of the book/project *Hadoop Illuminated*. He has authored and co-authored books and patents.

I would like to acknowledge the help of my colleagues, in particular Sujee Maniyam, and last but not least, my multitalented family.

Harvinder Singh Saluja has over 20 years of software architecture and development experience, and is the co-founder of MindTelligent, Inc. He works as Oracle SOA, Fusion MiddleWare, and Oracle Identity and Access Manager, and Oracle Big Data Specialist and Chief Integration Specialist at MindTelligent, Inc. Harvinder's strengths include his experience with strategy, concepts, and logical and physical architecture and development using Java/JEE/ADF/SEAM, SOA/AIA/OSB/OSR/OER, and OIM/OAM technologies.

He leads and manages MindTelligent's onshore and offshore and Oracle SOA/OSB/AIA/OSB/OER/OIM/OAM engagements. His specialty includes the AIA Foundation Pack – development of custom PIPS for Utilities, Healthcare, and Energy verticals. His integration engagements include CC&B (Oracle Utilities Customer Care and Billing), Oracle Enterprise Taxation and Policy, Oracle Utilities Mobile Workforce Management, Oracle Utilities Meter Data Management, Oracle eBusiness Suite, Siebel CRM, and Oracle B2B for EDI – X12 and EDIFACT.

His strengths include enterprise-wide security using Oracle Identity and Access Management, OID/OVD/ODSM/OWSM, including provisioning, workflows, reconciliation, single sign-on, SPML API, Connector API, and Web Services message and transport security using OWSM and Java cryptography.

He was awarded JDeveloper Java Extensions Developer of the Year award in 2003 by Oracle magazine.

www.PacktPub.com

Support files, eBooks, discount offers and more

You might want to visit www.PacktPub.com for support files and downloads related to your book.

Did you know that Packt offers eBook versions of every book published, with PDF and ePub files available? You can upgrade to the eBook version at www.PacktPub.com and as a print book customer, you are entitled to a discount on the eBook copy. Get in touch with us at service@packtpub.com for more details.

At www.PacktPub.com, you can also read a collection of free technical articles, sign up for a range of free newsletters and receive exclusive discounts and offers on Packt books and eBooks.

http://PacktLib.PacktPub.com

Do you need instant solutions to your IT questions? PacktLib is Packt's online digital book library. Here, you can access, read and search across Packt's entire library of books.

Why Subscribe?
- Fully searchable across every book published by Packt
- Copy and paste, print and bookmark content
- On demand and accessible via web browser

Free Access for Packt account holders

If you have an account with Packt at www.PacktPub.com, you can use this to access PacktLib today and view nine entirely free books. Simply use your login credentials for immediate access.

Table of Contents

Preface

Today, many organizations are facing the Big Data problem. Managing and processing Big Data can incur a lot of challenges for traditional data processing platforms such as relational database systems. Hadoop was designed to be a distributed and scalable system for dealing with Big Data problems. A Hadoop-based Big Data platform uses Hadoop as the data storage and processing engine. It deals with the problem by transforming the Big Data input into expected output.

Hadoop Operations and Cluster Management Cookbook provides examples and step-by-step recipes for you to administrate a Hadoop cluster. It covers a wide range of topics for designing, configuring, managing, and monitoring a Hadoop cluster. The goal of this book is to help you manage a Hadoop cluster more efficiently and in a more systematic way.

In the first three chapters, you will learn practical recipes to configure a fully distributed Hadoop cluster. The subsequent management, hardening, and performance tuning chapters will cover the core topics of this book. In these chapters, you will learn practical commands and best practices to manage a Hadoop cluster. The last important topic of the book is the monitoring of a Hadoop cluster. And, we will end this book by introducing steps to build a Hadoop cluster using the AWS cloud.

What this book covers

Chapter 1, Big Data and Hadoop, introduces steps to define a Big Data problem and outlines steps to build a Hadoop-based Big Data platform.

Chapter 2, Preparing for Hadoop Installation, describes the preparation of a Hadoop cluster configuration. Topics include choosing the proper cluster hardware, configuring the network, and installing the Linux operating system.

Chapter 3, Configuring a Hadoop Cluster, introduces recipes to configure a Hadoop cluster in pseudo-distributed mode as well as in fully distributed mode. We will also describe steps to verify and troubleshoot a Hadoop cluster configuration.

Chapter 4, Managing a Hadoop Cluster, shows you how to manage a Hadoop cluster. We will learn cluster maintenance tasks and practical steps to do the management. For example, we will introduce the management of an HDFS filesystem, management of MapReduce jobs, queues and quota, and so on.

Chapter 5, Hardening a Hadoop Cluster, introduces recipes to secure a Hadoop cluster. We will show you how to configure ACL for authorization and Kerberos for authentication, configure NameNode HA, recover from a failed NameNode, and so on.

Chapter 6, Monitoring a Hadoop Cluster, explains how to monitor a Hadoop cluster with various tools, such as Ganglia and Nagios.

Chapter 7, Tuning a Hadoop Cluster for Best Performance, introduces best practices to tune the performance of a Hadoop cluster. We will tune the memory profile, the MapReduce scheduling strategy, and so on to achieve best performance for a Hadoop cluster.

Chapter 8, Building a Hadoop Cluster with Amazon EC2 and S3, shows you how to configure a Hadoop cluster in the Amazon cloud. We will explain steps to register, connect, and start VM instances on EC2. We will also show you how to configure a customized AMI for a Hadoop cluster on EC2.

What you need for this book

This book is written to be as self-contained as possible. Each chapter and recipe has its specific prerequisites introduced before the topic.

In general, in this book, we will use the following software packages:

- CentOS 6.3
- Oracle JDK (Java Development Kit) SE 7
- Hadoop 1.1.2
- HBase 0.94.5
- Hive 0.9.0
- Pig 0.10.1
- ZooKeeper 3.4.5
- Mahout 0.7

Who this book is for

This book is for Hadoop administrators and Big Data architects. It can be a helpful book for Hadoop programmers.

You are not required to have solid knowledge about Hadoop to read this book, but you are required to know basic Linux commands and have a general understanding of distributed computing concepts.

Conventions

In this book, you will find a number of styles of text that distinguish between different kinds of information. Here are some examples of these styles, and an explanation of their meaning.

Code words in text, database table names, folder names, filenames, file extensions, pathnames, dummy URLs, user input, and Twitter handles are shown as follows: "Open the file `$HADOOP_HOME/conf/mapred-site.xml` with your favorite text editor."

A block of code is set as follows:

```
<property>
  <name>fs.default.name</name>
  <value>hdfs://master:54310</value>
</property>
```

When we wish to draw your attention to a particular part of a code block, the relevant lines or items are set in bold:

```
<property>
  <name>fs.default.name</name>
  <value>hdfs://master:54310</value>
</property>
```

Any command-line input or output is written as follows:

```
hadoop namenode -format
```

New terms and **important words** are shown in bold. Words that you see on the screen, in menus or dialog boxes for example, appear in the text like this: "By clicking on the link **Analyze This Job**, we will go to a web page."

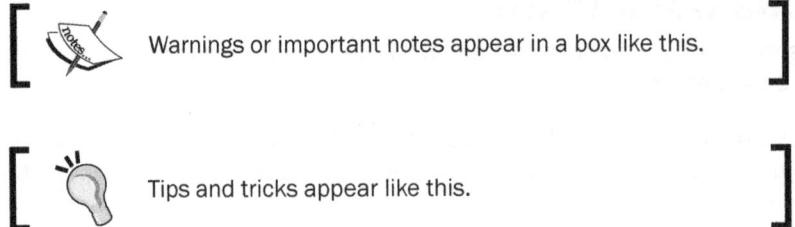

Warnings or important notes appear in a box like this.

Tips and tricks appear like this.

Reader feedback

Feedback from our readers is always welcome. Let us know what you think about this book—what you liked or may have disliked. Reader feedback is important for us to develop titles that you really get the most out of.

To send us general feedback, simply send an e-mail to feedback@packtpub.com, and mention the book title via the subject of your message.

If there is a topic that you have expertise in and you are interested in either writing or contributing to a book, see our author guide on www.packtpub.com/authors.

Customer support

Now that you are the proud owner of a Packt book, we have a number of things to help you to get the most from your purchase.

Errata

Although we have taken every care to ensure the accuracy of our content, mistakes do happen. If you find a mistake in one of our books—maybe a mistake in the text or the code—we would be grateful if you would report this to us. By doing so, you can save other readers from frustration and help us improve subsequent versions of this book. If you find any errata, please report them by visiting http://www.packtpub.com/submit-errata, selecting your book, clicking on the **errata submission form** link, and entering the details of your errata. Once your errata are verified, your submission will be accepted and the errata will be uploaded on our website, or added to any list of existing errata, under the Errata section of that title. Any existing errata can be viewed by selecting your title from http://www.packtpub.com/support.

Piracy

Piracy of copyright material on the Internet is an ongoing problem across all media. At Packt, we take the protection of our copyright and licenses very seriously. If you come across any illegal copies of our works, in any form, on the Internet, please provide us with the location address or website name immediately so that we can pursue a remedy.

Please contact us at copyright@packtpub.com with a link to the suspected pirated material.

We appreciate your help in protecting our authors, and our ability to bring you valuable content.

Questions

You can contact us at questions@packtpub.com if you are having a problem with any aspect of the book, and we will do our best to address it.

1
Big Data and Hadoop

In this chapter, we will cover:

▸ Defining a Big Data problem

▸ Building a Hadoop-based Big Data platform

▸ Choosing from Hadoop alternatives

Introduction

Today, many organizations are facing the **Big Data** problem. Managing and processing Big Data can incur a lot of challenges for traditional data processing platforms such as relational database systems. Hadoop was designed to be a **distributed** and **scalable** system for dealing with Big Data problems.

The design, implementation, and deployment of a Big Data platform require a clear definition of the Big Data problem by system architects and administrators. A Hadoop-based Big Data platform uses Hadoop as the data storage and processing engine. It deals with the problem by transforming the Big Data input into the expected output. On one hand, the Big Data problem determines how the Big Data platform should be designed, for example, which modules or subsystems should be integrated into the platform and so on. On the other hand, the architectural design of the platform can determine complexity and efficiency of the platform.

Different Big Data problems have different properties. A Hadoop-based Big Data platform is capable of dealing with most of the Big Data problems, but might not be good fit for others. Because of these and many other reasons, we need to choose from Hadoop alternatives.

Defining a Big Data problem

Generally, the definition of Big Data is data in large sizes that go beyond the ability of commonly used software tools to **collect**, **manage**, and **process** within a tolerable elapsed time. More formally, the definition of Big Data should go beyond the size of the data to include other properties. In this recipe, we will outline the properties that define Big Data in a formal way.

Getting ready

Ideally, data has the following three important properties: **volume**, **velocity**, and **variety**. In this book, we treat the **value** property of Big Data as the fourth important property. And, the value property also explains the reason why the Big Data problem exists.

How to do it...

Defining a Big Data problem involves the following steps:

1. Estimate the volume of data. The volume should not only include the current data volume, for example in gigabytes or terabytes, but also should include the expected volume in the future.

   There are two types of data in the real world: **static** and **nonstatic** data. The volume of static data, for example national census data and human genomic data, will not change over time. While for nonstatic data, such as streaming log data and social network streaming data, the volume increases over time.

2. Estimate the velocity of data. The velocity estimate should include how much data can be generated within a certain amount of time, for example during a day. For static data, the velocity is zero.

   The velocity property of Big Data defines the speed that data can be generated. This property will not only affect the volume of data, but also determines how fast a data processing system should handle the data.

3. Identify the data variety. In other words, the data variety means the different sources of data, such as web click data, social network data, data in relational databases, and so on.

   Variety means that data differs syntactically or semantically. The difference requires specifically designed modules for each data variety to be integrated into the Big Data platform. For example, a web crawler is needed for getting data from the Web, and a data translation module is needed to transfer data from relational databases to a nonrelational Big Data platform.

4. Define the expected value of data.

The value property of Big Data defines what we can potentially derive from and how we can use Big Data. For example, frequent item sets can be mined from online click-through data for better marketing and more efficient deployment of advertisements.

How it works...

A Big Data platform can be described with the IPO (`http://en.wikipedia.org/wiki/IPO_Model`) model, which includes three components: **input**, **process**, and **output**. For a Big Data problem, the volume, velocity, and variety properties together define the input of the system, and the value property defines the output.

See also

▸ The *Building a Hadoop-based Big Data platform* recipe

Building a Hadoop-based Big Data platform

Hadoop was first developed as a Big Data processing system in 2006 at Yahoo! The idea is based on Google's MapReduce, which was first published by Google based on their proprietary MapReduce implementation. In the past few years, Hadoop has become a widely used platform and runtime environment for the deployment of Big Data applications. In this recipe, we will outline steps to build a Hadoop-based Big Data platform.

Getting ready

Hadoop was designed to be **parallel** and **resilient**. It redefines the way that data is managed and processed by leveraging the power of computing resources composed of commodity hardware. And it can automatically recover from failures.

How to do it...

Use the following steps to build a Hadoop-based Big Data platform:

1. Design, implement, and deploy **data collection** or **aggregation** subsystems. The subsystems should transfer data from different data sources to Hadoop-compatible data storage systems such as **HDFS** and **HBase**.

The subsystems need to be designed based on the input properties of a Big Data problem, including volume, velocity, and variety.

2. Design, implement, and deploy Hadoop Big Data processing platform. The platform should consume the Big Data located on HDFS or HBase and produce the expected and valuable output.

3. Design, implement, and deploy result delivery subsystems. The delivery subsystems should transform the analytical results from a Hadoop-compatible format to a proper format for end users. For example, we can design web applications to visualize the analytical results using charts, graphs, or other types of dynamic web applications.

How it works...

The architecture of a Hadoop-based Big Data system can be described with the following chart:

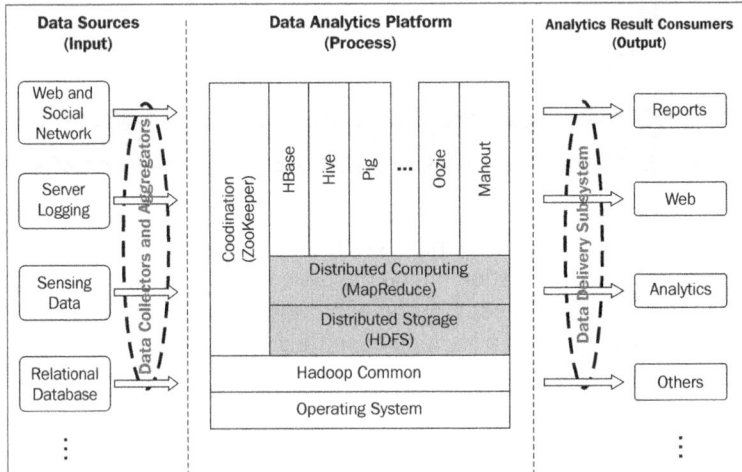

Although Hadoop borrows its idea from Google's MapReduce, it is more than MapReduce. A typical Hadoop-based Big Data platform includes the **Hadoop Distributed File System** (**HDFS**), the parallel computing framework (**MapReduce**), common utilities, a column-oriented data storage table (**HBase**), high-level data management systems (**Pig** and **Hive**), a Big Data analytics library (**Mahout**), a distributed coordination system (**ZooKeeper**), a workflow management module (**Oozie**), data transfer modules such as **Sqoop**, data aggregation modules such as **Flume**, and data serialization modules such as **Avro**.

HDFS is the default filesystem of Hadoop. It was designed as a distributed filesystem that provides high-throughput access to application data. Data on HDFS is stored as data blocks. The data blocks are replicated on several computing nodes and their checksums are computed. In case of a checksum error or system failure, erroneous or lost data blocks can be recovered from backup blocks located on other nodes.

MapReduce provides a programming model that transforms complex computations into computations over a set of **key-value** pairs. It coordinates the processing of tasks on a cluster of nodes by scheduling jobs, monitoring activity, and re-executing failed tasks.

In a typical MapReduce job, multiple map tasks on slave nodes are executed in parallel, generating results buffered on local machines. Once some or all of the map tasks have finished, the **shuffle** process begins, which aggregates the map task outputs by sorting and combining key-value pairs based on keys. Then, the shuffled data partitions are copied to reducer machine(s), most commonly, over the network. Then, reduce tasks will run on the shuffled data and generate final (or intermediate, if multiple consecutive MapReduce jobs are pipelined) results. When a job finishes, final results will reside in multiple files, depending on the number of reducers used in the job. The anatomy of the job flow can be described in the following chart:

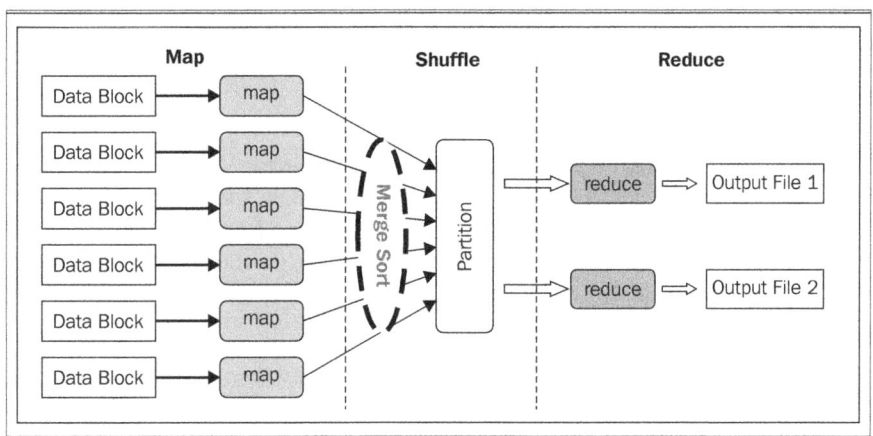

There's more...

HDFS has two types of nodes, **NameNode** and **DataNode**. A NameNode keeps track of the filesystem metadata such as the locations of data blocks. For efficiency reasons, the metadata is kept in the main memory of a master machine. A DataNode holds physical data blocks and communicates with clients for data reading and writing. In addition, it periodically reports a list of its hosting blocks to the NameNode in the cluster for verification and validation purposes.

The MapReduce framework has two types of nodes, **master** node and **slave** node. **JobTracker** is the daemon on a master node, and **TaskTracker** is the daemon on a slave node. The master node is the manager node of MapReduce jobs. It splits a job into smaller tasks, which will be assigned by the JobTracker to TaskTrackers on slave nodes to run. When a slave node receives a task, its TaskTracker will fork a Java process to run the task. Meanwhile, the TaskTracker is also responsible for tracking and reporting the progress of individual tasks.

Hadoop common

Hadoop common is a collection of components and interfaces for the foundation of Hadoop-based Big Data platforms. It provides the following components:

- Distributed filesystem and I/O operation interfaces
- General parallel computation interfaces
- Logging
- Security management

Apache HBase

Apache HBase is an open source, distributed, versioned, and column-oriented data store. It was built on top of Hadoop and HDFS. HBase supports random, real-time access to Big Data. It can scale to host very large tables, containing billions of rows and millions of columns. More documentation about HBase can be obtained from `http://hbase.apache.org`.

Apache Mahout

Apache Mahout is an open source scalable machine learning library based on Hadoop. It has a very active community and is still under development. Currently, the library supports four use cases: **recommendation mining**, **clustering**, **classification**, and **frequent item set mining**. More documentation of Mahout can be obtained from `http://mahout.apache.org`.

Apache Pig

Apache Pig is a high-level system for expressing Big Data analysis programs. It supports Big Data by compiling the Pig statements into a sequence of MapReduce jobs. Pig uses **Pig Latin** as the programming language, which is extensible and easy to use. More documentation about Pig can be found from `http://pig.apache.org`.

Apache Hive

Apache Hive is a high-level system for the management and analysis of Big Data stored in Hadoop-based systems. It uses a SQL-like language called **HiveQL**. Similar to Apache Pig, the Hive runtime engine translates HiveQL statements into a sequence of MapReduce jobs for execution. More information about Hive can be obtained from `http://hive.apache.org`.

Apache ZooKeeper

Apache ZooKeeper is a centralized coordination service for large scale distributed systems. It maintains the configuration and naming information and provides distributed synchronization and group services for applications in distributed systems. More documentation about ZooKeeper can be obtained from `http://zookeeper.apache.org`.

Apache Oozie

Apache Oozie is a scalable **workflow management** and **coordination service** for Hadoop jobs. It is data aware and coordinates jobs based on their dependencies. In addition, Oozie has been integrated with Hadoop and can support all types of Hadoop jobs. More information about Oozie can be obtained from `http://oozie.apache.org`.

Apache Sqoop

Apache Sqoop is a tool for moving data between Apache Hadoop and structured data stores such as relational databases. It provides command-line suites to transfer data from relational database to HDFS and vice versa. More information about Apache Sqoop can be found at `http://sqoop.apache.org`.

Apache Flume

Apache Flume is a tool for collecting log data in distributed systems. It has a flexible yet robust and fault tolerant architecture that streams data from log servers to Hadoop. More information can be obtained from `http://flume.apache.org`.

Apache Avro

Apache Avro is a fast, feature rich data serialization system for Hadoop. The serialized data is coupled with the data schema, which facilitates its processing with different programming languages. More information about Apache Avro can be found at `http://avro.apache.org`.

Choosing from Hadoop alternatives

Although Hadoop has been very successful for most of the Big Data problems, it is not an optimal choice in many situations. In this recipe, we will introduce a few Hadoop alternatives.

Getting ready

Hadoop has the following drawbacks as a Big Data platform:

- As an open source software, Hadoop is difficult to configure and manage, mainly due to the instability of the software and lack of properly maintained documentation and technical support
- Hadoop is not an optimal choice for real-time, responsive Big Data applications
- Hadoop is not a good fit for large graph datasets

Because of the preceding drawbacks as well as other reasons, such as special data processing requirements, we need to make an alternative choice.

Hadoop is not a good choice for data that is not categorized as Big Data; for example, data that has the following properties: small datasets and datasets with processing that requires transaction and synchronization.

How to do it...

We can choose Hadoop alternatives using the following guidelines:

1. Choose Enterprise Hadoop if there is no qualified Hadoop administrator and there is sufficient budget for deploying a Big Data platform.

2. Choose Spark or Storm if an application requires real-time data processing.

3. Choose GraphLab if an application requires handling of large graph datasets.

How it works...

Enterprise Hadoop refers to Hadoop distributions by some Hadoop-oriented companies. Compared with the community Hadoop releases, Enterprise Hadoop distributions are enterprise ready, easy to configure, and sometimes new features are added. In addition, the training and support services provided by these companies make it much easier for organizations to adopt the Hadoop Big Data platform. Famous Hadoop-oriented companies include: **Cloudera**, **Horntonworks**, **MapR**, **Hadapt**, and so on.

▶ **Cloudera** is one of the most famous companies that delivers Enterprise Hadoop Big Data solutions. It provides Hadoop consulting, training, and certification services. It is also one of the biggest contributors of the Hadoop codebase. Their Big Data solution uses Cloudera Desktop as the cluster management interface. You can learn more from www.cloudera.com.

▶ **Hortonworks** and **MapR** both provide featured Hadoop distributions and Hadoop-based Big Data solutions. You can get more details from www.hortonworks.com and www.mapr.com.

▶ **Hadapt** differentiates itself from the other Hadoop-oriented companies by the goal of integrating structured, semi-structured, and unstructured data into a uniform data operation platform. Hadapt unifies SQL and Hadoop and makes it easy to handle different varieties of data. You can learn more at http://hadapt.com/.

- **Spark** is a real-time in-memory Big Data processing platform. It can be up to 40 times faster than Hadoop. So it is ideal for iterative and responsive Big Data applications. Besides, Spark can be integrated with Hadoop, and the Hadoop-compatible storage APIs enable it to access any Hadoop-supported systems. More information about Spark can be learned from `http://spark-project.org/`.

- **Storm** is another famous real-time Big Data processing platform. It is developed and open sourced by Twitter. For more information, please check `http://storm-project.net/`.

- **GraphLab** is an open source distributed system developed at *Carnegie Mellon University*. It was targeted for handling **sparse iterative** graph algorithms. For more information, please visit: `http://graphlab.org/`.

> The MapReduce framework parallels computation by splitting data into a number of distributed nodes. Some large natural graph data, such as social network data, has the problem of being hard to partition and thus, hard to split for Hadoop parallel processing. The performance can be severely panelized if Hadoop is used.

- Other Hadoop-like implementations include **Phoenix** (`http://mapreduce.stanford.edu/`), which is a shared memory implementation of the MapReduce data processing framework, and **Haloop** (`http://code.google.com/p/haloop/`), which is a modified version of Hadoop for iterative data processing.

> Phoenix and Haloop do not have an active community and they are not recommended for production deployment.

There's more...

As the Big Data problem floods the whole world, many systems have been designed to deal with the problem. Two such famous systems that do not follow the MapReduce route are **Message Passing Interface** (**MPI**) and **High Performance Cluster Computing** (**HPCC**).

MPI

MPI is a library specification for message passing. Different from Hadoop, MPI was designed for high performance on both massively parallel machines and on workstation clusters. In addition, MPI lacks fault tolerance and performance will be bounded when data becomes large. More documentation about MPI can be found at `http://www.mpi-forum.org/`.

HPCC

HPCC is an open source Big Data platform developed by HPCC systems, which was acquired by LexisNexis Risk Solutions. It achieves high performance by clustering commodity hardware. The system includes configurations for both parallel batch processing and high performance online query applications using indexed data files. The HPCC platform contains two cluster processing subsystems: **Data Refinery** subsystem and **Data Delivery** subsystem. The Data Refinery subsystem is responsible for the general processing of massive raw data, and the Data Delivery subsystem is responsible for the delivery of clean data for online queries and analytics. More information about HPCC can be found at `http://hpccsystems.com/`.

2
Preparing for Hadoop Installation

In this chapter, we will cover:

- ▶ Choosing hardware for cluster nodes
- ▶ Designing the cluster network
- ▶ Configuring the cluster administrator machine
- ▶ Creating the kickstart file and boot media
- ▶ Installing the Linux operating system
- ▶ Installing Java and other tools
- ▶ Configuring SSH

Introduction

The configuration of a Hadoop cluster is a systematic project, especially, due to its large scale and distributed property. Efforts are needed in choosing the proper storage and computing hardware, designing the interconnected network, installing and configuring the operating system, and so on.

In a Hadoop cluster, different types of nodes may require different hardware configurations. For example, the **JobTracker** on a **master** node schedules jobs and assigns tasks to proper **slave** nodes for execution, and the **NameNode** on the master node manages the metadata for files and data blocks. In addition, the master node is a critical failure point in a default cluster configuration, which configures only one master node. A critical requirement for the master node is to be responsive and reliable. On the other hand, a slave node is responsible for hosting data blocks and running tasks upon the data blocks. Because of the built-in cluster-level-failure resilience, the reliability requirement for a slave node is not as strict as a master node. But a slave node should have enough storage space and computing power to satisfy the storage and computing requirements.

Similarly, different Hadoop cluster sizes may have different configuration requirements. For example, for a small to medium-sized cluster with up to a hundred slave nodes, the NameNode, JobTracker, and SecondaryNameNode daemons can be put on the same master machine. When the cluster size grows up to hundreds or even thousands of slave nodes, it becomes advisable to put these daemons on different machines. In this book, we assume to build a cluster with five slave nodes, which makes it reasonable to put the NameNode, JobTracker, and SecondaryNameNode daemons on the same physical machine.

Nodes in a Hadoop cluster are interconnected through network devices such as switches and routers. Data will be transferred from one node to another over the network during different phases of a MapReduce job. There are many factors that can affect the performance of a Hadoop cluster, some of which have greater influence than others. For example, network segmentation caused by device failures can greatly degrade the cluster performance, while network speed and latency have much smaller influence comparatively. So, a highly available and resilient network architecture is crucial for a Hadoop cluster.

Hadoop runs on Linux (although Windows operating systems are supported, it is still not stable at the time of writing this book). We need to install and configure Linux on all cluster nodes before the Hadoop installation process. If you have experience working with Linux, you may know that installing Linux on a single machine is straightforward by following the installation instructions. For example, we can burn the downloaded operating system ISO image onto a DVD optical disk and then boot and install the operating system using this DVD. However, the simple and straightforward installation method is too inefficient to be practical for a Hadoop cluster with a large number of nodes. We are going to explore more practical and efficient installation methods in this chapter.

Some operating system configuration is needed after installing the Linux operating system. For example, we need to configure users, groups, and system security, such as firewalls and SELinux. We also need to install the required Hadoop dependency software, Java, and some optional tools that can improve cluster management efficiency.

Choosing hardware for cluster nodes

A Hadoop cluster contains two types of nodes: a master node and a slave node. By default, the NameNode, SecondaryNameNode, and JobTracker daemons reside on a master node, and DataNode and TaskTracker daemons reside on slave nodes. Properly selecting hardware for these computing and storage nodes can maximize the efficiency of a Hadoop cluster. In this recipe, we will list suggestions on hardware selection for a computing node.

How to do it...

Although special requirements exist for a master node and a slave node, there is no gold standard for choosing optimal hardware for both types of nodes. It is reasonable to say that the hardware configuration is closely related to the properties of Big Data to be processed. In addition, the choice of hardware is an empirical and adaptive process with the changing requirements on a Hadoop cluster. For example, if the requirements for the throughput of a Hadoop cluster are high, we might need to choose high-end CPUs and hard drives. If we have a large number of potential Hadoop users, we may need to upgrade the hardware configuration for both the master node and the slave nodes.

Empirically, we recommend the following configurations for a small to medium-sized Hadoop cluster:

Node type	Node components	Recommended specification
Master node	CPU	2 Quad Core, 2.0GHz
	RAM (main memory)	16 GB
	Hard drive	2 x 1TB SATA II 7200 RPM HDD or SSD*
	Network card	1GBps Ethernet
Slave node	CPU	2 Quad Core
	RAM (main memory)	16 GB
	Hard drive	4 x 1TB HDD
	Network card	1GBps Ethernet
		*HDD stands for Hard Disk Drive and SSD stands for Solid State Drive

How it works...

On a Hadoop master node, the NameNode keeps the metadata, such as permissions of each file, in main memory. The amount of memory needed by a master node depends on the number of file system objects (for example, numbers of files and block replicas) to be created and tracked. The memory requirement will be high when the cluster is large. The SecondaryNameNode keeps a backup for the latest filesystem checkpoint mirrored from the NameNode, so its memory requirement is similar to the NameNode.

> In default configuration, the master node is a single failure point. High-end computing hardware and secondary power supplies are suggested.

In Hadoop, each slave node simultaneously executes a number of map or reduce tasks. The maximum number of parallel map/reduce tasks are known as map/reduce slots, which are configurable by a Hadoop administrator. Each slot is a computing unit consisting of CPU, memory and disk I/O resources. When a slave node was assigned a task by the JobTracker, its TaskTracker will fork a JVM for that task, allocating a preconfigured amount of computing resources. In addition, each forked JVM also will incur a certain amount of memory requirements. Empirically, a Hadoop job can consume 1 GB to 2 GB of memory for each CPU core. Higher data throughput requirement can incur higher I/O operations for the majority of Hadoop jobs. That's why higher end and parallel hard drives can help boost the cluster performance. To maximize parallelism, it is advisable to assign two slots for each CPU core. For example, if our slave node has two quad-core CPUs, we can assign `2 x 4 x 2 = 16` (map only, reduce only, or both) slots in total for this node.

> In the simple equation, the first `2` stands for the number of CPUs of the slave node, the number `4` represents the number of cores per CPU, and the other `2` means the number of slots per CPU core.

See also

- ▶ The *Designing the cluster network* recipe in *Chapter 2, Preparing for Hadoop Installation*
- ▶ The *Managing the HDFS cluster* recipe in *Chapter 4, Managing a Hadoop Cluster*
- ▶ *Chapter 7, Tuning Hadoop Cluster for Best Performance*

Designing the cluster network

The network is the backbone of a Hadoop cluster. Its stability is critical for the performance of the cluster. In this recipe, we will outline a few general rules for designing a Hadoop cluster network.

How to do it...

The network architecture for a small to medium-sized cluster can be as simple as connecting the cluster nodes with one or more switches. Connection redundancy can add reliability to the network.

Warning!

Computing nodes in a Hadoop cluster should be configured within the same network segment (**Local Area Network** (**LAN**)). Advanced features such as VLANs that can cause overhead are not recommended. Connecting nodes with a router is also not recommended.

The network architecture for the Hadoop clusters with hundreds or thousands of nodes is much more complex. In a large cluster, the physical nodes are usually so small, for example, a blade server, that they can be mounted on racks. Each rack has a local switch that interconnects nodes on the same rack. These racks are then interconnected with more advanced switches.

Nodes on the same rack can be interconnected with a 1 GBps (Gigabyte per second) Ethernet switch. Cluster level switches then connect the rack switches with faster links, such as 10 GBps optical fiber links, and other networks such as InfiniBand. The cluster-level switches may also interconnect with other cluster-level switches or even uplink to another higher level of switching infrastructure. With the increasing size of a cluster, the network, at the same time, will become larger and more complex. Connection redundancies for network high availability can also increase its complexity. In this book, we assume to discuss the basic network architecture design method. If you want to learn more advanced network design techniques, please refer to related books and online materials.

In general, the network architecture of a medium-sized cluster can be described with the following diagram:

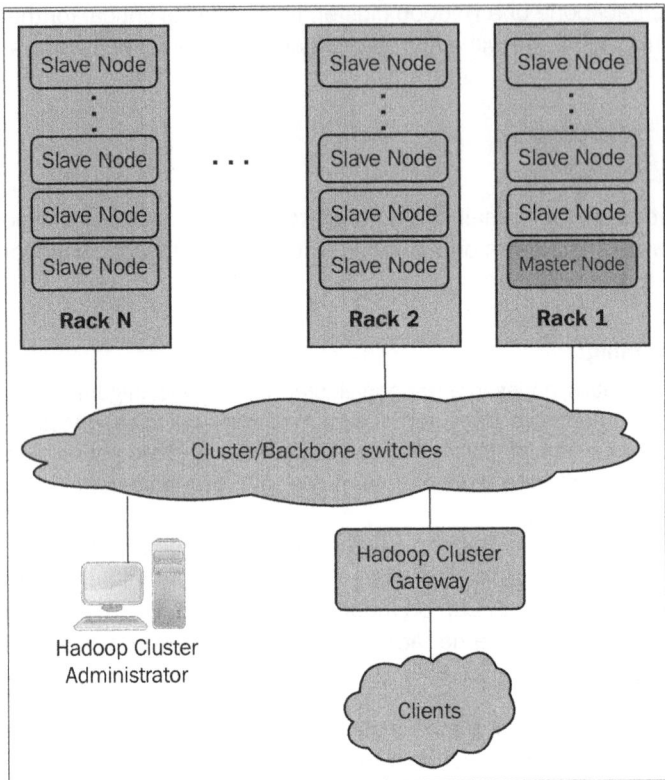

In this diagram, we assume there is a Hadoop cluster administrator machine and the clients connect to the cluster through a gateway, through which Hadoop jobs can be submitted.

How it works...

The increasing bandwidth of network devices makes it possible for Hadoop to load and replicate large datasets across interconnected nodes. Resilient and scalable network architecture can secure the high data throughput and performance requirements for a Hadoop cluster.

Configuring the cluster administrator machine

As we have mentioned previously, the most efficient way to install Linux on a large number of machines is to install over the network. In this book, we assume to use the administrator machine as the installation server. We will learn steps to configure this server, including the configuration of the following two services: DHCP and FTP.

Getting ready

Before getting started, we assume that the cluster administrator machine has a 64 bit Red Hat compatible Linux operating system installed. The hostname of the machine is `hadoop.admin` and an administrative user `hdadmin` has been created. This user should have `sudo` privileges to install software packages, configure system services, and so on. We also assume administrative tools such as a command-line text editor has been installed on this machine. We will use these tools and commands directly in the upcoming recipes.

> In this book, we assume to use **CentOS 6.3** (which corresponds to Red Hat Enterprise Linux (RHEL) 6.3) as the Linux distribution. We will follow the Red Hat syntax for all the administrative commands. If you are using a Linux distribution other than CentOS, such as Debian, please refer to corresponding documentation.

1. Log in to the administrator machine as `hdadmin` and change the hostname of the machine with the following command:

   ```
   sudo sed -i 's/^HOSTNAME.
   *$/HOSTNAME=hadoop.admin/' /etc/sysconfig/network
   ```

2. Create directories with the following command:

   ```
   mkdir -v ~/mnt ~/isoimages ~/repo
   ```

>  We will use directory `~/mnt` as the mount point for ISO images. The `~/isoimages` directory will be used to contain the original image files and the `~/repo` directory will be used as the repository folder for network installation.

3. Install the DHCP and FTP servers on the machine with the following commands:

   ```
   sudo yum -y install dhcp
   sudo yum -y install vsftpd
   ```

We will use the DHCP server to assign IP addresses and bootstrap the operating system in the installation process, and use the FTP server to host the installation packages.

4. Download the latest ISO image from a mirror.

The CentOS official site provides a worldwide mirrors list, including North America, European countries, South America, Asia, Oceania, Middle East, Africa, and other regions.

After selecting the nearest mirror, we can use either HTTP or FTP to download the image. Let's choose FTP as the download method by clicking on the link in the corresponding line of the selected mirror. Then select **6.3 | isos | x86_64** consecutively. In this directory, as shown in the following screenshot, we choose to download two ISO image files. The image file `CentOS-6.3-x86_64-minimal.iso` contains all the necessary installation packages. And the `CentOS-6.3-x86_64-netinstall.iso` image file contains PXE network booting files used for booting over the network.

Index of /mirror/centos/6.3/isos/x86_64

Name	Last modified	Size	Description
Parent Directory		-	
0_README.txt	06-Jul-2012 06:01	2.0K	
CentOS-6.3-x86_64-LiveCD.iso	07-Jul-2012 13:26	692M	
CentOS-6.3-x86_64-LiveCD.torrent	09-Jul-2012 14:03	217K	
CentOS-6.3-x86_64-LiveDVD.iso	06-Jul-2012 09:07	1.6G	
CentOS-6.3-x86_64-LiveDVD.torrent	09-Jul-2012 13:50	263K	
CentOS-6.3-x86_64-bin-DVD1.iso	06-Jul-2012 06:20	4.0G	
CentOS-6.3-x86_64-bin-DVD1to2.torrent	09-Jul-2012 14:15	217K	
CentOS-6.3-x86_64-bin-DVD2.iso	06-Jul-2012 06:20	1.4G	
CentOS-6.3-x86_64-minimal-EFI.iso	21-Aug-2012 14:30	364M	
CentOS-6.3-x86_64-minimal.iso	06-Jul-2012 06:23	330M	
CentOS-6.3-x86_64-netinstall-EFI.iso	18-Sep-2012 05:39	234M	
CentOS-6.3-x86_64-netinstall.iso	06-Jul-2012 06:14	200M	
md5sum.txt	18-Sep-2012 17:31	734	
md5sum.txt.asc	18-Sep-2012 17:31	1.6K	
sha1sum.txt	18-Sep-2012 17:31	822	

If you are not sure about the architecture of the cluster machines, please refer to the product hardware menu.

Alternatively, we can use the following `rsync` to download the image:

```
rsync rsync://mirror.its.dal.ca/centos/6.3/isos/x86_64/CentOS-6.3-
x86_64-netinstall.iso ~/isoimages
```

We can also use the following `wget` command to download the image file:

```
wget http://mirror.its.dal.ca/centos/6.3/isos/x86_64/CentOS-6.3-
x86_64-netinstall.iso -P ~/isoimages
```

5. Mount the image file with the following command:

```
sudo mount ~/isoimages/ CentOS-6.3-x86_64-minimal.iso ~/mnt
```

6. Copy all the files to the `~/repo` directory for FTP hosting with the following command:

```
cp -r ~/mnt/* ~/repo
```

7. Unmount the ISO image with the following command:

```
sudo umount ~/mnt
```

The directory tree of the minimal image is similar to the following:

```
├── EFI
│   ├── BOOT
│   │   ├── BOOTX64.conf
│   │   ├── BOOTX64.efi
│   │   ├── splash.xpm.gz
│   │   └── TRANS.TBL
│   └── TRANS.TBL
├── images
│   ├── efiboot.img
│   ├── efidisk.img
│   ├── install.img
│   ├── TRANS.TBL
│   └── updates.img
├── isolinux
│   ├── boot.msg
```

```
|   ├── grub.conf
|   ├── initrd.img
|   ├── isolinux.bin
|   ├── isolinux.cfg
|   ├── memtest
|   └── vmlinuz
├── Packages
|   ├── ...
├── ...
```

The directory tree of the `netinstall` image is similar to the following:

```
├── images
|   ├── install.img
|   ├── pxeboot
|   |   ├── initrd.img
|   |   ├── TRANS.TBL
|   |   └── vmlinuz
|   └── TRANS.TBL
└── isolinux
    ├── boot.msg
    ├── grub.conf
    ├── initrd.img
    ├── isolinux.bin
    ├── isolinux.cfg
    ├── memtest
    ├── ...
    └── vmlinuz
```

```
3 directories, 16 files
```

We can see from the directory trees that the minimal installation image file contains packages and boot images for system installation. The `netinstall` package only contains files for booting, including network booting files in the `images/pxeboot` directory.

How to do it...

The following recipe will explain how to configure the DHCP server:

1. Use your favorite text editor to open the file `/etc/dhcp/dhcpd.conf` and change the following content:

    ```
    # Domain name
    option domain-name "hadoop.cluster";

    # DNS hostname or IP address
    option domain-name-servers
    dlp.server.world;

    # Default lease time
    default-lease-time 600;

    # Maximum lease time
    max-lease-time 7200;

    # Declare the DHCP server to be valid.
    authoritative;

    # Network address and subnet mask
    subnet 10.0.0.0 netmask 255.255.255.0 {

    # Range of lease IP address, should be based
        # on the size of the network
        range dynamic-bootp 10.0.0.200 10.0.0.254;

        # Broadcast address
        option broadcast-address 10.0.0.255;

        # Default gateway
        option routers 10.0.0.1;
    }
    ```

2. Start the DHCP server with the following command:

    ```
    sudo service dhcpd start
    ```

 The DHCP server starts with the following message:
Starting dhcpd: [OK]

3. Make the DHCP server to survive a system reboot:

```
sudo chkconfig dhcpd --level 3 on
```

Use the following recipe to configure the FTP server:

1. Open the file /etc/vsftpd/vsftpd.conf with your favorite text editor and change the content according to the following list:

```
# The FTP server will run in standalone mode.
listen=YES

# Use Anonymous user.
anonymous_enable=YES

# Disable change root for local users.
chroot_local_user=NO

# Disable uploading and changing files.
write_enable=NO

# Enable logging of uploads and downloads.
xferlog_enable=YES

# Enable port 20 data transfer.
connect_from_port_20=YES

# Specify directory for hosting the Linux installation packages.
anon_ropot=~/repo
```

2. Start the FTP server with the following command:

```
$ sudo service vsftpd start
```

 The server will start with the following message:
Starting vsftpd: [OK]

3. Verify the FTP configuration with the following command:

```
$ ftp hadoop.admin
```

The configuration is successful if we get the following message:

Trying 10.0.0.1...

Connected to hadoop.admin (10.0.0.1).

220 (vsFTPd 3.0.0)

Name (knoesis157:hdadmin):

See also

▶ The *Creating the kickstart file and boot media* recipe in *Chapter 2, Preparing for Hadoop Installation*.

▶ The *Installing the Linux operating system* recipe in *Chapter 2, Preparing for Hadoop installation*.

Creating the kickstart file and boot media

Installing Linux on a large number of nodes with a kickstart file has a few advantages. For example, the installation process can be automated by specifying a list of to-be installed packages and configuring system settings for the post-installation process.

In this section, we will cover steps of creating a kickstart file and a USB boot media with the operating system image.

Getting ready

A kickstart file is a plain text file used for the automatic installation of Linux.

1. Prepare a USB flash drive with storage capacity larger than 512MB. The drive should have a single `vfat` filesystem partition. We can use the following command to check the filesystem type:

   ```
   blkid
   ```

We should see a message similar to the following:

/dev/sdb1 SEC_TYPE="msdos" LABEL="LIVE" UUID="07D9-051C" TYPE="vfat"

2. If the `TYPE` attribute is other than `vfat`, use the following command to clear the first few blocks of the drive:

   ```
   dd if=/dev/zero of=/dev/sdb1 bs=1M count=100
   ```

3. Log in to the administrative machine using the following command:

    ssh hdadmin@hadoop.admin

How to do it...

We will use the following steps to create a kickstart file:

1. Install the `kickstart` file with the command:

    sudo yum install system-config-kickstart

2. Use your favorite text editor to create a `ks.cfg` file with the following content:

```
#!/bin/bash
# Kickstart for CentOS 6.3 for Hadoop cluster.

# Install system on the machine.
install

# Use ftp as the package repository
url --url ftp://hadoop.admin/repo

# Use the text installation interface.
text

# Use UTF-8 encoded USA English as the language.
lang en_US.UTF-8

# Configure time zone.
timezone America/New_York

# Use USA keyboard.
keyboard us

# Set bootloader location.
bootloader --location=mbr --driveorder=sda rhgb quiet

# Set root password
rootpw  --password=hadoop

################################
# Partion the hard disk
################################
```

```
# Clear the master boot record on the hard drive.
zerombr yes

# Clear existing partitions.
clearpart --all --initlabel

# Create /boot partition, size is in MB.
part /boot --fstype ext3 --size 128

# Create / (root) partition.
part / --fstype ext3 --size 4096 --grow --maxsize 8192

# Create /var partition.
part /var --fstype ext3 --size 4096 --grow --maxsize 8192

# Create Hadoop data storage directory.
part /hadoop --fstype ext3 --grow

# Create swap partition, 16GB, double size of the main memory.
# Change size according to your hardware memory configuration.
part swap --size 16384


###################################
# Configure Network device.
###################################

# Use DHCP and disable IPv6.
network --onboot yes --device eth0 --bootproto dhcp --noipv6

# Disable firewall.
firewall --disabled

# Configure authorization.
authconfig --enableshadow

# Put Selinux in permissive mode.
selinux --permissive


###############################################
# Specify packages to install.
###############################################


# Automatically resolve package dependencies,
```

```
# exclude installation of documents and ignore missing packages.
%packages --resolvedeps --excludedocs --ignoremissing

# Install core packages.
@Base

# Don't install OpenJDK.
-java

# Install wget.
wget

# Install the vim text editor.
vim

# Install the Emacs text editor.
emacs

# Install rsync.
rsync

# install nmap network mapper.
nmap

%end

####################################
# Post installation configuration.
####################################

# Enable post process logging.
%post --log=~/install-post.log

# Create Hadoop user hduser with password hduser.
useradd -m -p hduser hduser

# Create group Hadoop.
groupadd hadoop

# Change user hduser's current group to hadoop.
usermod -g hadoop hduser
```

```
# Tell the nodes hostname and ip address of the admin machine.
echo "10.0.0.1 hadoop.admin" >> /etc/hosts


# Configure administrative privilege to hadoop group.


# Configure the kernel settings.
ulimit -u


###########################
# Startup services.
###########################


service sshd start
chkconfig sshd on


%end


# Reboot after installation.
reboot


# Disable first boot configuration.
firstboot --disable
```

3. Put the kickstart file into the root directory of the FTP server with the command:

   cp ks.cfg ~/repo

   This will make the kickstart file available during the installation process.

We will now create a USB boot media using the following recipe:

1. Use a text editor to open the file `~/isolinux/grub.conf` and add the following content:

   default=0

   splashimage=@SPLASHPATH@

   timeout 0

   hiddenmenu

   title @PRODUCT@ @VERSION@

   kernel @KERNELPATH@ ks=ftp://hadoop.admin/ks.cfg

   initrd @INITRDPATH@

2. Make an ISO file from the `isolinux` directory using the following commands:

```
mkisofs -o CentOS6.3-x86_64-boot.iso \
-b ~/repo/isolinux/isolinux.bin \
-c ~/repo/isolinux/boot.cat \
-no-emul-boot \
-boot-load-size 4
```

3. Plug in a USB flash drive on the administrator machine and write the bootable ISO image into the USB flash drive with the following command (assuming the USB drive corresponds to the `/dev/sdb` device file):

```
dd if=~/CentOS6.3-x86_64-boot.iso of=/dev/sdb
```

> **Warning!**
> Make sure you have a backup of the data on the USB flash drive, all the information will be wiped out when we write the ISO image file into the drive.

How it works...

A kickstart file specifies a number of installation options, such as installation media, networking configuration, firewall configuration, and so on. Lines that start with # are treated as comments.

The file contains a `%packages` section, which specifies the packages to be installed. In this section, both specific packages and package groups can be specified to install. For example, in our kickstart file, we configure to install the Linux base package with `@Base`. In addition, if a package is not intended to be installed, we can add a dash symbol before the package. For example, if we don't want to install OpenJDK, we can specify this with `-java`.

> For a Hadoop cluster, basic packages are enough, so we have ignored the unnecessary packages in the kickstart file.

The `%post` section allows us to specify configurations and commands after installation. This is very helpful when we need to do some administrative configurations after installing the operating system. For example, we might want to create a regular user for Hadoop with privileges to run Hadoop commands and to configure system services such as SSHD and FTP.

The USB boot media was used to boot a system and start the installation process automatically. We can specify the following kernel start up option in the `grub.conf` file:

```
ks=ftp://hadoop.admin/ks.cfg
```

This option tells the location of the kickstart file. Once the kickstart file is located and transferred to the local machine, automatic installation will start.

There's more...

There are other installation methods other than FTP, for example, we can also use NFS and HTTP. The difference of these methods from FTP lies only in the configuration of the corresponding repository URL. For example, if we want to use an HTTP server, we can make the following two changes in our configuration:

▸ In the kickstart file, change `url --url ftp://hadoop.admin/repo` to `url --url http://hadoop.admin:80/repo`.

▸ In the `grub.conf` file, change the kernel option from `ks=ftp://hadoop.admin/ks.cfg` to `ks=http://hadoop.admin:80/ks.cfg`.

See also

▸ The *Installing the Linux operating system* recipe in *Chapter 2, Preparing for Hadoop installation*

Installing the Linux operating system

Although there are many ways to install Linux on a machine, installing over the network with the help of a kickstart file is the most efficient option. The installation process can be automated requiring minimal human intervention. A kickstart file can be kept on a server and read by individual machines during the installation process. In the recipe, we will outline steps to install Linux on a number of Hadoop nodes over the network.

Getting ready

Before getting started, we need to verify that the DHCP server and FTP server are running correctly on the administrative machine.

Use the following command on the administrator machine to check if the DHCP server is working properly:

```
ps -ef | grep dhcp
```

If this command gives non-empty output, then it is working correctly, otherwise, we need to start the service with the following command:

```
sudo service dhcpd start
```

Similarly, the following command can be used to check the FTP server on the administrator machine:

```
ftp hadoop.admin
```

We should be able to log in anonymously and list the kickstart file and installation packages in the root directory.

In addition, we assume that the cluster nodes have been physically configured. For example, racks and networking devices are all working without any issues.

How to do it...

Use the following recipe to install Linux on a machine:

1. Plug in the USB flash drive boot media and power on the computer.
2. Press *F9* to select the boot device.

 Different BIOS versions may have different shortcut keys. If *F9* does not work, please refer to the related product manual.

3. From the list of boot devices, choose **USB** or **Removable Devices**.
4. When the installation starts, you can remove the boot media and start the installation on the next machine.

How it works...

The Linux system was designed to be flexible. Its booting process is composed of the following stages:

- Switch on physical machine
- Choose the boot media
- Stage 1 - boot loader
- Stage 2 - boot loader
- Load the kernel image
- System initialization

After we power on the machine and select as the boot media, the boot loader, grub in our case, will start to work. Grub contains two boot loading stages. In stage 1, an executable program will run and load stage 2. Then, stage 2 will load the kernel, which resides on boot media. When installing the operating system, the kernel has very limited functionality to start the installation process, for example, finding the location of software packages. In our case, the kernel option kickstart file contains all the specification for the installation process. Thus, everything will be automated after booting from the USB boot media.

One advantage of separating the boot media from the installation package repository is that the installation on multiple machines can be paralleled to reduce the total installation time.

There's more...

With the help of a kickstart file, we can automate the installation of Linux on a number of machines. One disadvantage of this method is that we need to manually boot each machine. This is tedious and requires a lot of repetitive work. Even worse, in reality, we may find that a lot of servers don't even have a monitor or video card installed. This makes it impractical to use this method. So, we need to explore alternative methods.

In this part, we will introduce the steps to automate the installation process with the help of DHCP and TFTP servers. A DHCP server is configured as a booting server, which serves similarly as a USB drive boot media, and the TFTP is configured to host the actual operating system packages.

Configuring DHCP for network booting

We have mentioned the basic configuration of a DHCP server in the previous section. To enable network booting for DHCP, we will use the **Preboot Execution Environment** (**PXE**) method of TFTP.

Create the configuration file /etc/dhcpd.conf for DHCP with the following content:

```
option domain-name "hadoop.cluster";

default-lease-time 5000;

max-lease-time 7200;

# Enable network booting and bootp protocol.
allow booting;
allow bootp;
```

```
# IP address allocations.
subnet 10.0.0.0 netmask 255.255.255.0 {

  range 10.0.0.200 10.0.0.253;

  option broadcast-address 10.0.0.255;

  # Gateway address
  option routers 10.0.0.1;

  # indicate the dns you want to use
  option domain-name-servers 10.0.0.1;
}

group {
  next-server 10.0.0.1;

  host tftpclient {

  # tftp client hardware address
  hardware ethernet  00:10:DC:27:6C:15;

  filename "/pxelinux.0";
  }
}
```

Configuring TFTP for network booting:

1. Log in to the administrator machine with the command:

   ssh hdadmin@hadoop.admin

2. Install the TFTP server with the command:

   sudo yum install tftpd

3. Open the file /etc/xinetd.d/tftpd with your favorite text editor and edit the content to be similar to the following:

```
service tftp
{
    socket_type   = dgram
    protocol      = udp
    wait          = yes
    user          = hdadmin
    server        = /usr/sbin/in.tftpd
    server_args   = -c -s /tftpboot
```

```
disable        = no
per_source     = 11
cps            = 100 2
}
```

 In this file, we enabled the TFTP service by setting the `disable` primitive to be `no`.

4. Create the TFTP boot image directory with the following command:

   `mkdir -p ~/tftp/boot/centos6.3`

5. Mount the net install ISO image with the following command:

   `sudo mount ~/isoimages/CentOS-6.3-x86_64-netinstall.iso ~/mnt`

6. Copy PXE boot files to the boot image directory with the following command:

   `cp ~/mnt/images/pxeboot/* ~/tftp/boot/centos6.3`

7. Start the TFTP server with the following command:

   `sudo service tftpd start`

8. Test the TFTP configuration with the following command:

   `tftp hadoop.admin`

 If we can log in and list files, the TFTP has been configured correctly.

9. Start the installation process by powering on the cluster machines.

Installing Java and other tools

Hadoop was built using Java, so Java is required before installing Hadoop.

Getting ready

Under Linux, OpenJDK provides an open source Java implementation. But if we use OpenJDK for Hadoop, it will cause low level and hard to tackle problems. So, OpenJDK is not recommended for the Hadoop installation. Instead, Java from Oracle is recommended.

1. Check if OpenJDK has been installed in the system with the command:

   `rpm -qa | grep openjdk`

If no output is given, it means OpenJDK has not been installed.

2. If Java has been installed in the system, we can check its version with:

```
java -version
```

3. If OpenJDK is used, we should be able to get output similar to the following:

```
java version "1.7.0_09-icedtea"
OpenJDK Runtime Environment (fedora-2.3.4.fc17-x86_64)
OpenJDK 64-Bit Server VM (build 23.2-b09, mixed mode)
```

4. After confirming whether we are using OpenJDK, we need to remove the package and reinstall the version downloaded from Oracle's official website.

5. To remove OpenJDK, we can use the following command:

```
sudo yum uninstall java-1.x.y-openjdk
```

In this command, `1.x.y` is the version of the OpenJDK to be removed, for example 1.7.0.

Warning!

This command can be destructive, especially, when some dependent software packages have been installed. In such a case, it will prompt you to confirm the removal of OpenJDK together with the depending software packages. If you don't want all the packages to be removed, answer **NO** to the question.

6. Alternatively, we can use the following `rpm` command to remove the package:

```
sudo rpm -e java-1.x.y-openjdk
```

This command will only remove the OpenJDK package, regardless of the dependent software packages.

Note that this command can break software package dependencies, causing dependent software not working properly.

7. As another alternative method, we can tweak the `PATH` environment variable to let both Java versions co-exist on the system while let the system to prefer the Java from Oracle.

8. Suppose we have both OpenJDK and Oracle Java installed in `/usr/openjdk` and `/usr/jdk` respectively. We can set the `PATH` environment variable to be the following:

   `PATH=/usr/jdk/bin:/usr/openjdk/bin:$PATH`

   Or, if we would like to only use the Oracle Java, we can set PATH to be:

   `PATH=/usr/jdk/bin:$PATH`

9. To download Java from Oracle, please visit: `http://www.oracle.com/technetwork/java/javase/downloads/index.html`.

10. Select **Java SE Development Kit 7 Downloads**, which is Java 1.7.x (Hadoop can work with Java with a version greater or equal to 1.6.0).

11. Next, click on the **Accept License Agreement** radio button and choose **jdk-7u11-linux-x64.rpm** for a 64 bit Linux machine.

12. The preceding operations are shown in the following screenshot:

Java SE Development Kit 7u11
You must accept the Oracle Binary Code License Agreement for Java SE to download this software.

Accept License Agreement ◉ Decline License Agreement

Product / File Description	File Size	Download
Linux x86	106.61 MB	jdk-7u11-linux-i586.rpm
Linux x86	92.95 MB	jdk-7u11-linux-i586.tar.gz
Linux x64	104.75 MB	jdk-7u11-linux-x64.rpm
Linux x64	91.7 MB	jdk-7u11-linux-x64.tar.gz
Mac OS X x64	143.72 MB	jdk-7u11-macosx-x64.dmg
Solaris x86 (SVR4 package)	135.54 MB	jdk-7u11-solaris-i586.tar.Z
Solaris x86	91.92 MB	jdk-7u11-solaris-i586.tar.gz
Solaris x64 (SVR4 package)	22.52 MB	jdk-7u11-solaris-x64.tar.Z
Solaris x64	14.95 MB	jdk-7u11-solaris-x64.tar.gz
Solaris SPARC (SVR4 package)	135.87 MB	jdk-7u11-solaris-sparc.tar.Z
Solaris SPARC	95.25 MB	jdk-7u11-solaris-sparc.tar.gz
Solaris SPARC 64-bit (SVR4 package)	22.77 MB	jdk-7u11-solaris-sparcv9.tar.Z
Solaris SPARC 64-bit	17.49 MB	jdk-7u11-solaris-sparcv9.tar.gz
Windows x86	88.77 MB	jdk-7u11-windows-i586.exe
Windows x64	90.41 MB	jdk-7u11-windows-x64.exe

How to do it...

Use the following recipe to install Java and other tools:

1. Install Oracle Java with the following command (assuming we saved the downloaded Java package to the home directory:

   ```
   sudo yum localinstall ~/java-package-*.rpm
   ```

2. Verify the installation with the following command:

   ```
   java -version
   ```

   If Java is correctly installed, the output should be similar to the following:

   ```
   java version "1.6.0_33"
   Java(TM) SE Runtime Environment (build 1.6.0_33-b04)
   Java HotSpot(TM) 64-Bit Server VM (build 20.8-b03, mixed mode)
   ```

3. Use the following command to install necessary tools:

   ```
   sudo yum -y install wget rsync nmap
   ```

    If these packages have been specified in the installation kickstart file, this step will be optional.

How it works...

GNU wget is a software tool used for transferring files using HTTP, HTTPS, and FTP protocols. It is not interactive and can be used from command line and scripts for file download. For more information please visit http://www.gnu.org/software/wget/.

rsync is an open source tool that provides fast and incremental file transfers. It is widely used for file copying and synchronization under Linux. For more information about rsync, please visit http://rsync.samba.org/.

Network Mapper (nmap) is a famous tool for network exploration and security auditing. We can use nmap to scan large networks and identify security problems. For example, to scan the service on a local machine, we can use the following command:

```
nmap localhost
```

We get an output similar to the following:

```
Starting Nmap 6.01 ( http://nmap.org ) at 2013-01-26 23:52 EST
Nmap scan report for localhost (127.0.0.1)
Host is up (0.0021s latency).
rDNS record for 127.0.0.1: localhost.localdomain
Not shown: 995 closed ports
PORT     STATE SERVICE
21/tcp   open  ftp
22/tcp   open  ssh
25/tcp   open  smtp
111/tcp  open  rpcbind
631/tcp  open  ipp

Nmap done: 1 IP address (1 host up) scanned in 0.14 seconds
```

 The output tells us that the local machine has the following services running: `ftp`, `ssh`, `smtp`, `rpcbind` (service for remote procedure calls), and `jpp` (service for Java packaging).

Similarly, we can use the following command to scan the IP segment `10.0.1.*`:

```
nmap 10.0.0.*
```

The command will give us service information of each host under the IP segment from `10.0.0.1` to `10.0.0.255`.

There's more...

Under Linux, we can use the `man` command to get the usage of a command. For example, to get usage of `wget`, we can use `man wget`.

If more detailed information about a command is desired, we can use the `info` command. For example, the command `info wget` gives more details about the `wget` command.

Configuring SSH

SSH is the de facto standard protocol for secure data connection and remote command execution. Proper configuration of SSH is required for Hadoop installation. In this section, we are going to learn how to configure SSH on the cluster nodes. Specifically, we are discussing how to configure SSH for a passwordless login to a remote machine.

Getting ready

Start up the SSHD service on all the cluster nodes (both the slave nodes and the master node) with the following command:

```
sudo service sshd start
```

Make the service survive system reboot with the command:

```
sudo chkconfig sshd on
```

Verify whether sshd works properly with the command from the master node:

```
ssh hduser@slave1
```

If it is the first time of logging into to the host, we will get a message similar to the following:

```
The authenticity of host 'hdslave.host(10.0.0.1)' can't be established.
RSA key fingerprint is 7c:e0:61:3b:b6:70:07:ab:65:f9:bf:2d:90:77:1b:57.
Are you sure you want to continue connecting (yes/no)?
```

We need to type in yes and then provide the password for the user hduser to log in to the host.

How to do it...

Use the following recipe to configure a passwordless login:

1. Log in to the master node from the cluster administrator machine with the following command:

   ```
   ssh hduser@master
   ```

2. Use a text editor to modify the SSHD service configuration file /etc/ssh/ssh_config by changing the following line:

   ```
   #    StrictHostKeyChecking ask
   ```

   to:

   ```
   StrictHostKeyChecking no
   ```

3. Restart the SSHD server with the following command:

   sudo service sshd restart

4. Generate private and public keys with the command:

   ssh-keygen

   Press *Enter* three times until this command finishes. A public key file ~/.ssh/id_rsa.pub and a private key file ~/.ssh/id_rsa will be generated.

5. Copy the public key file to the remote machine with the following command:

   ssh-copy-id slave1

6. Test the configuration with the following command:

   ssh hduser@slave1

 If we can log in without entering the password, then the configuration is successful!

How it works...

When we run the command ssh-copy-id hdslave.host, we actually append the content of the public key file on the local machine into the file ~/.ssh/authorized_keys on the remote machine. Next time we log in, the public key string in the file ~/.ssh/authorized_keys on the remote machine and local private key will be used for the login authentication process.

There's more...

Configuration of a passwordless login failure can be caused by many reasons, for example, the configuration of the firewall (or iptables, to be more specific), SELinux, and even the SSHD server itself. We will discuss methods to deal with these potential problems.

Erroneous SSH settings

If the /etc/ssh_config file contains the following lines:

```
RSAAuthentication no
PubkeyAuthentication no
```

It means that the public key authorization has been disabled. We need to change these two lines to the following:

```
RSAAuthentication yes
PubkeyAuthentication yes
```

Make sure that the SSHD service has been successfully restarted on the remote machine with the following command:

```
sudo service sshd restart
```

Manually check the ~/.ssh/authorized_hosts file on the remote host and see if the local machine's public key string has been appended. If not, we can manually append the local machine's public key to the ~/.ssh/authorized_hosts on the remote machine with the following commands:

```
scp ~/.ssh/id_rsa.pub hduser@hdslave.host:~/
ssh hduser@hdslave.host -C "cat ~/id_rsa.pub >> ~/.ssh/authorized_hosts"
```

Log out of the remote machine and log in again, if the problem persists, go to the next section.

Erroneous iptables configuration

Check the status of iptables with the following command:

```
sudo iptables -L
```

If no rules are printed, go to the next step, otherwise, disable iptables by flushing all the existing rules with the following command:

```
sudo iptables -F
```

If the problem persists, go to the next section.

Erroneous SELinux configuration

Security Enhanced Linux (**SELinux**) is a Linux feature that provides the mechanism for supporting access control security policies. SELinux that is in enforcing mode can block the passwordless login operation. We can check the current SELinux status with the following command:

```
getenforce
```

If we get an output similar to the following:

```
Enforcing
```

The output means SELinux is currently in enforcing mode, we need to put it in permissive mode with command:

`sudo setenforce 0`

Alternatively, we can disable SELinux by editing the `/etc/selinux/config` file and change `SELINUX=enforcing` to `SELINUX=disabled`. Note that system reboot is required for the changes to take effect in this method.

See also

> ▸ The Creating the kickstart file and boot media recipe

3
Configuring a Hadoop Cluster

In this chapter, we will cover:

- ▶ Choosing a Hadoop version
- ▶ Configuring Hadoop in pseudo-distributed mode
- ▶ Configuring Hadoop in fully-distributed mode
- ▶ Validating Hadoop installation
- ▶ Configuring ZooKeeper
- ▶ Installing HBase
- ▶ Installing Hive
- ▶ Installing Pig
- ▶ Installing Mahout

Introduction

After finishing all the preparing tasks, we are ready to configure a Hadoop cluster in this chapter. First, we will give you some tips on choosing a proper Hadoop release version. Then we will show you how to configure a Hadoop cluster in pseudo-distributed and fully-distributed mode. Pseudo-distributed mode is a very good starting point if you have no experience configuring a Hadoop cluster. In this mode, we will configure all the Hadoop daemons to run on a single machine, which can give us the first feeling of a working Hadoop cluster while minimizing configuration difficulties. Next, we will show you how to validate a Hadoop cluster. The importance of validating a Hadoop cluster configuration will never be overemphasized. We typically use this step to confirm that the Hadoop cluster is running as expected. The last few recipes will show you how to install a few components in the cluster.

Choosing a Hadoop version

As an open source project, Hadoop has been under active development over the past few years. New versions are being released regularly. These new releases either fix bugs contributed by the community, leading to a more stable Hadoop software stack, or add new features for the purpose of more full-fledged and enterprise-level distribution.

In this section, we are going to review the history of releases of Hadoop, pointing out features of these releases. More importantly, we will give tips on choosing a proper Hadoop distribution.

Getting ready

In general, the **release version number** of a Hadoop distribution consists of three parts: the **version** number, the **major revision** number, and the **minor revision** number.

 Sometimes the revision number can have a fourth part, for example, 0.20.203.0, but this is relatively rare.

A Hadoop release name can be described with the following figure:

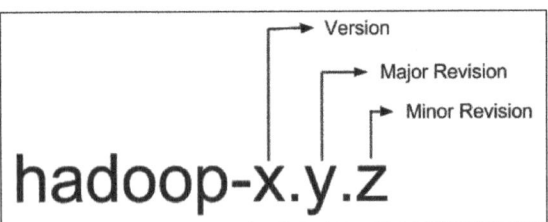

How to do it...

The following table shows features of major Hadoop releases:

Feature\Version	2.0.x	1.1.x	0.23.x	0.20.x
Stable		Yes		Yes
MRv1		Yes		Yes
MRv2	Yes		Yes	
Kerberos security	Yes	Yes	Yes	
HDFS federation	Yes		Yes	

Feature\Version	2.0.x	1.1.x	0.23.x	0.20.x
NameNode HA	Yes		Yes	
HDFS append	Yes	Yes	Yes	
HDFS symbolic links	Yes	Yes	Yes	

The table tells us that Hadoop is evolving rapidly, with new features such as security, **HDFS federation**, and **NameNode HA** being added over time. Another lesson we can learn from the table is that the most recent stable release, Version 1.1.x, does not contain all the features. And although release Version 2.0.x is the most feature-rich Hadoop release, it is still in alpha state requiring further improvements.

So, which version should you choose for your deployment? Generally, we need to consider two properties: stability and features. For a production deployment, we definitely want to deploy a stable release and we want to use the release that contains all the required features. Clearly, our current optimal and only choice is Version 1.1.x or specifically Version 1.1.2 as of this book's writing.

See also

▸ More information about Hadoop releases can be found at `http://hadoop.apache.org/releases.html`

Configuring Hadoop in pseudo-distributed mode

Pseudo-distributed mode refers to a Hadoop cluster configuration that contains only one node. This mode can be helpful for debugging and validation purposes. In this recipe, we will outline steps to configure Hadoop in pseudo-distributed mode.

Getting ready

Before configuring Hadoop in pseudo-distributed mode, we assume that we have a machine, for example, the master node of the Hadoop cluster, with Linux installed. We also assume that all the necessary tools have been installed and properly configured.

▸ The most important dependent software is Java, which is the programming language and library that Hadoop is based on. To check that Java has been properly installed, we can use the following command:

```
$ java -version
```

You should have output similar to the following:

```
java version "1.7.0_13"

Java(TM) SE Runtime Environment (build 1.7.0_13-b20)

Java HotSpot(TM) 64-Bit Server VM (build 23.7-b01, mixed mode)
```

▶ If you have installed OpenJDK other than the Oracle's official Java, the output will be similar to the following:

```
Java version "1.7.0_09-icedtea"

OpenJDK Runtime Environment (fedora-2.3.4.fc17-x86_64)

OpenJDK 64-Bit Server VM (build 23.2-b09, mixed mode)
```

 If you have installed OpenJDK, please refer to the *Installing Java and other tools* recipe from *Chapter 2, Preparing for Hadoop installation*.

▶ Download the desired Hadoop distribution. In this book, we assume that we're using Hadoop release 1.1.2. To download a Hadoop release, please visit the following URL:

```
http://www.apache.org/dyn/closer.cgi/hadoop/common/
```

Choose the proper mirror site (or use the suggested link on top of the mirror). Start downloading by clicking on the proper Hadoop release. We suggest downloading a `.gzip` archived file with the filename ending with `tar.gz`.

▶ Alternatively, we can download a Hadoop release with the following command under Linux:

```
wget http://mirror.quintex.com/apache/hadoop/common/hadoop-1.1.2/
hadoop-1.1.2.tar.gz -P ~
```

▶ Last, we assume that the `ssh` password-less login has been properly configured.

How to do it...

Perform the following steps to configure Hadoop in pseudo-distributed mode:

1. Copy the Hadoop archive to the `/usr/local` directory:

    ```
    sudo cp hadoop-1.1.2.tar.gz /usr/local
    ```

2. Decompress the Hadoop package archive:

    ```
    cd /usr/local
    sudo tar xvf hadoop-1.1.2.tar.gz
    ```

The uncompressed archive file will contain the following files and folders:

`CHANGES.txt` `lib`	`c++`	`hadoop-examples-1.1.2.jar`
`LICENSE.txt` `libexec`	`conf`	`hadoop-minicluster-1.1.2.jar`
`NOTICE.txt` `sbin`	`contrib`	`hadoop-test-1.1.2.jar`
`README.txt` `share`	`hadoop-ant-1.1.2.jar`	`hadoop-tools-1.1.2.jar`
`bin` `src`	`hadoop-client-1.1.2.jar`	`ivy`
`build.xml` `webapps`	`hadoop-core-1.1.2.jar`	`ivy.xml`

The folder contains several `.jar` files and folders such as `bin`, `sbin`, and `conf`. The `.jar` files `hadoop-core-1.1.2.jar` and `hadoop-tools-1.1.2.jar` contain the core classes of Hadoop. The files `hadoop-examples-1.1.2.jar` and `hadoop-test-1.1.2.jar` contain sample MapReduce jobs.

The `conf` folder contains cluster configuration files, the `bin` folder contains commands and scripts to start and stop a cluster, and the `sbin` folder contains scripts to perform specific tasks.

3. Make a soft link for Hadoop root directory:

```
sudo ln -s hadoop-1.1.2 hadoop
```

4. Use your favorite text editor to open the file `~/.bashrc` and add the following contents:

```
export JAVA_HOME=/usr/java/latest
export HADOOP_HOME=/usr/local/hadoop
export PATH=$PATH:$JAVA_HOME/bin:HADOOP_HOME/bin
```

We are assuming Oracle Java has been installed under the `/usr/java/latest` directory.

5. Reload the configuration file `~/.bashrc` with the following command:

```
. ~/.bashrc
```

6. Use your favorite text editor to open the file `$HADOOP_HOME/conf/hadoop-env.sh`, and change the `JAVA_HOME` environment variable to the following:

```
export JAVA_HOME=/usr/Java/latest
```

7. Use your favorite text editor to open the file $HADOOP_HOME/conf/core-site.xml, and add the following content:

```
<configuration>
  <property>
    <name>fs.default.name</name>
    <value>hdfs://localhost:54310</value>
  </property>

  <property>
    <name>mapred.job.tracker</name>
    <value>localhost:54311</value>
  </property>

  <property>
    <name>hadoop.tmp.dir</name>
    <value>/hadoop/tmp/</value>
  </property>
</configuration>
```

8. Use your favorite text editor to open the file $HADOOP_HOME/conf/hdfs-site.xml, and add the following content to the file:

```
<configuration>
  <property>
    <name>dfs.replication</name>
    <value>2</value>
  </property>

  <property>
    <name>dfs.data.dir</name>
    <value>/hadoop/data/</value>
  </property>
</configuration>
```

9. Use your favorite text editor to open the file $HADOOP_HOME/conf/mapred-site.xml, and add the following content:

```
<configuration>
  <property>
    <name>mapred.system.dir</name>
    <value>/hadoop/mapred</value>
  </property>
</configuration>
```

10. Ask `localhost` to run the SecondaryNameNode daemon with the following command:

    ```
    sudo echo "localhost" > $HADOOP_HOME/conf/masters
    ```

11. Configure `localhost` as the single slave node with the following command:

    ```
    sudo echo "localhost" > $HADOOP_HOME/conf/slaves
    ```

Use the following steps to start and stop a Hadoop cluster:

1. Format the HDFS filesystem from NameNode with the following command:

   ```
   hadoop namenode -format
   ```

   We will get output similar to the following:

   ```
   13/02/14 01:43:12 INFO namenode.NameNode: STARTUP_MSG:
   /************************************************************
   STARTUP_MSG: Starting NameNode
   STARTUP_MSG:   host = localhost/127.0.0.1
   STARTUP_MSG:   args = [-format]
   STARTUP_MSG:   version = 1.1.2
   STARTUP_MSG:   build = https://svn.apache.org/repos/asf/hadoop/
   common/branches/branch-1.0 -r 1393290; compiled by 'hortonfo' on
   Wed Oct  3 05:13:58 UTC 2012
   ************************************************************/
   13/02/14 01:43:13 INFO util.GSet: VM type        = 64-bit
   13/02/14 01:43:13 INFO util.GSet: 2% max memory = 17.77875 MB
   13/02/14 01:43:13 INFO util.GSet: capacity       = 2^21 = 2097152
   entries
   13/02/14 01:43:13 INFO util.GSet: recommended=2097152,
   actual=2097152
   13/02/14 01:43:13 INFO namenode.FSNamesystem: fsOwner=shumin
   13/02/14 01:43:13 INFO namenode.FSNamesystem:
   supergroup=supergroup
   13/02/14 01:43:13 INFO namenode.FSNamesystem:
   isPermissionEnabled=true
   13/02/14 01:43:13 INFO namenode.FSNamesystem: dfs.block.
   invalidate.limit=100
   13/02/14 01:43:13 INFO namenode.FSNamesystem:
   isAccessTokenEnabled=false accessKeyUpdateInterval=0 min(s),
   accessTokenLifetime=0 min(s)
   ```

```
13/02/14 01:43:13 INFO namenode.NameNode: Caching file names
occuring more than 10 times

13/02/14 01:43:13 INFO common.Storage: Image file of size 112
saved in 0 seconds.

13/02/14 01:43:14 INFO common.Storage: Storage directory /hadoop/
tmp/dfs/name has been successfully formatted.

13/02/14 01:43:14 INFO namenode.NameNode: SHUTDOWN_MSG:

/***********************************************************

SHUTDOWN_MSG: Shutting down NameNode at localhost/127.0.0.1

***********************************************************/
```

2. Start the HDFS daemons with the following command:

    `start-dfs.sh`

    We will get output similar to the following:

    ```
    starting namenode, logging to /usr/local/hadoop/libexec/../logs/
    hadoop-hduser-namenode-localhost.out

    localhost: starting datanode, logging to /usr/local/hadoop/Hadoop/
    libexec/../logs/hadoop-hduser-datanode-localhost.out

    localhost: starting secondarynamenode, logging to /usr/local/
    hadoop/libexec/../logs/hadoop-hduser-secondarynamenode-localhost.
    out
    ```

     The output shows that the following HDFS daemons have been started: NameNode, DataNode, and SecondaryNameNode.

3. Start the MapReduce daemons with the following command:

    `start-mapred.sh`

    The output will be similar to the following:

    ```
    starting jobtracker, logging to /usr/local/hadoop/libexec/../logs/
    hadoop-hduser-jobtracker-localhost.out

    localhost: starting tasktracker, logging to /usr/local/hadoop/
    libexec/../logs/hadoop-hduser-tasktracker-localhost.out
    ```

     The output shows that the JobTracker and TaskTracker MapReduce daemons have been started.

4. With the `jps` command, we can get a list of all running daemons as follows:

   ```
   10984 SecondaryNameNode
   11272 TaskTracker
   11144 JobTracker
   26966 NameNode
   10855 DataNode
   27183 Jps
   ```

>  So far, all the Hadoop daemons have been started.

5. Stop the MapReduce daemons with the following command:

   stop-mapred.sh

6. Stop the HDFS daemons with the following command:

   stop-hdfs.sh

How it works...

Under Unix-like operating systems, system runtime configurations and environment variables are specified via plain text files. These files are called run configuration files, meaning that they provide configurations when the program runs. For example, the `.bashrc` file under a user's home directory is the run configuration file for bash shell. It will be sourced (loaded) automatically every time when a bash terminal is opened. So, in this file, we can specify commands and environment variables for a running bash environment.

> **.bashrc OR .bash_profile**
>
> 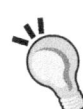 Under Linux, the bash shell has two run configuration files for a user, `.bashrc` and `.bash_profile`. The difference between the two files is that `.bash_profile` is executed for login shells, while `.bashrc` is for interactive, non-login shells. More specifically, when we log in to the system by entering username and password either locally or from a remote machine, `.bash_profile` will be executed, and a bash shell process is initialized. On the other hand, if we open a new bash terminal after logging into a machine or type the `bash` command from command line, the `.bashrc` file will be used for initialization before we see the command prompt on the terminal window. In this recipe, we used the `.bashrc` file, so that new configurations will be available after opening a new bash process. Alternatively, we can manually source a configuration file after it is created or changed with the `source` command.

The following table shows configuration files for configuring a Hadoop cluster in pseudo-distributed mode:

File	Description
`hadoop-env.sh`	Configures the environment variable used by Hadoop
`core-site.xml`	Configures parameters for the whole Hadoop cluster
`hdfs-site.xml`	Configures parameters for HDFS and its clients
`mapred-site.xml`	Configures parameters for MapReduce and its clients
`masters`	Configures host machines for SecondaryNameNode
`slaves`	Configures a list of slave node hosts

The following list explains the configuration files:

- `hadoop-env.sh` specifies environment variables for running Hadoop. For example, the home directory of Java installation `JAVA_HOME`, those related to Hadoop runtime options and cluster logging, and so on.

- `core-site.xml` specifies the URI of HDFS NameNode and MapReduce JobTracker. The `hdfs://localhost:54310` value of the `fs.default.name` property specifies the location of the default filesystem as HDFS on `localhost` using port `54310`. We can specify other filesystem schemes such as a local filesystem with `file:///home/hduser/hadoop`, Amazon web service S3 with `s3://a-bucket/hadoop`, and so on. The `localhost:54311` value of the `mapred.job.tracker` property specifies the URI of the cluster's JobTracker.

- `hdfs-site.xml` specifies the HDFS-related configurations. For example, `dfs.replication` configures the replication factor of data blocks on HDFS. For example, the value 2 specifies that each data block will be replicated twice on the filesystem. The `dfs.data.dir` property specifies the location of the data directory on the host Linux filesystem.

- `mapred-site.xml` specifies configurations for the MapReduce framework. For example, we can configure the total number of the `jvm` tasks, the number of the `map` slots, and reduce slots on a slave node, reduce the amount of memory for each task, and so on.

- The `masters` file specifies hosts that will run a SecondaryNameNode daemon. In our single node configuration, we put `localhost` in this file. A SecondaryNameNode daemon will be started on `localhost`, which has been verified with the `jps` command.

- The `slaves` file specifies slave nodes that run tasks controlled by task trackers. In our pseudo-distributed mode configuration, `localhost` is the only slave node in the cluster.

Hadoop provides a number of bash scripts for convenience of starting and stopping a cluster. The following table shows these scripts:

Script	Description
`start-dfs.sh`	This is the script to start HDFS daemons, including NameNode, SecondaryNameNode, and DataNode. A PID file will be created for each daemon process under the default folder `${hadoop.tmp.dir}`. For example, if the user `hduser` is used to run the script, the `/hadoop/tmp/hadoop-hduser-namenode.pid` file will be created for the NameNode daemon process.
`stop-dfs.sh`	This is the script to stop HDFS daemons. This command will try to find the PID files of the HDFS daemons, and kill the processes with the PID files. So, if the PID file is missing, this script will not work.
`start-mapred.sh`	This is the script to start MapReduce daemons, including the JobTracker and TaskTracker daemons. Similar to `start-hdfs.sh` script, PID files will be created for each daemon process.
`stop-mapred.sh`	This is the script to stop Hadoop MapReduce daemons. Similar to `stop-dfs.sh` script, the script will try to find the PID files and then kill those processes.
`start-all.sh`	It is equal to `start-dfs.sh` plus `start-mapred.sh`.
`stop-all.sh`	It is equal to `stop-dfs.sh` plus `stop-mapred.sh`.

There's more...

Currently, Hadoop is also available in the `rpm` format. So, we can use the following command to install Hadoop:

```
sudo rpm -ivh http://www.poolsaboveground.com/apache/hadoop/common/
stable/hadoop-1.1.2-1.x86_64.rpm
```

The locations of installed files will be different from the tarball method, and we can check the file layout with the following command:

```
rpm -ql hadoop
```

Then we can use the following command to configure a Hadoop cluster in single node:

```
sudo hadoop-setup-single-node.sh
```

See also

▶ The *Configuring Hadoop in fully distributed mode* recipe in *Chapter 3, Configuring a Hadoop Cluster*

▶ The *Validating Hadoop installation* recipe in *Chapter 3, Configuring a Hadoop Cluster*

Configuring Hadoop in fully-distributed mode

To configure a Hadoop cluster in **fully-distributed mode**, we need to configure all the master and slave machines. Although different from the pseudo-distributed mode, the configuration experience will be similar. In this recipe, we will outline steps to configure Hadoop in fully-distributed mode.

Getting ready

In this book, we propose to configure a Hadoop cluster with one master node and five slave nodes. The hostname of the `master` node is `1` and the hostnames of the slave nodes are `slave1`, `slave2`, `slave3`, `slave4`, and `slave5`.

Before getting started, we assume that Linux has been installed on all the cluster nodes and we should validate password-less login with the following commands on the master node:

```
ssh hduser@slave1
ssh hduser@slave2
...
```

> Unlike the pseudo-distributed mode, configuring a Hadoop cluster in fully-distributed mode requires the successful configuration of all the nodes in the cluster. Otherwise, the cluster will not work as expected.
>
> We should be cautious about the interconnection of the cluster nodes. Connection problems might be caused by configurations of firewalls, network, and so on.

Assuming the `$HADOOP_HOME/conf/slaves` file contains hostnames of the slave nodes, we can use the following command to check the password-less login to all slave nodes from the master node:

```
for host in 'cat $HADOOP_HOME/conf/slaves'; do
  echo 'Testing ssh from master to node ' $host
  ssh hduser@$host
done
```

How to do it...

Use the following recipe to configure Hadoop in fully-distributed mode:

1. Log in to the master node from the administrator machine with the following command:
    ```
    ssh hduser@master
    ```

2. Copy the Hadoop archive to the /usr/local directory:

```
sudo cp hadoop-1.1.2.tar.gz /usr/local
```

3. Decompress the Hadoop archive:

```
cd /usr/local
sudo tar xvf hadoop-1.1.2.tar.gz
```

4. Make a proper soft link for Hadoop root directory:

```
sudo ln -s hadoop-1.1.2 hadoop
```

5. Use your favorite text editor to open the ~/.bashrc file, and add the following content:

```
export JAVA_HOME=/usr/java/latest
export HADOOP_HOME=/usr/local/Hadoop
export PATH=$PATH:$JAVA_HOME/bin:HADOOP_HOME/bin
```

6. Open the $HADOOP_HOME/conf/hadoop-env.sh file with your favorite text editor and add the following content:

```
export JAVA_HOME=/usr/java/latest
```

7. Open the $HADOOP_HOME/conf/core-site.xml file with your favorite text editor and add the following content:

```
<configuration>
  <property>
    <name>fs.default.name</name>
    <value>hdfs://master:54310</value>
  </property>

  <property>
    <name>mapred.job.tracker</name>
    <value>master:54311</value>
  </property>
</configuration>
```

8. Open the $HADOOP_HOME/conf/hdfs-site.xml file with your favorite text editor and add the following content into the file:

```
<configuration>
  <property>
    <name>dfs.replication</name>
    <value>2</value>
  </property>

  <property>
    <name>dfs.data.dir</name>
```

```
        <value>/hadoop/data/</value>
    </property>

    <property>
        <name>hadoop.tmp.dir</name>
        <value>/hadoop/tmp/</value>
    </property>
</configuration>
```

9. Open the $HADOOP_HOME/conf/mapred-site.xml file with your favorite text editor and add the following content:

```
<configuration>
    <property>
        <name>mapred.tasktracker.map.tasks.maximum</name>
        <value>6</value>
    </property>

    <property>
        <name>mapred.tasktracker.reduce.tasks.maximum</name>
        <value>6</value>
    </property>

    <property>
        <name>mapred.map.child.java.opts</name>
        <value>-Xmx512m</value>
    </property>

    <property>
        <name>mapred.reduce.child.java.opts</name>
        <value>-Xmx512m</value>
    </property>

</configuration>
```

10. Configure the $HADOOP_HOME/conf/masters file with the following command:

```
sudo echo "master" > $HADOOP_HOME/conf/masters
```

This will configure the master node to run SecondaryNameNode.

11. Open the $HADOOP_HOME/conf/slaves file with your favorite text editor and add all the slave node hostnames into the file similar to the following:

```
slave1

slave2

slave3

...
```

12. Copy the configured Hadoop directory to all the slave nodes with the following command:

```
for host in 'cat $HADOOP_HOME/conf/slaves
    do
    echo 'Configuring hadoop on slave node ' $host
    sudo scp -r /usr/local/hadoop-1.1.2 hduser@$host:/usr/local/
    echo 'Making symbolic link for Hadoop home directory on host '
$host
    sudo ssh hduser@$host -C "ln -s /usr/local/hadoop-1.1.2 /usr/
local/hadoop"
    done
```

> The for-loop command will recursively copy the /usr/local/
> hadoop-1.1.2 directory to each node specified in the $HADOOP_HOME/
> conf/slaves file, and a symbolic link is made on each node for the Hadoop
> directory. We can get the following output information:
>
> ```
> Configuring hadoop on slave node slave1
> Making symbolic link for Hadoop home directory on host
> host slave1
> Configuring hadoop on slave node slave2
> Making symbolic link for Hadoop home directory on host
> host slave2
> Configuring hadoop on slave node slave3
> Making symbolic link for Hadoop home directory on host
> host slave3
> Configuring hadoop on slave node slave4
> Making symbolic link for Hadoop home directory on host
> host slave4
> ...
> ```

13. Copy the bash configuration file to each slave node with the following command:

```
for host in cat $HADOOP_HOME/conf/slaves; do
    echo 'Copying local bash run configuration file to host ' $host
    sudo cp ~/.bashrc $host:~/
    done
```

The `for-loop` command copies the bash run configuration file from the master node to all the slave nodes in the cluster. We can get the following output message:

```
Copying local bash run configuration file to host slave1
Copying local bash run configuration file to host slave2
Copying local bash run configuration file to host slave3
...
```

Use the following recipe to start a Hadoop cluster:

1. Format the HDFS filesystem on the master node with the following command:

```
hadoop namenode -format
```

If this is the first time to format the HDFS, the command should finish automatically. If you are reformatting an existing filesystem, it will ask you for permission to format the filesystem. For example, the output information will contain a message similar to the following:

```
Re-format filesystem in /tmp/hadoop-shumin/dfs/name ?
(Y or N)
```

In such a case, we need to press *Y* to confirm the reformatting of the filesystem. Be cautious that all the data will be wiped out after you hit the *Enter* key.

2. Check the directory structure of the formatted NameNode with the following command:

```
tree /hadoop/dfs/
```

The output will be similar to the following:

```
/hadoop/dfs/
└── name
    ├── current
    │   ├── edits
    │   ├── fsimage
    │   ├── fstime
    │   └── VERSION
    └── image
        └── fsimage


3 directories, 5 files
```

The tree listing shows the directory structure of a formatted HDFS filesystem which contains the filesystem `image` (in the `/hadoop/dfs/name/image` directory) and the current live `image` (mirrored to the `/hadoop/dfs/name/current` folder) in the main memory.

3. Start HDFS cluster daemons with the following command:

```
start-dfs.sh
```

We will get output similar to the following:

```
starting namenode, logging to /usr/local/hadoop/logs/hadoop-hdu
ser-namenode-master.out
```

```
slave1: starting datanode, logging to /usr/local/hadoop/logs/h
adoop-hduser-datanode-sslave1.out
```

```
slave2: starting datanode, logging to /usr/local/hadoop/logs/
hadoop-hduser-datanode-slave2.out
```

```
slave3: starting datanode, logging to /usr/local/hadoop/logs/
hadoop-hduser-datanode-slave3.out
```

```
slave4: starting datanode, logging to /usr/local/hadoop/logs/
hadoop-hduser-datanode-slave4.out
```

```
slave5: starting datanode, logging to /usr/local/hadoop/logs/
hadoop-hduser-datanode-slave5.out
```

```
master: starting secondarynamenode, logging to /usr/local/hadoop/
logs/hadoop-hduser-secondarynamenode-hadoop-master.out
```

 The output message shows that NameNode and SecondaryNameNode daemons are started on the master node, and a DataNode daemon is started on each slave node.

4. Start the MapReduce cluster daemons with the following command:

```
start-mapred.sh
```

The output will be similar to the following:

```
starting jobtracker, logging to /usr/local/hadoop/logs/hadoop-
hduser-jobtracker-master.out
```

```
slave1: starting tasktracker, logging to /usr/local/Hadoop/logs/
hadoop-hduser-tasktracker-slave1.out
```

```
slave2: starting tasktracker, logging to /usr/local/Hadoop/logs/
hadoop-hduser-tasktracker-slave2.out
```

```
slave3: starting tasktracker, logging to /usr/local/Hadoop/logs/
hadoop-hduser-tasktracker-slave3.out
```

```
slave4: starting tasktracker, logging to /usr/local/Hadoop/logs/
hadoop-hduser-tasktracker-slave4.out

slave5: starting tasktracker, logging to /usr/local/Hadoop/logs/
hadoop-hduser-tasktracker-slave5.out
```

 The output message shows that a JobTracker daemon is started on the master node and a TaskTracker daemon is started on each slave node.

5. On the master node, check the status of the Hadoop daemons with the following command:

    `jps`

    The output will be similar to the following:

    ```
    19512 NameNode
    19930 JobTracker
    19708 SecondaryNameNode
    20276 Jps
    ```

6. On a slave node, we can check the status of the daemon processes with the same command, and the output will be similar to the following:

    ```
    3949 Jps
    3639 TaskTracker
    3501 DataNode
    ```

 The highlighted daemons in the previous two steps must be present. Otherwise there will be configuration problems. You can review the recipe *Validating Hadoop installation* for troubleshooting and debugging suggestions.

7. List all the available TaskTrackers with the following command:

    `hadoop job -list-active-trackers`

    The output message will be similar to the following:

    ```
    tracker_slave1:slave1/10.0.0.2:38615
    tracker_slave2:slave2/10.0.0.3:39618
    tracker_slave3:slave3/10.0.0.4:48228
    tracker_slave4:slave4/10.0.0.5:42954
    tracker_slave5:slave5/10.0.0.6:43858
    ```

8. Check the status of each node in the HDFS cluster with the following command:

    ```
    hadoop dfsadmin -report
    ```

    The output message will be similar to the following:

    ```
    Configured Capacity: 13500319031296 (12.28 TB)
    Present Capacity: 12015141961728 (10.93 TB)
    DFS Remaining: 4067084627968 (3.7 TB)
    DFS Used: 7948057333760 (7.23 TB)
    DFS Used%: 66.15%
    Under replicated blocks: 0
    Blocks with corrupt replicas: 0
    Missing blocks: 0


    -------------------------------------------------

    Datanodes available: 5 (5 total, 0 dead)


    Name: 192.168.1.14:50010
    Decommission Status : Normal
    Configured Capacity: 964306395136 (898.08 GB)
    DFS Used: 590553788416 (550 GB)
    Non DFS Used: 97300185088 (90.62 GB)
    DFS Remaining: 276452421632(257.47 GB)
    DFS Used%: 61.24%
    DFS Remaining%: 28.67%
    Last contact: Sat Feb 16 00:34:17 EST 2013


    ...


    Name: 192.168.1.17:50010
    Decommission Status : Normal
    Configured Capacity: 964262363136 (898.04 GB)
    DFS Used: 617057673216 (574.68 GB)
    Non DFS Used: 81531011072 (75.93 GB)
    DFS Remaining: 265673678848(247.43 GB)
    DFS Used%: 63.99%
    DFS Remaining%: 27.55%
    Last contact: Sat Feb 16 00:34:15 EST 2013
    ```

> The output shows that there are 5 DataNodes in the cluster, and the status of each DataNode such as capacity and percentage of usage is reported.

Use the following two steps to stop a running Hadoop cluster:

1. Stop the MapReduce daemons with the following command on the master node:

   `stop-mapred.sh`

   We will get an output message similar to the following:

   ```
   stopping jobtracker
   slave3: stopping tasktracker
   slave2: stopping tasktracker
   slave5: stopping tasktracker
   slave4: stopping tasktracker
   slave1: stopping tasktracker
   ```

> The output shows that the JobTracker daemon on the master node and TaskTracker daemons on the slave nodes are being stopped.

2. Stop the HDFS daemons with the following command on the master node:

   `stop-dfs.sh`

   The output message will be similar to the following:

   ```
   stopping namenode
   slave3: stopping datanode
   slave4: stopping datanode
   slave2: stopping datanode
   slave1: stopping datanode
   slave5: stopping datanode
   localhost: stopping secondarynamenode
   ```

> The output shows that the NameNode and SecondaryNameNode daemons on the master node and the DataNode daemons on the slave nodes are being stopped.

How it works...

The following table shows the properties used in this recipe:

Property	Description
`fs.default.name`	The URI of the default filesystem.
`mapred.job.tracker`	The URI of the JobTracker, for example, `localhost:54310`.
`dfs.replication`	Specifies how many nodes a block should be replicated to. The default value of this property is 3.
`dfs.data.dir`	The local storage directory of data blocks on DataNodes.
`hadoop.tmp.dir`	A base directory for a number of other directories.
`mapred.tasktracker.map.tasks.maximum`	Max number of parallel map tasks that a TaskTracker daemon can run.
`mapred.tasktracker.reduce.tasks.maximum`	Max number of parallel reduce tasks that a TaskTracker daemon can run.
`mapred.map.child.java.opts`	The Java options for the `map` task child processes.
`mapred.reduce.child.java.opts`	The Java options for the reduce task child processes.

There's more...

Alternatively, we can use the following steps to configure a fully-distributed Hadoop cluster:

1. Download Hadoop `rpm` package on the administrator machine with the following command:

   ```
   wget http://www.poolsaboveground.com/apache/hadoop/common/stable/
   hadoop-1.1.2-1.x86_64.rpm -P ~/repo
   ```

2. Log in to the master node with the following command:

   ```
   ssh hduser@master
   ```

3. Use the following commands to install Hadoop on all nodes:

```
for host in master slave1 slave2 slave3 slave4 slave5; do
    echo 'Installing Hadoop on node: ' $host
    sudo rpm -ivh ftp://hadoop.admin/repo/hadoop-1.1.2-1.x86_64.rpm
done
```

4. Configure the Hadoop cluster by modifying the configuration files located in the `/etc/hadoop` folder.

See also

▶ The *Configuring Hadoop in pseudo-distributed mode* recipe in *Chapter 3, Configuring a Hadoop Cluster*

▶ The *Validating Hadoop installation* recipe in *Chapter 3, Configuring a Hadoop cluster*

Validating Hadoop installation

The configuration of a Hadoop cluster is not done before the validation step. Validation plays an important role in the configuration of a Hadoop cluster; for example, it can help us figure out configuration problems.

The most straightforward way to validate a Hadoop cluster configuration is to run a MapReduce job from the master node. Alternatively, there are two methods to validate the cluster configuration. One is from web interface and the other is from the command line. In this recipe, we will list steps to validate the configuration of a Hadoop cluster.

Getting ready

To validate the configuration from the web interface, a web browser such as Firefox or Google Chrome is needed. Sometimes if a GUI web browser is not available, we can use a command line based web browser such as `elinks` and `lynx`. In this book, we assume to use `elinks` for illustration purpose.

We assume that `elinks` has been installed with the following command:

```
sudo yum install elinks
```

Start all the Hadoop daemons with the following commands:

```
start-dfs.sh
```

```
start-mapred.sh
```

How to do it...

Use the following steps to run a MapReduce job:

1. Log in to the master node with the following command:

   ssh hduser@master

2. Run a sample MapReduce job with the following command:

   hadoop jar $HADOOP_HOME/hadoop-examples*.jar pi 20 100000

> In this command, hadoop-examples*jar is a .jar file that
> contains a few sample MapReduce jobs such as pi. Option 20
> is the number of tasks to run and 100000 specifies the size of
> the sample for each task.
>
> If this job finishes without any problem, we can say that the
> Hadoop cluster is working. But this is not enough, because we
> also need to make sure all the slave nodes are available for
> running tasks.

Use the following steps to validate Hadoop cluster configuration through a web user interface:

1. Open the master:50030/jobtracker.jsp URL with a web browser. The web
   page will be similar to the following screenshot:

   ### master Hadoop Map/Reduce Administration

   State: RUNNING
   Started: Sat Feb 16 02:19:09 EST 2013
   Version: 1.1.1, r1411108
   Compiled: Mon Nov 19 10:48:11 UTC 2012 by hortonfo
   Identifier: 201302160219
   SafeMode: OFF

   #### Cluster Summary (Heap Size is 56.75 MB/1.89 GB)

Running Map Tasks	Running Reduce Tasks	Total Submissions	Nodes	Occupied Map Slots
0	0	0	5	0

   #### Scheduling Information

Queue Name	State	Scheduling Information
default	running	N/A

   Filter (Jobid, Priority, User, Name)
   Example: 'user:smith 3200' will filter by 'smith' only in the user field and '3200' in all fields

   #### Running Jobs

   #### Retired Jobs

   #### Local Logs

   Log directory, Job Tracker History

   This is Apache Hadoop release 1.1.1

2. Check the status of each slave node by clicking on the link, which leads us to a web page similar to the following screenshot:

master Hadoop Machine List

Active Task Trackers

							Task Trackers									
Name	Host	# running tasks	Max Map Tasks	Max Reduce Tasks	Task Failures	Directory Failures	Node Health Status	Seconds Since Node Last Healthy	Total Tasks Since Start	Succeeded Tasks Since Start	Total Tasks Last Day	Succeeded Tasks Last Day	Total Tasks Last Hour	Succeeded Tasks Last Hour	Seconds since heartbeat
tracker_slave1:localhost/127.0.0.1:53431	slave1	0	6	6	0	0	N/A	0	0	0	0	0	0	0	0
tracker_slave4:localhost/127.0.0.1:52644	slave4	0	6	6	0	0	N/A	0	0	0	0	0	0	0	0
tracker_slave3:localhost/127.0.0.1:37775	slave3	0	6	6	0	0	N/A	0	0	0	0	0	0	0	0
tracker_slave2:localhost/127.0.0.1:56074	slave2	0	6	6	0	0	N/A	0	0	0	0	0	0	0	0
tracker_slave5:localhost/127.0.0.1:43541	slave5	0	6	6	0	0	N/A	0	0	0	0	0	0	0	0

This is Apache Hadoop release 1.1.1

From this screenshot, we can easily check the status of the active TaskTrackers on the slave nodes. For example, we can see the count of failed tasks, the number of MapReduce slots, the heart beat seconds, and so on.

3. Check the status of slave DataNodes by opening the `master:50070` URL. The web page will be similar to the following screenshot:

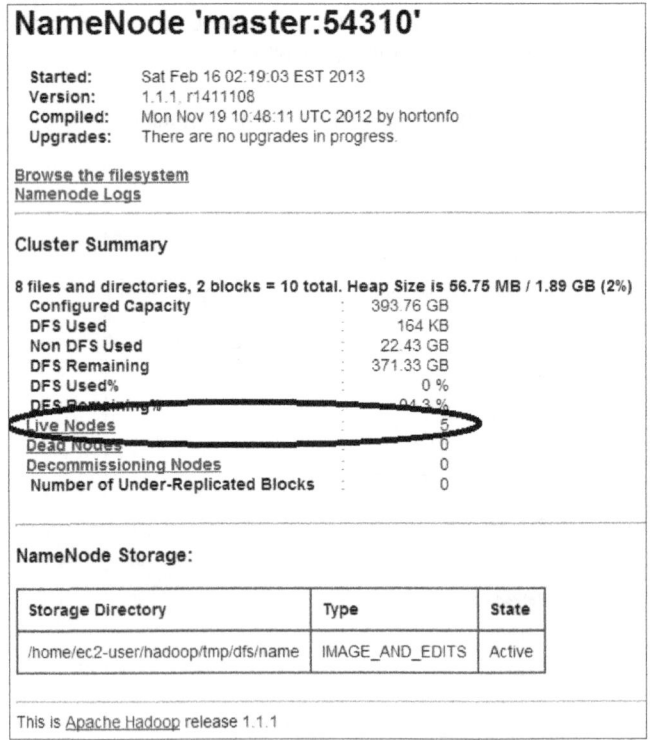

NameNode 'master:54310'

Started: Sat Feb 16 02:19:03 EST 2013
Version: 1.1.1, r1411108
Compiled: Mon Nov 19 10:48:11 UTC 2012 by hortonfo
Upgrades: There are no upgrades in progress.

Browse the filesystem
Namenode Logs

Cluster Summary

8 files and directories, 2 blocks = 10 total. Heap Size is 56.75 MB / 1.89 GB (2%)

Configured Capacity	:	393.76 GB
DFS Used	:	164 KB
Non DFS Used	:	22.43 GB
DFS Remaining	:	371.33 GB
DFS Used%	:	0 %
DFS Remaining%	:	94.3 %
Live Nodes	:	5
Dead Nodes	:	0
Decommissioning Nodes	:	0
Number of Under-Replicated Blocks	:	0

NameNode Storage:

Storage Directory	Type	State
/home/ec2-user/hadoop/tmp/dfs/name	IMAGE_AND_EDITS	Active

This is Apache Hadoop release 1.1.1

4. By clicking on the **Live Nodes** link we can see the details of each node as shown in the following screenshot:

NameNode 'master:54310'

Started: Sat Feb 16 02:19:03 EST 2013
Version: 1.1.1, r1411108
Compiled: Mon Nov 19 10:48:11 UTC 2012 by hortonfo
Upgrades: There are no upgrades in progress.

Browse the filesystem
Namenode Logs
Go back to DFS home

Live Datanodes : 5

Node	Last Contact	Admin State	Configured Capacity (GB)	Used (GB)	Non DFS Used (GB)	Remaining (GB)	Used (%)	Used (%)	Remaining (%)	Blocks
slave1	3	In Service	78.75	0.63	4.51	73.61	0.8		93.47	14
slave2	2	In Service	78.75	0.48	4.64	73.63	0.61		93.5	14
slave3	2	In Service	78.75	0.5	4.59	73.66	0.64		93.53	16
slave4	0	In Service	78.75	0.65	4.49	73.61	0.83		93.47	17
slave5	2	In Service	78.75	0.55	4.66	73.55	0.69		93.39	14

This is Apache Hadoop release 1.1.1

5. Run an example `teragen` job to generate 10 GB data on the HDFS with the following command:

```
hadoop jar $HADOOP_HOME/hadoop-examples-1.1.2.jar teragen
$((1024*1024*1024* 10/100)) teraout
```

In this command, `hadoop-examples-1.1.2.jar` is the Java archive file which provides a number of Hadoop examples. The option `$((1024*1024*1024* 10/100))` tells us how many lines of data will be generated with the total data size 10 GB.

6. When the job is running, we can check the status of the job by opening the following URL:

```
http://master:50030/jobdetails.jsp?jobid=job_201302160219_0003&
refresh=30
```

In this URL, `job_201302160219_0003` is the job ID and `refresh=30` tells how often the web page should be refreshed.

The job status web page will be similar to the following screenshot:

Hadoop job_201302160219_0003 on <u>master</u>

User: ec2-user
Job Name: TeraGen
Job File: <u>hdfs://master:54310/user/ec2-user/.staging/job_201302160219_0003/job.xml</u>
Submit Host: master
Submit Host Address: 10.144.150.104
Job-ACLs: All users are allowed
Job Setup: <u>Successful</u>
Status: Running
Started at: Sat Feb 16 02:46:33 EST 2013
Running for: 3mins, 32sec
Job Cleanup: Pending

Kind	% Complete	Num Tasks	Pending	Running	Complete	Killed	Failed/Killed Task Attempts
<u>map</u>	65.63%	12	0	<u>11</u>	<u>1</u>	0	0 / 0
<u>reduce</u>	0.00%	0	0	0	0	0	0 / 0

	Counter	Map	Reduce	Total
File Input Format Counters	Bytes Read	0	0	0
Job Counters	SLOTS_MILLIS_MAPS	0	0	210,672
	Launched map tasks	0	0	16
File Output Format Counters	Bytes Written	3,191,878,700	0	3,191,878,700
FileSystemCounters	HDFS_BYTES_READ	1,025	0	1,025
	FILE_BYTES_WRITTEN	289,682	0	289,682
	HDFS_BYTES_WRITTEN	3,567,423,770	0	3,567,423,770
Map-Reduce Framework	Map input records	35,674,895	0	35,674,895
	Physical memory (bytes) snapshot	881,270,784	0	881,270,784
	Spilled Records	0	0	0
	Total committed heap usage (bytes)	714,080,256	0	714,080,256
	CPU time spent (ms)	89,680	0	89,680
	Map input bytes	35,674,895	0	35,674,895
	Virtual memory (bytes) snapshot	23,136,190,464	0	23,136,190,464
	SPLIT_RAW_BYTES	1,025	0	1,025
	Map output records	35,674,887	0	35,674,887

Map Completion Graph - <u>close</u>

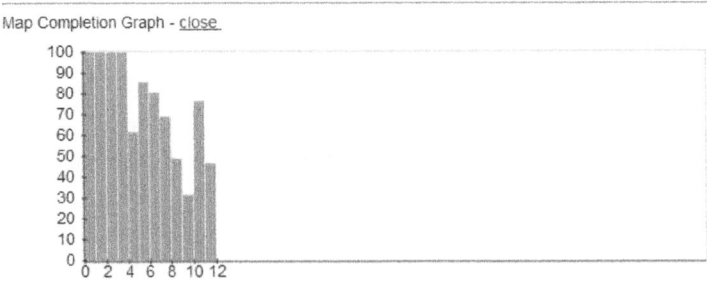

Go back to JobTracker

7. After the `teragen` job finishes, we can check the node storage space usage by opening the URL `http://master:50070/dfsnodelist.jsp?whatNodes=LIVE`. The web page will be similar to the following screenshot:

NameNode 'master:54310'

Started: Sat Feb 16 02:19:03 EST 2013
Version: 1.1.1, r1411108
Compiled: Mon Nov 19 10:48:11 UTC 2012 by hortonfo
Upgrades: There are no upgrades in progress

Browse the filesystem
Namenode Logs
Go back to DFS home

Live Datanodes : 5

Node	Last Contact	Admin State	Configured Capacity (GB)	Used (GB)	Non DFS Used (GB)	Remaining (GB)	Used (%)	Used (%)	Remaining (%)	Blocks
slave1	1	In Service	78.75	2.73	4.27	71.74	3.47		91.1	69
slave2	2	In Service	78.75	2.76	4.25	71.75	3.5		91.1	74
slave3	2	In Service	78.75	3.3	4.42	71.04	4.19		90.2	71
slave4	1	In Service	78.75	2.88	4.45	71.43	3.65		90.7	60
slave5	2	In Service	78.75	3.38	4.23	71.14	4.29		90.34	66

This is Apache Hadoop release 1.1.1

Sometimes, a command-line based web browser can be handier than a GUI browser. For example, we can use the `elinks master:50030` command to check the status of MapReduce on the master node and use the `elinks master:50070` command to check the status of HDFS.

Use the following steps to validate the configuration of a Hadoop cluster from command line:

1. List all available TaskTrackers with the following command:

   `hadoop job -list-active-trackers`

   Example output is similar to the following:

   ```
   tracker_slave1:localhost/127.0.0.1:53431
   tracker_slave4:localhost/127.0.0.1:52644
   tracker_slave3:localhost/127.0.0.1:37775
   tracker_slave2:localhost/127.0.0.1:56074
   tracker_slave5:localhost/127.0.0.1:43541
   ```

 The output confirms that all the configured TaskTrackers are active in the Hadoop cluster.

2. Check the status of the HDFS cluster with the following command:

   `hadoop fsck /`

The output will be similar to the following:

```
FSCK started by hduser from /10.0.0.1 for path / at Sat Feb 16
03:03:44 EST 2013
.............................Status: HEALTHY
 Total size:     7516316665 B
 Total dirs:     15
 Total files:    31
 Total blocks (validated):      125 (avg. block size 60130533 B)
 Minimally replicated blocks:   125 (100.0 %)
 Over-replicated blocks:        0 (0.0 %)
 Under-replicated blocks:       0 (0.0 %)
 Mis-replicated blocks:         0 (0.0 %)
 Default replication factor:    2
 Average block replication:     2.0
 Corrupt blocks:                0
 Missing replicas:              0 (0.0 %)
 Number of data-nodes:          5
 Number of racks:               1
FSCK ended at Sat Feb 16 03:03:44 EST 2013 in 12 milliseconds


The filesystem under path '/' is HEALTHY
```

 The output gives us the same information as from the web interface, and the last line tells us that the root filesystem is HEALTHY.

How it works...

Hadoop provides commands and web interfaces for system administrators to check the status of the cluster. When we start Hadoop daemons, a built-in web server will be started and a number of prewritten .jsp script files are used to respond to the user's requests from a web browser. The .jsp files can be found under the $HADOOP_HOME/webapps directory. If you have programming experience, you can take advantage of the .jsp files to develop personalized Hadoop cluster management tools.

There's more...

In this part, we list a few typical Hadoop configuration problems and give suggestions on dealing with these problems.

Can't start HDFS daemons

There are many possible reasons that can cause this problem. For example, the NameNode on the master node has not been formatted, in which case, we can format the HDFS before starting the cluster with the following command:

```
hadoop namenode -format
```

> **Warning!**
> Be cautious when formatting the filesystem with this command. It will erase all the data on the filesystem. Always try other methods before using this one.

More generically, to troubleshoot this problem, we need to check that HDFS has been properly configured and daemons are running. This can be done with the following command:

```
jps
```

> If the output of this command does not contain the NameNode and SecondaryNameNode daemons, we need to check the configuration of HDFS.

To troubleshoot the HDFS startup problem, we can open a new terminal and monitor the NameNode logfile on the master node with the following command:

```
tail -f $HADOOP_HOME/logs/hadoop-hduser-namenode-master.log
```

This command will show the content of the logfile in a dynamic way when a new log is appended to the file. If an error happens, we can get error messages similar to the following:

```
2013-02-16 11:44:29,860 ERROR org.apache.hadoop.hdfs.server.namenode.
NameNode: java.net.UnknownHostException: Invalid hostname for server:
master1
        at org.apache.hadoop.ipc.Server.bind(Server.java:236)
        at org.apache.hadoop.ipc.Server$Listener.<init>(Server.java:302)
        at org.apache.hadoop.ipc.Server.<init>(Server.java:1488)
        at org.apache.hadoop.ipc.RPC$Server.<init>(RPC.java:560)
        at org.apache.hadoop.ipc.RPC.getServer(RPC.java:521)
```

```
        at org.apache.hadoop.hdfs.server.namenode.NameNode.
initialize(NameNode.java:295)
        at org.apache.hadoop.hdfs.server.namenode.
NameNode.<init>(NameNode.java:529)
        at org.apache.hadoop.hdfs.server.namenode.NameNode.
createNameNode(NameNode.java:1403)
        at org.apache.hadoop.hdfs.server.namenode.NameNode.main(NameNode.
java:1412)


2013-02-16 11:44:29,865 INFO org.apache.hadoop.hdfs.server.namenode.
NameNode: SHUTDOWN_MSG:
/************************************************************
SHUTDOWN_MSG: Shutting down NameNode at master/10.144.150.104
************************************************************/
```

Alternatively, the following command will give the same error:

```
hadoop jobtracker
```

 The previous message shows that the hostname of the NameNode is wrong. It should be `master` instead of `master1`.

Cluster is missing slave nodes

Most likely, this problem is caused by hostname resolution. To confirm, we can check the content of the `/etc/hosts` file with the following command:

```
cat /etc/hosts
```

The output should be similar to the following:

```
10.0.0.1   master
10.0.0.2   slave1
10.0.0.3   slave2
10.0.0.4   slave3
10.0.0.5   slave4
10.0.0.6   slave5
```

 If the IP address and hostname mapping does not exist or has been erroneously specified in this file, correcting the error can solve this problem.

MapReduce daemons can't be started

The following two reasons can cause this problem:

> ▸ The HDFS daemons are not running, which can cause the MapReduce daemons to ping the NameNode daemon at a regular interval, which can be illustrated with the following log output:

```
13/02/16 11:32:19 INFO ipc.Client: Retrying connect to server:
master/10.0.0.1:54310. Already tried 0           time(s); retry
policy is RetryUpToMaximumCountWithFixedSleep(maxRetries=10,
sleepTime=1 SECONDS)

13/02/16 11:32:20 INFO ipc.Client: Retrying connect to server:
master/10.0.0.1:54310. Already tried 1 time(s); retry policy is
RetryUpToMaximumCountWithFixedSleep(maxRetries=10, sleepTime=1
SECONDS)

13/02/16 11:32:21 INFO ipc.Client: Retrying connect to server:
master/10.0.0.1:54310. Already tried 2 time(s); retry policy is
RetryUpToMaximumCountWithFixedSleep(maxRetries=10, sleepTime=1
SECONDS)

13/02/16 11:32:22 INFO ipc.Client: Retrying connect to server:
master/10.0.0.1:54310. Already tried 3 time(s); retry policy is
RetryUpToMaximumCountWithFixedSleep(maxRetries=10, sleepTime=1
SECONDS)

13/02/16 11:32:23 INFO ipc.Client: Retrying connect to server:
master/10.0.0.1:54310. Already tried 4 time(s); retry policy is
RetryUpToMaximumCountWithFixedSleep(maxRetries=10, sleepTime=1
SECONDS).
```

 To troubleshoot this problem, we can refer to tips from the *Can't start HDFS daemons* section.

> ▸ Configuration problems of MapReduce can cause the `MapReduce daemons can't be started` problem. Recall that we have configurations for the number of the `map` slots and reduce slots as well as the amount of memory in the `$HADOOP_HOME/conf/mapred-site.xml` file. Before starting a cluster, we need to make sure that the total amount of configured memory should be smaller than the total amount of system memory.

For example, suppose a slave host has 4 GB of memory, and we have configured six map slots, and six reduce slots with 512 MB of memory for each slot. So, we can compute the total configured task memory with the following formula:

6 x 512 + 6 x 512 = 6 GB

As 6 GB is larger than the system memory of 4 GB, the system will not start. To clear this problem, we can decrease the number of the map slots and reduce slots from six to three. This configuration gives us a total configured memory of 3 GB, which is smaller than the system total memory 4 GB, thus the MapReduce daemons should be able to start successfully.

See also

▶ The *Configuring Hadoop in pseudo-distributed mode* recipe in *Chapter 3, Configuring a Hadoop Cluster*

▶ The *Configuring Hadoop in fully-distributed mode* recipe in *Chapter 3, Configuring a Hadoop Cluster*

Configuring ZooKeeper

ZooKeeper provides highly reliable centralized service for maintaining configuration information, naming, and providing distributed synchronization and group services. In this recipe, we will outline steps to install ZooKeeper.

Getting ready

Make sure Hadoop has been properly configured. Please refer to the previous recipes in this chapter about installation of Hadoop on a cluster.

Log in to the master node from the Hadoop administrator machine as hduser with the following command:

```
ssh hduser@master
```

Download the ZooKeeper archive file with the following commands:

```
wget http://www.gtlib.gatech.edu/pub/apache/zookeeper/stable/zookeeper-3.4.5.tar.gz -P ~/repo
```

How to do it...

Use the following steps to configure ZooKeeper:

1. Log in to the master node with the following command:

   `ssh hduser@master`

2. Copy the downloaded archive to `/usr/local` with the following command:

   `sudo wget ftp://hadoop.admin/repo/zookeeper-3.4.5.tar.gz -P /usr/local`

3. Decompress the file with the following command:

   `cd /usr/local/`

   `sudo tar xvf zookeeper-3.4.5.tar.gz`

4. Create a symbolic link with the following command:

   `sudo ln -s /usr/local/zookeeper-3.4.5 /usr/local/zookeeper`

5. Open the `~/.bashrc` file and add the following lines:

   ```
   ZK_HOME=/usr/local/zookeeper
   export PATH=$ZK_HOME/bin:$PATH
   ```

6. Load the configuration file with the following command:

   `. ~/.bashrc`

7. Create data and log directories for ZooKeeper with the following command:

   `sudo mkdir -pv /hadoop/zookeeper/{data,log}`

8. Create Java configuration file `$ZK_HOME/conf/java.env` with the following content:

   ```
   JAVA_HOME=/usr/java/latest
   export PATH=$JAVA_HOME/bin:$PATH
   ```

 The filename `java.env` is mandatory. It will be loaded by ZooKeeper.

9. Create the `$ZK_HOME/conf/zookeeper.cfg` file and add the following lines to it:

   ```
   tickTime=2000
   clientPort=2181
   initLimit=5
   ```

```
syncLimit=2
server.1=master:2888:3888
server.2=slave1:2888:3888
server.3=slave2:2888:3888
server.4=slave3:2888:3888
server.5=slave4:2888:3888
server.6=slave5:2888:3888
dataDir=/hadoop/zookeeper/data
dataLogDir=/hadoop/zookeeper/log
```

> The highlighted section makes every node know the other nodes in the ZooKeeper ensemble.

10. Configure ZooKeeper on all slave nodes with the following command:

```
for host in cat $HADOOP_HOME/conf/slaves; do
  echo 'Configuring ZooKeeper on ' $host
  scp ~/.bashrc hduser@$host:~/
  sudo scp -r /usr/local/zookeeper-3.4.5 hduser@$host:/usr/local/
  echo 'Making symbolic link for ZooKeeper home directory on '
$host
  sudo ssh hduser@$host -C "ln -s /usr/local/zookeeper-3.4.5 /usr/
local/zookeeper"
done
```

11. Start ZooKeeper on master node with the following command:

```
zkServer.sh start
```

12. Verify ZooKeeper configuration with the following command:

```
zkCli.sh -server master:2181
```

13. Stop ZooKeeper with the following command:

```
zkServer.sh stop
```

See also

▶ The *Installing HBase* recipe in *Chapter 3, Configuring a Hadoop Cluster*

▶ Get more documentation about ZooKeeper from `http://zookeeper.apache.org/doc/r3.4.5/zookeeperAdmin.html`

Installing HBase

HBase is the database based on Hadoop. It is a distributed, scalable Big Data storage system. In this section, we are going to list steps about installing HBase in our Hadoop cluster.

Getting ready

To install HBase, we assume that Hadoop has been configured without any issues.

Download HBase from a mirror site. Similar to downloading Hadoop, HBase is hosted on mirrors all over the world. Visit the link `http://www.apache.org/dyn/closer.cgi/hbase/`, and select the nearest mirror (the suggested mirror on the top is the optimal choice). After selecting the mirror, follow the link to select the HBase version; we suggest the stable version. For example, follow the link `http://mirror.quintex.com/apache/hbase/stable/` and you can see the downloadable files as shown in the following screenshot:

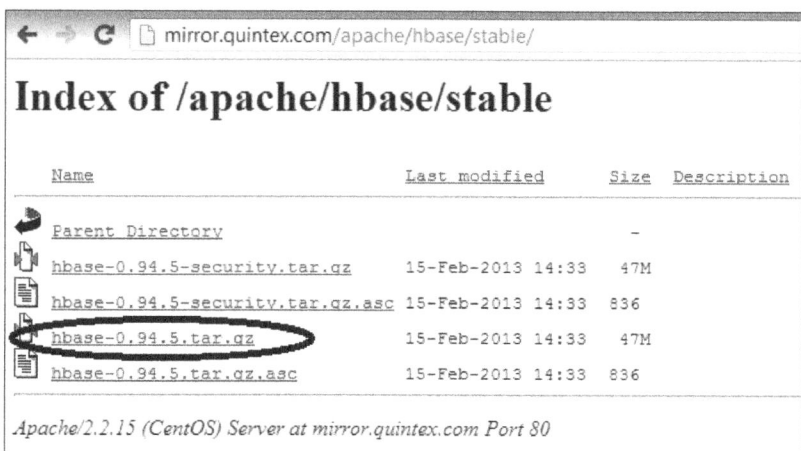

Click on the file link `hbase-0.94.5.tar.gz` to download the file to the administrator machine. Then, copy the file to the FTP repository with the following command:

```
cp hbase-0.94.5.tar.gz ~/repo
```

Alternatively, we can download the file with the following command:

```
wget http://mirror.quintex.com/apache/hbase/stable/hbase-0.94.5.tar.gz -P ~/repo
```

How to do it...

Use the following recipe to install HBase:

1. Log in to the master node from the administrator machine with the following command:

    ```
    ssh hduser@master
    ```

2. Decompress the HBase archive with the following commands:

    ```
    cd /usr/local
    sudo wget ftp://hadoop.admin/repo/hbase-0.94.5.tar.gz -P /usr/
    local
    sudo tar xvf hbase-0.94.5.tar.gz
    ```

3. Create a symbolic link with the following command:

    ```
    ln -s hbase-0.94.5 hbase
    ```

4. Use your favorite text editor to open the ~/.bashrc file and append the following lines into the file:

    ```
    export HBASE_HOME=/usr/local/hbase
    export PATH=$HBASE_HOME/bin:$PATH
    ```

5. Open the $HBASE_HOME/conf/hbase-env.sh file and set JAVA_HOME as:

    ```
    export JAVA_HOME=/usr/java/latest
    ```

6. Open the $HBASE_HOME/conf/hbase-site.xml file with your favorite text editor and add the following contents to the file:

    ```xml
    <?xml version="1.0"?>
    <?xml-stylesheet type="text/xsl" href="configuration.xsl"?>
    <configuration>
      <property>
        <name>hbase.rootdir</name>
        <value>hdfs://master:54310/hbase</value>
      </property>

      <property>
        <name>hbase.cluster.distributed</name>
        <value>true</value>
      </property>

      <property>
        <name>hbase.tmp.dir</name>
        <value>/hadoop/hbase</value>
      </property>
    ```

```
<property>
  <name>hbase.ZooKeeper.quorum</name>
  <value>master</value>
</property>

<property>
  <name>hbase.zookeeper.property.dataDir</name>
  <value>/hadoop/zookeeper</value>
</property>
</configuration>
```

7. Open the `$HBASE_HOME/conf/regionservers` file and add the following lines:

```
slave1
slave2
slave3
slave4
slave5
```

8. Link the HDFS configuration file to the HBase configuration directory with the following command:

```
sudo ln -s $HADOOP_HOME/conf/hdfs-site.xml $HBASE_HOME/conf/hdfs-site.xml
```

9. Replace the dependent `.jar` files for HBase with the following commands:

```
rm -i $HBASE_HOME/lib/hadoop-core*.jar $HBASE_HOME/lib/zookeeper-*.jar
```

```
cp -i $HADOOP_HOME/hadoop-core*.jar $HADOOP_HOME/lib/commons-*.jar $ZK_HOME/zookeeper-*.jar $HBASE_HOME/lib/
```

10. Configure all the slave nodes with the following commands:

```
for host in 'cat $HBASE_HOME/conf/regionservers'; do
  echo 'Configuring HBase on ' $host
  scp ~/.bashrc hduser@$host:~/
  sudo scp -r /usr/local/hbase-0.94.5 hduser@$host:/usr/local/
  echo 'Making symbolic link for HBase home directory on ' $host
  sudo ssh hduser@$host -C "ln -s /usr/local/hbase-0.94.5 /usr/local/hbase"
  echo 'Making symbolic link for hdfs-site.xml to the HBase configuration directory on ' $host
  sudo ssh hduser@$host -C "ln -s /usr/local/hadoop-1.1.2/conf/hdfs-site.xml /usr/local/hbase-0.94.5/conf/hdfs-site.xml"
done
```

11. Start HBase daemons with the following command:

```
start-hbase.sh
```

12. Connect to the running HBase with the following command:

```
hbase shell
```

13. Verify the HBase installation with the following HBase shell commands:

```
hbase(main):001:0> create 'test', 'c'
0 row(s) in 0.2410 seconds


hbase(main):001:0> put 'test', 'r1', 'c:a', 'v1'
0 row(s) in 0.0320 seconds


hbase(main):003:0> scan 'test'
ROW COLUMN+CELL row1 column=c:a, timestamp=124455459102, value=v1
r1
1 row(s) in 0.2130 seconds


hbase(main):006:0> disable 'test'
0 row(s) in 9.4210 seconds


hbase(main):007:0> drop 'test'
0 row(s) in 8.3412 seconds


hbase(main):010:0> exit
```

14. To stop HBase, use the following command:

```
stop-hbase.sh
```

The following message will be given:

```
stopping hbase...............
```

How it works...

In the configuration, the `hbase.rootdir` property specifies the root directory of the HBase data storage, and the `hbase.zookeeper.property.dataDir` property specifies the root directory of the ZooKeeper data storage.

See also

▶ The *Installing ZooKeeper* recipe in *Chapter 3, Configuring a Hadoop Cluster*

▶ More documentation about HBase can be found at: `http://wiki.apache.org/hadoop/Hbase`

Installing Hive

As a top-level abstraction language, **Hive** provides a handy tool for manipulating data storage on HDFS with SQL-like language. In this section, we will talk about installing Hive on our Hadoop cluster.

Getting ready

Before we install Hive, we need to make sure Hadoop has been properly installed. Please refer to the previous sections about the configuration of a Hadoop cluster.

Download Hive from a mirror site with a command similar to the following on the administrator machine:

```
wget http://apache.osuosl.org/hive/stable/hive-0.9.0.tar.gz -P ~/repo
```

How to do it...

Use the following steps to install Hive:

1. Log in to the master node from the Hadoop administrator machine as `hduser` with the following command:

   ```
   ssh hduser@master
   ```

2. Copy the archive to `/usr/local` with the following command:

   ```
   sudo wget ftp://hadoop.admin/repo/hive-0.9.0.tar.gz /usr/local
   ```

3. Decompress the Hive archive with the following command:

   ```
   cd /usr/local
   tar xvf hive-0.9.0.tar.gz
   ```

4. Create a symbolic link with the following command:

   ```
   ln -s /usr/local/hive-0.9.0 /usr/local/hive
   ```

5. Use your favorite text editor to open the ~/.bashrc file and add the following lines to this file:

    ```
    export HIVE_HOME=/usr/local/hive
    export PATH=$HIVE_HOME/bin:$PATH
    ```

6. Start Hive with the following command:

    ```
    hive
    ```

See also

▸ The *Installing Pig* recipe in *Chapter 3, Configuring a Hadoop Cluster*

▸ Get more documentation about Hive from `https://cwiki.apache.org/confluence/display/Hive/Home`

Installing Pig

Similar to Hive, **Pig** provides a handy tool for manipulating Hadoop data. In this recipe, we are going to discuss the installation of Apache Pig.

Getting ready

Before we install Pig, we need to make sure Hadoop has been properly installed. Please refer to the previous sections about the configuration of a Hadoop cluster.

Download the Pig archive file from a mirror site with the following command on the administrator machine:

```
wget http://www.motorlogy.com/apache/pig/stable/pig-0.10.1.tar.gz
~/repo
```

How to do it...

Use the following steps to configure Pig:

1. Log in to the master node from the Hadoop administrator machine as hduser with the following command:

    ```
    ssh hduser@master
    ```

2. Copy the archive to /usr/local with the following command:

    ```
    sudo wget ftp://hadoop.admin/repo/pig-0.10.1.tar.gz /usr/local
    ```

3. Decompress the Pig archive file with the following command:

```
cd /usr/local
sudo tar xvf pig-0.10.1.tar.gz
```

4. Create a symbolic link to the Pig directory using the following command:

```
sudo ln -s /usr/local/pig-0.10.1 /usr/local/pig
```

5. Open the ~/.bashrc file with your favorite text editor and add the following lines into the file:

```
export PIG_HOME=/usr/local/pig
export PATH=$PIG_HOME/bin:$PATH
```

6. Run Pig in local mode with the following command:

```
pig -x local
```

7. Run Pig in MapReduce mode with the following command:

```
pig
```

8. Alternatively, we can use the following command:

```
pig -x mapreduce
```

 Pig that runs in MapReduce mode will utilizes the power of distributed computing provided by Hadoop.

See also

▶ The *Installing Hive* recipe in *Chapter 3, Configuring a Hadoop Cluster*

▶ More documentation about Pig can be obtained from: `http://pig.apache.org/docs/r0.10.0/`

Installing Mahout

Apache **Mahout** is a machine learning library that scales machine learning algorithms on Big Data. It is implemented on top of the Hadoop Big Data stack. It already implements a wide range of machine learning algorithms. In this recipe, we will outline steps to configure Apache Mahout.

Getting ready

Before we install Mahout, we need to make sure Hadoop has been properly installed.

Download Mahout from the mirror site with the following command on the master node:

```
wget http://www.eng.lsu.edu/mirrors/apache/mahout/0.7/mahout-
distribution-0.7.tar.gz -P ~/repo
```

How to do it...

Use the following recipe to install Mahout:

1. Log in to the master node from the Hadoop administrator machine as `hduser` with the following command:

   ```
   ssh hduser@master
   ```

2. Copy the archive to `/usr/local` with the following command:

   ```
   sudo wget ftp://hadoop.admin/repo/mahout-distribution-0.7.tar.gz /
   usr/local
   ```

3. Decompress the Mahout archive with the following commands:

   ```
   cd /usr/local
   ```

   ```
   sudo tar xvf mahout-distribution-0.7.tar.gz
   ```

4. Create a symbolic link to the Mahout directory with the following command:

   ```
   sudo ln -s /usr/local/mahout-distribution-0.7 /usr/local/mahout
   ```

5. Open the `~/.bashrc` file with your favorite text editor and add the following lines to the file:

   ```
   export MAHOUT_HOME=/usr/local/pig
   export PATH=$MAHOUT_HOME/bin:$PATH
   ```

6. Load the configuration with the following command:

   ```
   . ~/.bashrc
   ```

7. Install **Maven** with the following command:

   ```
   sudo yum install maven
   ```

8. Compile and install Mahout core with the following commands:

   ```
   cd $MAHOUT_HOME
   sudo mvn compile
   sudo mvn install
   ```

The `install` command will run all the tests by default; we can ignore the tests to speed up the installation process with command `sudo mvn -DskipTests install`.

9. Compile the Mahout examples with the following commands:

```
cd examples
sudo mvn compile
```

Use the following steps to verify Mahout configuration:

1. Download sample data with the following command:

```
wget http://archive.ics.uci.edu/ml/databases/synthetic_control/
synthetic_control.data -P ~/
```

2. Start the Hadoop cluster with commands:

```
start-dfs.sh
start-mapred.sh
```

3. Put the downloaded data into HDFS with the following commands:

```
hadoop fs -mkdir testdata
hadoop fs -put ~/synthetic_control.data testdata
```

4. Run the `kmeans` clustering with the following command:

```
mahout org.apache.mahout.clustering.syntheticcontrol.kmeans.Job
```

See also

▶ More documentation about Mahout can be obtained from
   https://cwiki.apache.org/confluence/display/MAHOUT/Mahout+Wiki.

4
Managing a Hadoop Cluster

In this chapter, we will cover:

- ▶ Managing the HDFS cluster
- ▶ Configuring SecondaryNameNode
- ▶ Managing the MapReduce cluster
- ▶ Managing TaskTracker
- ▶ Decommissioning DataNode
- ▶ Replacing a slave node
- ▶ Managing MapReduce jobs
- ▶ Checking job history from the web UI
- ▶ Importing data to HDFS
- ▶ Manipulating files on HDFS
- ▶ Configuring the HDFS quota
- ▶ Configuring CapacityScheduler
- ▶ Configuring Fair Scheduler
- ▶ Configuring Hadoop daemon logging
- ▶ Configuring Hadoop audit logging
- ▶ Upgrading Hadoop

Introduction

From the perspective of functionality, a Hadoop cluster is composed of an **HDFS** cluster and a **MapReduce** cluster. The HDFS cluster consists of the default filesystem for Hadoop. It has one or more **NameNodes** to keep track of the filesystem metadata, while actual data blocks are stored on distributed slave nodes managed by **DataNode**. Similarly, a **MapReduce** cluster has one **JobTracker** daemon on the master node and a number of **TaskTrackers** on the slave nodes. The JobTracker manages the life cycle of MapReduce jobs. It splits jobs into smaller tasks and schedules the tasks to run by the TaskTrackers. A TaskTracker executes tasks assigned by the JobTracker in parallel by forking one or a number of JVM processes. As a Hadoop cluster administrator, you will be responsible for managing both the HDFS cluster and the MapReduce cluster.

In general, system administrators should maintain the health and availability of the cluster. More specifically, for an HDFS cluster, it means the management of the NameNodes and DataNodes and the management of the JobTrackers and TaskTrackers for MapReduce. Other administrative tasks include the management of Hadoop jobs, for example configuring job scheduling policy with schedulers.

At the end of this chapter, we will cover topics for configuring Hadoop logging and doing a system upgrade. Logging provides insights for diagnosing cluster failure or performance problems, and system upgrade plays an important role in keeping the software up to date.

Managing the HDFS cluster

The health of HDFS is critical for a Hadoop-based Big Data platform. HDFS problems can negatively affect the efficiency of the cluster. Even worse, it can make the cluster not function properly. For example, DataNode's unavailability caused by network segmentation can lead to some under-replicated data blocks. When this happens, HDFS will automatically replicate those data blocks, which will bring a lot of overhead to the cluster and cause the cluster to be too unstable to be available for use. In this recipe, we will show commands to manage an HDFS cluster.

Getting ready

Before getting started, we assume that our Hadoop cluster has been properly configured and all the daemons are running without any problems.

Log in to the master node from the administrator machine with the following command:

```
ssh hduser@master
```

How to do it...

Use the following steps to check the status of an HDFS cluster with `hadoop fsck`:

1. Check the status of the root filesystem with the following command:

```
hadoop fsck /
```

We will get an output similar to the following:

```
FSCK started by hduser from /10.147.166.55 for path / at Thu Feb
28 17:14:11 EST 2013

. .

/user/hduser/.staging/job_201302281211_0002/job.jar:  Under
replicated blk_-665238265064328579_1016. Target Replicas is 10 but
found 5 replica(s).
...............................Status: HEALTHY
 Total size:      14420321969 B
 Total dirs:      22
 Total files:     35
 Total blocks (validated):       241 (avg. block size 59835360 B)
 Minimally replicated blocks:    241 (100.0 %)
 Over-replicated blocks:         0 (0.0 %)
 Under-replicated blocks:        2 (0.8298755 %)
 Mis-replicated blocks:          0 (0.0 %)
 Default replication factor:     2
 Average block replication:      2.0248964
 Corrupt blocks:                 0
 Missing replicas:               10 (2.0491803 %)
 Number of data-nodes:           5
 Number of racks:                1
FSCK ended at Thu Feb 28 17:14:11 EST 2013 in 28 milliseconds


The filesystem under path '/' is HEALTHY
```

The output shows that some percentage of data blocks is under-replicated. But because HDFS can automatically make duplication for those data blocks, the HDFS filesystem and the '/' directory are both HEALTHY.

2. Check the status of all the files on HDFS with the following command:

```
hadoop fsck / -files
```

We will get an output similar to the following:

```
FSCK started by hduser from /10.147.166.55 for path / at Thu Feb
28 17:40:35 EST 2013
/ <dir>
/home <dir>
/home/hduser <dir>
/home/hduser/hadoop <dir>
/home/hduser/hadoop/tmp <dir>
/home/hduser/hadoop/tmp/mapred <dir>
/home/hduser/hadoop/tmp/mapred/system <dir>
/home/hduser/hadoop/tmp/mapred/system/jobtracker.info 4 bytes, 1
block(s):  OK
/user <dir>
/user/hduser <dir>
/user/hduser/randtext <dir>
/user/hduser/randtext/_SUCCESS 0 bytes, 0 block(s):  OK
/user/hduser/randtext/_logs <dir>
/user/hduser/randtext/_logs/history <dir>
/user/hduser/randtext/_logs/history/job_201302281451_0002_13620904
21087_hduser_random-text-writer 23995 bytes, 1 block(s):  OK
/user/hduser/randtext/_logs/history/job_201302281451_0002_conf.xml
22878 bytes, 1 block(s):  OK
/user/hduser/randtext/part-00001 1102231864 bytes, 17 block(s):
OK
Status: HEALTHY
Hadoop will scan and list all the files in the cluster.
```

This command scans all files on HDFS and prints the size and status.

3. Check the locations of file blocks with the following command:

```
hadoop fsck / -files -locations
```

The output of this command will contain the following information:

```
/user/hduser/randtext/part-00000 1102227538 bytes, 17 block(s):  OK
0. blk_-6733127705602961004_1127 len=67108864 repl=2 [10.145.231.46:50010, 10.145.223.184:50010]
1. blk_-3499637928486209903_1131 len=67108864 repl=2 [10.152.166.137:50010, 10.145.223.184:50010]
2. blk_-7447070369089405151_1131 len=67108864 repl=2 [10.152.161.43:50010, 10.145.223.184:50010]
3. blk_-8073458631475956975_1131 len=67108864 repl=2 [10.152.161.43:50010, 10.145.223.184:50010]
4. blk_8203013555531589356_1131 len=67108864 repl=2 [10.152.161.43:50010, 10.145.223.184:50010]
5. blk_5527099832775272870_1131 len=67108864 repl=2 [10.145.223.184:50010, 10.152.175.122:50010]
6. blk_-7826017535334756187_1131 len=67108864 repl=2 [10.152.161.43:50010, 10.145.223.184:50010]
7. blk_-7133187333235954008_1131 len=67108864 repl=2 [10.152.161.43:50010, 10.145.223.184:50010]
8. blk_-7838247448397906386_1131 len=67108864 repl=2 [10.152.175.122:50010, 10.145.223.184:50010]
9. blk_5940231997120725764_1131 len=67108864 repl=2 [10.152.161.43:50010, 10.145.223.184:50010]
10. blk_-715734526286596755_1131 len=67108864 repl=2 [10.145.231.46:50010, 10.145.223.184:50010]
11. blk_-8274826271093781621_1131 len=67108864 repl=2 [10.152.161.43:50010, 10.145.223.184:50010]
12. blk_-68955761814105317_1131 len=67108864 repl=2 [10.152.166.137:50010, 10.145.223.184:50010]
13. blk_2458876183802132370_1131 len=67108864 repl=2 [10.152.166.137:50010, 10.145.223.184:50010]
14. blk_1416174925496285827_1131 len=67108864 repl=2 [10.152.166.137:50010, 10.145.223.184:50010]
15. blk_6231571904916249244_1131 len=67108864 repl=2 [10.145.223.184:50010, 10.152.166.137:50010]
16. blk_2311912184438150486_1131 len=28485714 repl=2 [10.145.231.46:50010, 10.145.223.184:50010]
```

The first line tells us that file `part-00000` has 17 blocks in total and each block has 2 replications (replication factor has been set to 2). The following lines list the location of each block on the DataNode. For example, block `blk_6733127705602961004_1127` has been replicated on hosts `10.145.231.46` and `10.145.223.184`. The number `50010` is the port number of the DataNode.

4. Check the locations of file blocks containing rack information with the following command:

    hadoop fsck / -files -blocks -racks

5. Delete corrupted files with the following command:

    hadoop fsck -delete

6. Move corrupted files to `/lost+found` with the following command:

    hadoop fsck -move

Use the following steps to check the status of an HDFS cluster with `hadoop dfsadmin`:

1. Report the status of each slave node with the following command:

    hadoop dfsadmin -report

    The output will be similar to the following:

    Configured Capacity: 422797230080 (393.76 GB)

    Present Capacity: 399233617920 (371.82 GB)

    DFS Remaining: 388122796032 (361.47 GB)

    DFS Used: 11110821888 (10.35 GB)

```
DFS Used%: 2.78%
Under replicated blocks: 0
Blocks with corrupt replicas: 0
Missing blocks: 0


-------------------------------------------------
Datanodes available: 5 (5 total, 0 dead)

Name: 10.145.223.184:50010
Decommission Status : Normal
Configured Capacity: 84559446016 (78.75 GB)
DFS Used: 2328719360 (2.17 GB)
Non DFS Used: 4728565760 (4.4 GB)
DFS Remaining: 77502160896(72.18 GB)
DFS Used%: 2.75%
DFS Remaining%: 91.65%
Last contact: Thu Feb 28 20:30:11 EST 2013


...
```

The first section of the output shows the summary of the HDFS cluster, including the configured capacity, present capacity, remaining capacity, used space, number of under-replicated data blocks, number of data blocks with corrupted replicas, and number of missing blocks.

The following sections of the output information show the status of each HDFS slave node, including the name (**ip:port**) of the DataNode machine, commission status, configured capacity, HDFS and non-HDFS used space amount, HDFS remaining space, and the time that the slave node contacted the master.

2. Refresh all the DataNodes using the following command:

```
hadoop dfsadmin -refreshNodes
```

3. Check the status of the **safe mode** using the following command:

```
hadoop dfsadmin -safemode get
```

We will be able to get the following output:

```
Safe mode is OFF
```

The output tells us that the NameNode is not in safe mode. In this case, the filesystem is both readable and writable. If the NameNode is in safe mode, the filesystem will be read-only (write protected).

4. Manually put the NameNode into safe mode using the following command:

    ```
    hadoop dfsadmin -safemode enter
    ```

    This command is useful for system maintenance.

5. Make the NameNode to leave safe mode using the following command:

    ```
    hadoop dfsadmin -safemode leave
    ```

    If the NameNode has been in safe mode for a long time or it has been put into safe mode manually, we need to use this command to let the NameNode leave this mode.

6. Wait until NameNode leaves safe mode using the following command:

    ```
    hadoop dfsadmin -safemode wait
    ```

    This command is useful when we want to wait until HDFS finishes data block replication or wait until a newly commissioned DataNode to be ready for service.

7. Save the metadata of the HDFS filesystem with the following command:

    ```
    hadoop dfsadmin -metasave meta.log
    ```

    The `meta.log` file will be created under the directory `$HADOOP_HOME/logs`. Its content will be similar to the following:

    ```
    21 files and directories, 88 blocks = 109 total
    Live Datanodes: 5
    Dead Datanodes: 0
    Metasave: Blocks waiting for replication: 0
    Metasave: Blocks being replicated: 0
    Metasave: Blocks 0 waiting deletion from 0 datanodes.
    Metasave: Number of datanodes: 5
    10.145.223.184:50010 IN 84559446016(78.75 GB) 2328719360(2.17 GB)
    2.75% 77502132224(72.18 GB) Thu Feb 28 21:43:52 EST 2013
    10.152.166.137:50010 IN 84559446016(78.75 GB) 2357415936(2.2 GB)
    2.79% 77492854784(72.17 GB) Thu Feb 28 21:43:52 EST 2013
    10.145.231.46:50010 IN 84559446016(78.75 GB) 2048004096(1.91 GB)
    2.42% 77802893312(72.46 GB) Thu Feb 28 21:43:54 EST 2013
    10.152.161.43:50010 IN 84559446016(78.75 GB) 2250854400(2.1 GB)
    2.66% 77600096256(72.27 GB) Thu Feb 28 21:43:52 EST 2013
    10.152.175.122:50010 IN 84559446016(78.75 GB) 2125828096(1.98 GB)
    2.51% 77724323840(72.39 GB) Thu Feb 28 21:43:53 EST 2013
    21 files and directories, 88 blocks = 109 total
    . . .
    ```

How it works...

The HDFS filesystem will be write protected when NameNode enters safe mode. When an HDFS cluster is started, it will enter safe mode first. The NameNode will check the replication factor for each data block. If the replica count of a data block is smaller than the configured value, which is 3 by default, the data block will be marked as under-replicated. Finally, an under-replication factor, which is the percentage of under-replicated data blocks, will be calculated. If the percentage number is larger than the threshold value, the NameNode will stay in safe mode until enough new replicas are created for the under-replicated data blocks so as to make the under-replication factor lower than the threshold.

We can get the usage of the `fsck` command using:

```
hadoop fsck
```

The usage information will be similar to the following:

```
Usage: DFSck <path> [-move | -delete | -openforwrite] [-files [-blocks
[-locations | -racks]]]
        <path>  start checking from this path
        -move   move corrupted files to /lost+found
        -delete delete corrupted files
        -files  print out files being checked
        -openforwrite   print out files opened for write
        -blocks print out block report
        -locations      print out locations for every block
        -racks print out network topology for data-node locations
        By default fsck ignores files opened for write, use
-openforwrite to report such files. They are usually tagged CORRUPT or
HEALTHY depending on their block allocation status.
```

We can get the usage of the `dfsadmin` command using:

```
hadoop dfsadmin
```

The output will be similar to the following:

```
Usage: java DFSAdmin
        [-report]
        [-safemode enter | leave | get | wait]
        [-saveNamespace]
        [-refreshNodes]
        [-finalizeUpgrade]
```

```
[-upgradeProgress status | details | force]
[-metasave filename]
[-refreshServiceAcl]
[-refreshUserToGroupsMappings]
[-refreshSuperUserGroupsConfiguration]
[-setQuota <quota> <dirname>...<dirname>]
[-clrQuota <dirname>...<dirname>]
[-setSpaceQuota <quota> <dirname>...<dirname>]
[-clrSpaceQuota <dirname>...<dirname>]
[-setBalancerBandwidth <bandwidth in bytes per second>]
[-help [cmd]]
```

There's more...

Besides using command line, we can use the web UI to check the status of an HDFS cluster. For example, we can get the status information of HDFS by opening the link `http://master:50070/dfshealth.jsp`.

We will get a web page that shows the summary of the HDFS cluster such as the configured capacity and remaining space. For example, the web page will be similar to the following screenshot:

By clicking on the **Live Nodes** link, we can check the status of each DataNode. We will get a web page similar to the following screenshot:

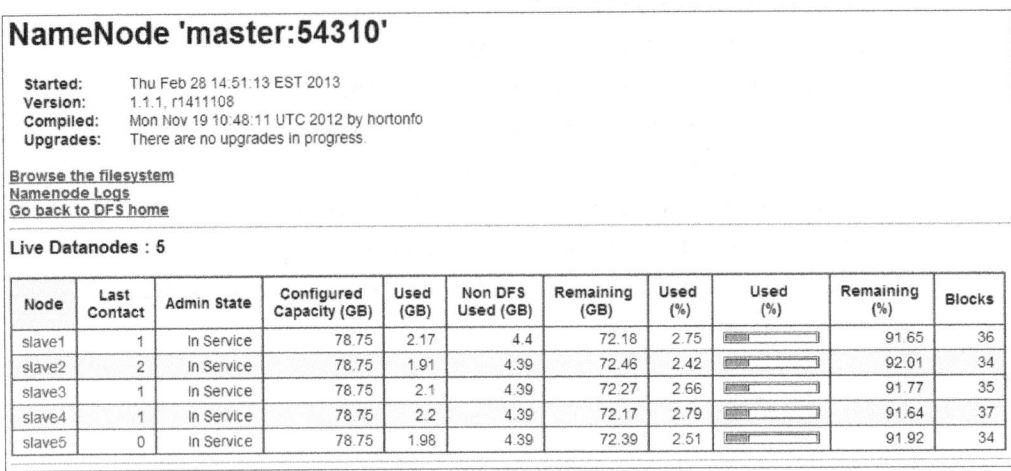

By clicking on the link of each node, we can browse the directory of the HDFS filesystem. The web page will be similar to the following screenshot:

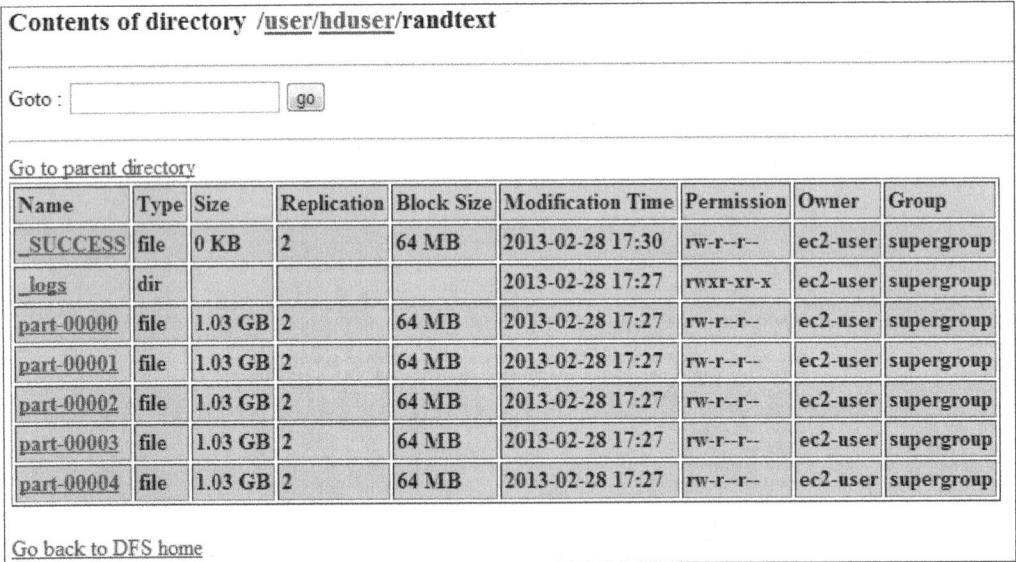

The web page shows that file `/user/hduser/randtext` has been split into five partitions. We can browse the content of each partition by clicking on the `part-0000x` link.

See also

▸ The *Validating Hadoop installation* recipe in *Chapter 3, Configuring a Hadoop cluster*

▸ The *Decommissioning DataNode* recipe

▸ The *Manipulating files on HDFS* recipe

Configuring SecondaryNameNode

Hadoop NameNode is a single point of failure. By configuring **SecondaryNameNode**, the filesystem image and edit log files can be backed up periodically. And in case of NameNode failure, the backup files can be used to recover the NameNode. In this recipe, we will outline steps to configure **SecondaryNameNode**.

Getting ready

We assume that Hadoop has been configured correctly.

Log in to the master node from the cluster administration machine using the following command:

```
ssh hduser@master
```

How to do it...

Perform the following steps to configure SecondaryNameNode:

1. Stop the cluster using the following command:

   ```
   stop-all.sh
   ```

2. Add or change the following into the file $HADOOP_HOME/conf/hdfs-site.xml:

   ```
   <property>
       <name>fs.checkpoint.dir</name>
    <value>/hadoop/dfs/namesecondary</value>
   </property>
   ```

   If this property is not set explicitly, the default checkpoint directory will be ${hadoop.tmp.dir}/dfs/namesecondary.

3. Start the cluster using the following command:

   ```
   start-all.sh
   ```

The tree structure of the NameNode data directory will be similar to the following:

```
${dfs.name.dir}/
├── current
│   ├── edits
│   ├── fsimage
│   ├── fstime
│   └── VERSION
├── image
│   └── fsimage
├── in_use.lock
└── previous.checkpoint
        ├── edits
        ├── fsimage
        ├── fstime
    └── VERSION
```

And the tree structure of the SecondaryNameNode data directory will be similar to the following:

```
${fs.checkpoint.dir}/
├── current
│   ├── edits
│   ├── fsimage
│   ├── fstime
│   └── VERSION
├── image
│   └── fsimage
└── in_use.lock
```

There's more...

To increase redundancy, we can configure NameNode to write filesystem metadata on multiple locations. For example, we can add an NFS shared directory for backup by changing the following property in the file $HADOOP_HOME/conf/hdfs-site.xml:

```
<property>
  <name>dfs.name.dir</name>
  <value>/hadoop/dfs/name,/nfs/name</value>
</property>
```

 `/nfs/name` is an NFS shared directory on a remote machine.

See also

▸ The *Managing the HDFS cluster* recipe

▸ The *Decommissioning DataNode* recipe

Managing the MapReduce cluster

A typical MapReduce cluster is composed of one master node that runs the JobTracker and a number of slave nodes that run TaskTrackers. The task of managing a MapReduce cluster includes maintaining the health as well as the membership between TaskTrackers and the JobTracker. In this recipe, we will outline commands to manage a MapReduce cluster.

Getting ready

We assume that the Hadoop cluster has been properly configured and running.

Log in to the master node from the cluster administration machine using the following command:

```
ssh hduser@master
```

How to do it...

Perform the following steps to manage a MapReduce cluster:

1. List all the active TaskTrackers using the following command:

   ```
   hadoop -job -list-active-trackers
   ```

    This command can help us check the registration status of the TaskTrackers in the cluster.

2. Check the status of the JobTracker safe mode using the following command:

   ```
   hadoop mradmin -safemode get
   ```

   We will get the following output:

   ```
   Safe mode is OFF
   ```

The output tells us that the JobTracker is not in safe mode. We can submit jobs to the cluster. If the JobTracker is in safe mode, no jobs can be submitted to the cluster.

3. Manually let the JobTracker enter safe mode using the following command:

    ```
    hadoop mradmin -safemode enter
    ```

    This command is handy when we want to maintain the cluster.

4. Let the JobTracker leave safe mode using the following command:

    ```
    hadoop mradmin -safemode leave
    ```

    When maintenance tasks are done, you need to run this command.

5. If we want to wait for safe mode to exit, the following command can be used:

    ```
    hadoop mradmin -safemode wait
    ```

6. Reload the MapReduce queue configuration using the following command:

    ```
    hadoop mradmin -refreshQueues
    ```

7. Reload active TaskTrackers using the following command:

    ```
    hadoop mradmin -refreshNodes
    ```

How it works...

Get the usage of the `mradmin` command using the following:

```
hadoop mradmin
```

The usage information will be similar to the following:

```
Usage: java MRAdmin
          [-refreshServiceAcl]
          [-refreshQueues]
          [-refreshUserToGroupsMappings]
          [-refreshSuperUserGroupsConfiguration]
          [-refreshNodes]
          [-safemode <enter | leave | get | wait>]
          [-help [cmd]]
...
```

The meaning of the command options is listed in the following table:

Option	Description
-refreshServiceAcl	Force JobTracker to reload service ACL.
-refreshQueues	Force JobTracker to reload queue configurations.
-refreshUserToGroupsMappings	Force JobTracker to reload user group mappings.
-refreshSuperUserGroupsConfiguration	Force JobTracker to reload super user group mappings.
-refreshNodes	Force JobTracker to refresh the JobTracker hosts.
-help [cmd]	Show the help information for a command or all commands.

See also

▸ The *Configuring SecondaryNameNode* recipe
▸ The *Managing MapReduce jobs* recipe

Managing TaskTracker

TaskTrackers are MapReduce daemon processes that run on slave nodes. They accept tasks assigned by the JobTracker on the master node and fork JVM processes/threads to run the tasks. TaskTracker is also responsible for reporting the progress of the tasks as well as its health status using heartbeat.

Hadoop maintains three lists for TaskTrackers: **blacklist**, **gray list**, and **excluded list**. TaskTracker black listing is a function that can blacklist a TaskTracker if it is in an unstable state or its performance has been downgraded. For example, when the ratio of failed tasks for a specific job has reached a certain threshold, the TaskTracker will be blacklisted for this job. Similarly, Hadoop maintains a gray list of nodes by identifying potential problematic nodes.

Sometimes, excluding certain TaskTrackers from the cluster is desirable. For example, when we debug or upgrade a slave node, we want to separate this node from the cluster in case it affects the cluster. Hadoop supports the live decommission of a TaskTracker from a running cluster.

Getting ready

We assume that Hadoop has been properly configured. MapReduce and HDFS daemons are running without any issues.

Log in to the cluster master node from the administrator machine using the following command:

```
ssh hduser@master
```

List the active trackers with the following command on the master node:

```
hadoop job -list-active-trackers
```

And the output should be similar to the following:

```
tracker_slave5:localhost/127.0.0.1:55590

tracker_slave1:localhost/127.0.0.1:47241

tracker_slave3:localhost/127.0.0.1:51187

tracker_slave4:localhost/127.0.0.1:60756

tracker_slave2:localhost/127.0.0.1:42939
```

How to do it...

Perform the following steps to configure the heartbeat interval:

1. Stop a MapReduce cluster with the following command:

    ```
    stop-dfs.sh
    ```

2. Open the file $HADOOP_HOME/conf/mapred-site.xml with your favorite text editor and add the following content into the file:

    ```
    <property>
      <name>mapred.tasktracker.expiry.interval</name>
    <value>600000</value>
      </property>
    ```

    The value is in milliseconds.

3. Copy the configuration into the slave nodes using the following command:

    ```
    for host in 'cat $HADOOP_HOME/conf/slaves'; do

      echo 'Copying mapred-site.xml to slave node ' $host

      sudo scp $HADOOP_HOME/conf/mapred-site.xml hduser@$host:$HADOOP_
    HOME/conf

      done
    ```

4. Start the MapReduce cluster with the following command:

```
start-mapred.sh
```

Perform the following steps to configure TaskTracker blacklisting:

1. Stop the MapReduce cluster with the following command:

```
stop-mapred.sh
```

2. Set the number of task failures for a job to blacklist a TaskTracker by adding or changing the following property in the file `$HADOOP_HOME/conf/hdfs-site.xml`:

```
<property>
  <name>mapred.max.tracker.failures</name>
<value>10</value>
</property>
```

3. Set the maximum number of successful jobs that can blacklist a TaskTracker by adding or changing the following property in the file `$HADOOP_HOME/conf/hdfs-site.xml`:

```
<property>
  <name>mapred.max.tracker.blacklists</name>
<value>5</value>
</property>
```

4. Copy the configuration file to the slave nodes using the following commands:

```
for host in 'cat $HADOOP_HOME/conf/slaves'; do
  echo 'Copying hdfs-site.xml to slave node ' $host
  sudo scp $HADOOP_HOME/conf/hdfs-site.xml hduser@$host:$HADOOP_
HOME/conf
done
```

5. Start the MapReduce cluster using the following command:

```
start-mapred.sh
```

6. List blacklisted TaskTrackers using the following command:

```
hadoop job -list-blacklisted-trackers
```

Perform the following steps to decommission TaskTrackers:

1. Set the TaskTracker exclude file by adding the following properties into the file:

```
<property>
  <name>mapred.hosts.exclude</name>
<value>$HADOOP_HOME/conf/mapred-exclude.txt</value>
</property>
```

The `$HADOOP_HOME/conf/mapred-exclude.txt` file will contain the excluding TaskTracker hostnames one per line. For example, the file should contain the following two lines if we want to exclude `slave1` and `slave3` from the cluster:

```
slave1
slave3
```

2. Force the JobTracker to reload the TaskTracker list with the following command:

    `hadoop mradmin -refreshNodes`

3. List all the active trackers again using the following command:

    `hadoop job -list-active-trackers`

    We will get the following output:

    ```
    tracker_slave5:localhost/127.0.0.1:55590
    tracker_slave4:localhost/127.0.0.1:60756
    tracker_slave2:localhost/127.0.0.1:42939
    ```

How it works...

TaskTrackers on slave nodes contact the JobTracker on the master node periodically. The interval between two consecutive contact communications is called a **heartbeat**. More frequent heartbeat configurations can incur higher loads to the cluster. The value of the heartbeat property should be set based on the size of the cluster.

The JobTracker uses TaskTracker blacklisting to remove those unstable TaskTrackers. If a TaskTracker is blacklisted, all the tasks currently running on the TaskTracker can still finish and the TaskTracker will continue the connection with JobTracker through the heartbeat mechanism. But the TaskTracker will not be scheduled for running future tasks. If a blacklisted TaskTracker is restarted, it will be removed from the blacklist.

 The total number of blacklisted TaskTrackers should not exceed 50 percent of the total number of TaskTrackers.

See also

▶ The *Managing the MapReduce cluster* recipe

▶ The *Managing MapReduce jobs* recipe

▶ The *Decommissioning DataNode* recipe

▶ The *Replacing a slave node* recipe

Decommissioning DataNode

Similar to TaskTracker, there are situations when we need to temporarily disable a DataNode from the cluster, for example, because the storage space of the DataNode has been used up. In this recipe, we will outline steps to decommission a DataNode from a live Hadoop cluster.

Getting ready

We assume that our Hadoop has been configured properly.

Log in to the master node from the cluster administrator machine with the following command:

ssh hduser@master

For illustration purpose, we assume to decommission DataNode on host slave1 from our running Hadoop cluster.

How to do it...

Perform the following steps to decommission a live DataNode:

1. Create the file $HADOOP_HOME/conf/dfs-exclude.txt with the following content:

    slave1

    The dfs-exclude.txt file contains the DataNode hostnames, one per line, that are to be decommissioned from the cluster.

2. Add the following property to the file $HADOOP_HOME/conf/hdfs-site.xml:

    ```
    <property>
      <name>dfs.hosts.exclude</name>
      <value>$HADOOP_HOME/conf/dfs-exclude.txt</value>
    </property>
    ```

3. Force the NameNode to reload the active DataNodes using the following command:

    hadoop dfsadmin -refreshNodes

4. Get a description report of each active DataNode:

    hadoop dfsadmin -report

How it works...

Cluster administrators can use the `dfsadmin` command to manage the DataNodes. We can get the usage of this command using the following:

```
hadoop dfsadmin
```

The usage information will be similar to the following:

```
Usage: java DFSAdmin
            [-report]
            [-safemode enter | leave | get | wait]
            [-saveNamespace]
            [-refreshNodes]
            [-finalizeUpgrade]
            [-upgradeProgress status | details | force]
            ...
```

See also

- ▶ The *Managing the HDFS cluster* recipe
- ▶ The *Configuring SecondaryNameNode* recipe
- ▶ The *Managing TaskTracker* recipe
- ▶ The *Replacing a slave node* recipe

Replacing a slave node

Sometimes, we need to replace a slave node with new hardware. For example, the slave node is not stable, more storage space or more powerful CPUs are desired, and so on. In this recipe, we will outline the steps to replace a slave node.

Getting ready

We assume that replacement hardware is ready for use. And for illustration purposes, we suppose `slave2` needs to be replaced in this book.

How to do it...

Perform the following steps to replace a slave node:

1. Decommission the TaskTracker on the slave node with the steps outlined in the *Managing TaskTracker* recipe of this chapter.

2. Decommission the DataNode on the slave node with the steps outlined in the *Decommission DataNode* recipe of this chapter.

3. Power off the slave node and replace it with the new hardware.

4. Install and configure the Linux operating system on the new node with the steps outlined in the *Installing the Linux operating system*, *Installing Java and other tools*, and *Configuring SSH recipes* of *Chapter 2, Preparing for Hadoop Installation*.

5. Install Hadoop on the new node by copying the Hadoop directory and configuration from the master node with the following commands:

   ```
   sudo scp -r /usr/local/hadoop-1.1.2 hduser@slave2:/usr/local/
   sudo ssh hduser@slave2 -C "ln -s /usr/local/hadoop-1.1.2 /usr/local/hadoop"
   sudo scp ~/.bashrc hduser@slave2:~/
   ```

6. Log in to `slave2` and start the DataNode and TaskTracker using the following commands:

   ```
   ssh hduser@slave2 -C "hadoop DataNode &"
   ssh hduser@slave2 -C "Hadoop TaskTracker &"
   ```

7. Refresh the DataNodes with the following command:

   ```
   hadoop dfsadmin -refreshNodes
   ```

8. Refresh the TaskTracker with the following command:

   ```
   hadoop mradmin -refreshNodes
   ```

9. Report the status of the live DataNodes with the following command:

   ```
   hadoop dfsadmin -report
   ```

10. Get all the active TaskTrackers with the following command:

    ```
    hadoop job -list-active-trackers
    ```

See also

> ▸ The *Installing the Linux operating system* recipe of *Chapter 2, Preparing for Hadoop Installation*

> ▸ The *Installing Java and other tools* recipe of *Chapter 2, Preparing for Hadoop Installation*

> ▸ The *Configuring SSH* recipe of *Chapter 2, Preparing for Hadoop installation*

> ▸ The *Configuring Hadoop in Fully-distributed Mode* recipe of *Chapter 3, Configuring a Hadoop Cluster*

> ▸ The *Managing TaskTracker* recipe

> ▸ The *Decommissioning DataNode* recipe

Managing MapReduce jobs

The Hadoop Big Data platform accepts jobs submitted by clients. In a multiuser environment, multiple jobs can be submitted and run simultaneously. The management of Hadoop jobs include checking job status, changing the priority of jobs, killing a running job, and so on. In this recipe, we will outline the steps to do these job management tasks.

Getting ready

We assume that our Hadoop cluster has been configured properly and all the Hadoop daemons are running without any issues. We also assume that a regular user can submit Hadoop jobs to the cluster.

Log in to the master node from the cluster administrator machine with the following command:

```
ssh hduser@master
```

How to do it...

Perform the following steps to check the status of Hadoop jobs:

1. List all the running jobs using the following command:

   ```
   hadoop job -list
   ```

   We will be able to get an output similar to the following:

   ```
   1 jobs currently running
   JobId    State    StartTime    UserName        Priority
   SchedulingInfo
   ```

```
job_201302152353_0001    4    1361405786524    hduser  NORMAL  NA
```

 The output message tells us that currently one job with `JobId` `job_201302152353_0001` is running on the cluster.

2. List all the submitted jobs since the start of the cluster with the following command:

   `hadoop job -list all`

   We will get output similar to the following:

   ```
   2 jobs submitted
   States are:
           Running : 1      Succeeded : 2      Failed : 3       Prep : 4
   JobId    State    StartTime    UserName          Priority
   SchedulingInfo
   job_201302152353_0001    2    1361405786524    hduser  NORMAL  NA
   job_201302152353_0002    4    1361405860611    hduser  NORMAL  NA
   ```

   The `State` column of the output message shows the status of jobs. For example, in the preceding output, two jobs have been submitted, the first job with `JobId` `job_201302152353_0001` is in the **succeeded** state and the second job with `JobId` `job_201302152353_0002` is in the **preparation** state. Both jobs have normal priority and don't have scheduling information.

3. We can check the status of the default queue with the following command:

   `hadoop queue -list`

   If no queues have been added, we will get an output similar to the following:

   ```
   Queue Name : default
   Queue State : running
   Scheduling Info : N/A
   ```

   Hadoop manages jobs using queues. By default, there is only one default queue. The output of the command shows the cluster has only one default queue, which in the running state with no scheduling information.

4. Check the status of a queue ACL with the following command:

   `hadoop queue -showacls`

   If no ACLs have been configured, we will get an output similar to the following:

   ```
   Queue acls for user :  hduser
   ```

```
Queue   Operations
=====================
default  submit-job,administer-jobs
```

The output shows that the user hduser can submit and administer jobs in the default queue.

5. Show all the jobs in the default queue using the following command:

```
hadoop queue -info default -showJobs
```

We will get an output similar to the following:

```
Queue Name : default
Queue State : running
Scheduling Info : N/A
Job List
JobId     State    StartTime      UserName    Priority    SchedulingInfo
job_201302152353_0001    2    1361405786524    hduser    NORMAL    NA
```

6. Check the status of a job with the following command:

```
hadoop job -status job_201302152353_0001
```

The output will be similar to the following:

```
Job: job_201302152353_0001
file: hdfs://master:54310/user/hduser/.staging/
job_201302152353_0001/job.xm                       1
tracking URL: http://master:50030/jobdetails.jsp?jobid=j
ob_201302152353_000                   1
map() completion: 1.0
reduce() completion: 1.0


Counters: 31
        Job Counters
                Launched reduce tasks=1
                SLOTS_MILLIS_MAPS=87845
                Total time spent by all reduces waiting after
reserving slots (ms)=0
                Total time spent by all maps waiting after
reserving slots (ms)= 0
                Rack-local map tasks=8
```

```
            Launched map tasks=10
            Data-local map tasks=2
            SLOTS_MILLIS_REDUCES=16263
    File Input Format Counters
            Bytes Read=1180
    File Output Format Counters
            Bytes Written=97
    FileSystemCounters
            FILE_BYTES_READ=226
            HDFS_BYTES_READ=2440
            FILE_BYTES_WRITTEN=241518
            HDFS_BYTES_WRITTEN=215
    Map-Reduce Framework
            Map output materialized bytes=280
            Map input records=10
            Reduce shuffle bytes=252
            Spilled Records=40
            Map output bytes=180
            Total committed heap usage (bytes)=2210988032
            CPU time spent (ms)=9590
            Map input bytes=240
            SPLIT_RAW_BYTES=1260
            Combine input records=0
            Reduce input records=20
            Reduce input groups=20
            Combine output records=0
            Physical memory (bytes) snapshot=2033074176
            Reduce output records=0
            Virtual memory (bytes) snapshot=5787283456
            Map output records=20
```

Change the status of a job by performing the following steps:

1. Set the job `job_201302152353_0001` to be on high priority using the following command:

```
hadoop job -set-priority job_201302152353_0003 HIGH
```

 Available priorities, in descending order, include: `VERY_HIGH`, `HIGH`, `NORMAL`, `LOW`, and `VERY_LOW`.

The priority of the job will be `HIGH` as shown in the following output:

```
4 jobs submitted
States are:
        Running : 1      Succeeded : 2     Failed : 3        Prep : 4
JobId    State    StartTime    UserName       Priority
SchedulingInfo
job_201302152353_0001    2    1361405786524    hduser   NORMAL   NA
job_201302152353_0002    2    1361405860611    hduser   NORMAL   NA
job_201302152353_0003    1    1361408177470    hduser   HIGH     NA
```

2. Kill the job `job_201302152353_0004` using the following command:

    ```
    hadoop job -kill job_201302152353_0004
    ```

    With the job status command, we will get the following output:

    ```
    3 jobs submitted
    States are:
     Running : 1     Succeeded : 2   Failed : 3    Prep : 4    Killed : 5
    JobId    State    StartTime    UserName       Priority
    SchedulingInfo
    job_201302152353_0001    2    1361405786524    hduser   NORMAL   NA
    job_201302152353_0002    2    1361405860611    hduser   NORMAL   NA
    job_201302152353_0003    1    1361408177470    hduser   HIGH     NA
    job_201302152353_0004    5    1361407740639    hduser   NORMAL   NA
    ```

 The `Killed : 5` information is not in the original output, I put it there according to the state of the killed job `job_201302152353_0004`.

Perform the following steps to submit a MapReduce job:

1. Create the job configuration file, `job.xml`, with the following content:

    ```xml
    <?xml version="1.0" encoding="UTF-8" standalone="no"?>
    <configuration>
      <property>
        <name>mapred.input.dir</name>
    ```

```
      <value>randtext</value>
    </property>

    <property>
      <name>mapred.output.dir</name>
      <value>output</value>
    </property>

    <property>
      <name>mapred.job.name</name>
      <value>wordcount</value>
    </property>

    <property>
      <name>mapred.mapper.class</name>
      <value>org.apache.hadoop.mapred.WordCount$Map</value>
    </property>

    <property>
      <name>mapred.combiner.class</name>
      <value>org.apache.hadoop.mapred.WordCount$Reduce</value>
    </property>

    <property>
      <name>mapred.reducer.class</name>
      <value>org.apache.hadoop.mapred.WordCount$Reduce</value>
    </property>

    <property>
      <name>mapred.input.format.class</name>
      <value>org.apache.hadoop.mapred.TextInputFormat</value>
    </property>

    <property>
      <name>mapred.output.format.class</name>
      <value>org.apache.hadoop.mapred.TextOutputFormat</value>
    </property>

</configuration>
```

The `job.xml` file is an XML file that specifies the configuration of a job. In this job configuration file, we specified the job name, the mapper class, the reducer class, the combiner class, the input format, and output format for the job. We have used `wordcount` as an example, so we also need to make sure `$HADOOP_HOME/hadoop-examples*.jar` is available in `CLASSPATH`.

2. Submit the job with the following command:

```
hadoop job -submit job.xml
```

And we will get an output similar to the following:

```
13/03/01 11:55:53 WARN mapred.JobClient: Use GenericOptionsParser
for parsing the arguments. Applications should implement Tool for
the same.
13/03/01 11:55:53 INFO util.NativeCodeLoader: Loaded the native-
hadoop library
13/03/01 11:55:53 WARN snappy.LoadSnappy: Snappy native library
not loaded
13/03/01 11:55:53 INFO mapred.FileInputFormat: Total input paths
to process : 5
Created job job_201302281451_0012
```

How it works...

The `queue` command is a wrapper command for the `JobQueueClient` class, and the `job` command is a wrapper command for the `JobClient` class.

We can get the usage of the `queue` command with the following:

```
hadoop queue
Usage: JobQueueClient <command> <args>
        [-list]
        [-info <job-queue-name> [-showJobs]]
        [-showacls]
```

Similarly, we can get the usage of the `job` command with the following:

```
hadoop job
```

The output will be similar to the following:

```
Usage: JobClient <command> <args>
        [-submit <job-file>]
        [-status <job-id>]
        [-counter <job-id> <group-name> <counter-name>]
        [-kill <job-id>]
        [-set-priority <job-id> <priority>]. Valid values for priorities
are: VERY_HIGH HIGH NORMAL LOW VERY_LOW
        [-events <job-id> <from-event-#> <#-of-events>]
        [-history <jobOutputDir>]
        [-list [all]]
```

```
[-list-active-trackers]
[-list-blacklisted-trackers]
[-list-attempt-ids <job-id> <task-type> <task-state>]
[-kill-task <task-id>]
[-fail-task <task-id>]
```

There's more...

We discussed the most useful commands for Hadoop job management. Actually, there are even more commands that are related to job management, and alternatively, we can use the web UI to manage Hadoop jobs.

More job management commands

1. Get the value of a counter:

    ```
    hadoop job -counter <job-id> <group-name> <counter-name>
    ```

    For example, we can get the counter HDFS_BYTES_WRITTEN of the counter group FileSystemCounters for the job job_201302281451_0002 with the following command:

    ```
    hadoop job -counter job_201302281451_0002 FileSystemCounters HDFS_
    BYTES_WRITTEN
    ```

2. Query events of a MapReduce job with the following command:

    ```
    hadoop job -events <job-id> <from-event-#> <#-of-events>
    ```

    For example, we can query the first 10 events of the job job_201302281451_0002 using the following command:

    ```
    hadoop job -events job_201302281451_0002 0 10
    ```

    We will get output similar to the following:

```
Task completion events for job_201302281451_0002
Number of events (from 0) are: 10
SUCCEEDED attempt_201302281451_0002_m_000006_0 http://slave1:50060/tasklog?plaintext=true&attemptid=attempt_201302281451_0002_m_000006_0
SUCCEEDED attempt_201302281451_0002_m_000000_0 http://slave1:50060/tasklog?plaintext=true&attemptid=attempt_201302281451_0002_m_000000_0
SUCCEEDED attempt_201302281451_0002_m_000004_0 http://slave5:50060/tasklog?plaintext=true&attemptid=attempt_201302281451_0002_m_000004_0
SUCCEEDED attempt_201302281451_0002_m_000003_0 http://slave2:50060/tasklog?plaintext=true&attemptid=attempt_201302281451_0002_m_000003_0
SUCCEEDED attempt_201302281451_0002_m_000001_0 http://slave3:50060/tasklog?plaintext=true&attemptid=attempt_201302281451_0002_m_000001_0
KILLED attempt_201302281451_0002_m_000004_1 http://slave4:50060/tasklog?plaintext=true&attemptid=attempt_201302281451_0002_m_000004_1
KILLED attempt_201302281451_0002_m_000003_1 http://slave5:50060/tasklog?plaintext=true&attemptid=attempt_201302281451_0002_m_000003_1
KILLED attempt_201302281451_0002_m_000001_1 http://slave1:50060/tasklog?plaintext=true&attemptid=attempt_201302281451_0002_m_000001_1
SUCCEEDED attempt_201302281451_0002_m_000002_0 http://slave4:50060/tasklog?plaintext=true&attemptid=attempt_201302281451_0002_m_000002_0
KILLED attempt_201302281451_0002_m_000002_1 http://slave3:50060/tasklog?plaintext=true&attemptid=attempt_201302281451_0002_m_000002_1
```

3. Get the job history including job details, failed and killed jobs, and so on with the following command:

    ```
    hadoop job -history
    ```

And we will get an output similar to the following:

```
Hadoop job: 0012_1362156954465_hduser

=====================================

Job tracker host name: job

job tracker start time: Tue May 18 17:18:01 EDT 1976

User: hduser

JobName: wordcount

JobConf: hdfs://master:54310/user/hduser/.staging/
job_201302281451_0012/job.xml

Submitted At: 1-Mar-2013 11:55:54

Launched At: 1-Mar-2013 11:55:54 (0sec)

Finished At: 1-Mar-2013 11:56:43 (48sec)

Status: FAILED

Counters:


|Group Name    |Counter name   |Map Value |Reduce Value|Total
Value|

-------------------------------------------------------------

=====================================


Task Summary

=============================

Kind    Total   Successful  Failed  Killed  StartTime
FinishTime


Setup  1  1  0  0  1-Mar-2013 11:55:46   1-Mar-2013 11:55:49
(2sec)

Map 45  0   38   7 1-Mar-2013 11:55:49   1-Mar-2013 11:56:34
(44sec)

Reduce  0    0     0        0

Cleanup 1  1  0   0  1-Mar-2013 11:56:33  1-Mar-2013 11:56:36
(3sec)

=============================


No Analysis available as job did not finish
```

```
KILLED SETUP task list for 0012_1362156954465_hduser

TaskId          StartTime       FinishTime      Error

==========================================================


FAILED MAP task list for 0012_1362156954465_hduser

TaskId          StartTime       FinishTime      Error
InputSplits

==========================================================

task_201302281451_0012_m_000000 1-Mar-2013 11:55:58    1-Mar-2013
11:56:33 (35sec)    /default-rack/slave2,/default-rack/slave1


...

FAILED task attempts by nodes

Hostname        FailedTasks

=================================

slave1  task_201302281451_0012_m_000000, task_201302281451_0012
_m_000001, task_201302281451_0012_m_000002, task_201302281451_0012
_m_000004, task_201302281451_0012_m_000005, task_201302281451_0012
_m_000008, task_201302281451_0012_m_000010, task_201302281451_0012
_m_000013,

slave2  task_201302281451_0012_m_000000, task_201302281451_0012
_m_000005, task_201302281451_0012_m_000008, task_201302281451_0012
_m_000010, task_201302281451_0012_m_000019, task_201302281451_0012
_m_000034, task_201302281451_0012_m_000036, task_201302281451_0012
_m_000039,

slave3  task_201302281451_0012_m_000000, task_201302281451_0012
_m_000001, task_201302281451_0012_m_000002, task_201302281451_0012
_m_000003, task_201302281451_0012_m_000004, task_201302281451_0012
_m_000010, task_201302281451_0012_m_000012, task_201302281451_0012
_m_000019,

slave4  task_201302281451_0012_m_000000, task_201302281451_0012
_m_000001, task_201302281451_0012_m_000003, task_201302281451_0012
_m_000004, task_201302281451_0012_m_000010, task_201302281451_0012
_m_000012, task_201302281451_0012_m_000013, task_201302281451_0012
_m_000034,

slave5  task_201302281451_0012_m_000002, task_201302281451_0012
_m_000003, task_201302281451_0012_m_000005, task_201302281451_0012
_m_000008, task_201302281451_0012_m_000012, task_201302281451_0012
_m_000013,
```

```
KILLED task attempts by nodes

Hostname         FailedTasks

=================================

slave1  task_201302281451_0012_m_000003, task_201302281451_0012
_m_000012,

slave2  task_201302281451_0012_m_000002, task_201302281451_0012
_m_000013,

slave3  task_201302281451_0012_m_000005,

slave5  task_201302281451_0012_m_000001, task_201302281451_0012
_m_000004,
```

Managing tasks

We will show you how to kill tasks, check task attempts, and so on.

1. Kill a task with the following command:

    ```
    hadoop job -kill-task <task-id>
    ```

    For example, to kill the task `task_201302281451_0013_m_000000`, we can use the following command:

    ```
    hadoop job -kill-task task_201302281451_0013_m_000000
    ```

    After the task is killed, the JobTracker will restart the task on a different node. The killed tasks can be viewed through the web UI as shown in the following screenshot:

Hadoop job_201302281451_0014 failures on master

Attempt	Task	Machine	State	Error	Logs
attempt_201302281451_0014_m_000071_0	task_201302281451_0014_m_000071	slave3	KILLED		Last 4KB Last 8KB All
attempt_201302281451_0014_m_000072_0	task_201302281451_0014_m_000072	slave3	KILLED		Last 4KB Last 8KB All
attempt_201302281451_0014_m_000081_1	task_201302281451_0014_m_000081	slave2	KILLED		Last 4KB Last 8KB All

Hadoop JobTracker can automatically kill tasks in the following situations:

- ❑ A task does not report progress after timeout
- ❑ Speculative execution can run one task on multiple nodes; if one of these tasks has succeeded, other attempts of the same task will be killed because the attempt results for those attempts will be useless
- ❑ Job/Task schedulers, such as fair scheduler and capacity scheduler, need empty slots for other pools or queues

2. In many situations, we need a task to fail, which can be done with the following command:

```
hadoop job -fail-task <task-id>
```

For example, to fail the task `task_201302281451_0013_m_000000`, we can use the following command:

```
hadoop -job -fail-task task_201302281451_0013_m_000000
```

3. List task attempts with the following command:

```
hadoop job -list-attempt-ids <job-id> <task-type> <task-state>
```

In this command, available task types are `map`, `reduce`, `setup`, and `clean`; available task states are `running` and `completed`.

For example, to list all the completed map attempts for the job `job_201302281451_0014`, the following command can be used:

```
hadoop job -list-attempt-ids job_201302281451_0014 map completed
```

We will get an output similar to the following:

```
attempt_201302281451_0014_m_000000_0
attempt_201302281451_0014_m_000001_0
attempt_201302281451_0014_m_000002_0
attempt_201302281451_0014_m_000009_0
attempt_201302281451_0014_m_000010_0
...
```

Managing jobs through the web UI

We will show job management from the web UI.

1. Check the status of a job by opening the JobTracker URL, `master:50030/jobtracker.jsp`.

    We will get a web page similar to the following screenshot:

Cluster Summary (Heap Size is 56.75 MB/1.89 GB)

Running Map Tasks	Running Reduce Tasks	Total Submissions	Nodes	Occupied Map Slots	Occupied Reduce Slots	Reserved Map Slots	Reserved Reduce Slots	Map Task Capacity
0	1	3	5	0	1	0	0	10

Scheduling Information

Queue Name	State	Scheduling Information
default	running	N/A

Filter (Jobid, Priority, User, Name)
Example: 'user:smith 3200' will filter by 'smith' only in the user field and '3200' in all fields

Running Jobs

Jobid	Started	Priority	User	Name	Map % Complete	Map Total	Maps Completed	Reduce % Complete	Reduc
job_201302281451_0004	Fri Mar 01 10:32:17 EST 2013	NORMAL	ec2-user	TableJoin	100.00%	86	86	33.33%	1

Completed Jobs

Jobid	Started	Priority	User	Name	Map % Complete	Map Total	Maps Completed	Reduce % Complet
job_201302281451_0001	Thu Feb 28 14:53:16 EST 2013	NORMAL	ec2-user	TableJoin	100.00%	52	52	100.00%
job_201302281451_0002	Thu Feb 28 17:27:01 EST 2013	NORMAL	ec2-user	random-text-writer	100.00%	5	5	100.00%

> From this web page, we can get the cluster summary information, the scheduling information, the running jobs list, the completed jobs list, and the retired jobs list. By clicking on a specific job link, we can check the details of a job, or we can open the URL, `http://master:50030/jobdetails.jsp?jobid=job_2013022814 51_0004&refresh=30`. By specifying the `refresh` parameter, we can tell the web page to refresh every 30 seconds.

2. Kill a job by opening the URL, `master:50030/jobdetails.jsp?jobid=job_201 302281451_0007&action=kill`.

After a while, the killed job will be listed in the **Failed Jobs** list as shown in the following screenshot:

Failed Jobs

Jobid	Started	Priority	User	Name	Map % Complete	Map Total	Maps Completed	Reduce % Complete
job_201302281451_0007	Fri Mar 01 11:08:55 EST 2013	NORMAL	hduser	random-text- writer	100.00%	5	0	100.00%

3. Change the job priority to be `HIGH` by opening the URL, `master:50030/jobdetails.jsp?jobid=job_201302281451_0007&action=changeprio&prio=HIGH`.

See also

▸ The *Validating Hadoop installation* recipe in *Chapter 3, Configuring a Hadoop Cluster*

▸ The *Managing the HDFS cluster* recipe

▸ The *Managing the MapReduce cluster* recipe

▸ Refer to `http://hadoop.apache.org/docs/r1.1.2/mapred_tutorial.html`

Checking job history from the web UI

Hadoop keeps track of all the submitted jobs in the logs directory. The job history logs contain information for each job such as the total run time and the run time of each task. In this section, we will show you how to check the job history logs through a web UI.

Getting ready

We assume that our Hadoop cluster has been properly configured and all daemons are running without any issues.

How to do it...

Perform the following steps to check job history logs from a web UI:

1. Open the job history URL, `http://master:50030/jobhistoryhome.jsp`.

We will be able to get a web page similar to the following screenshot:

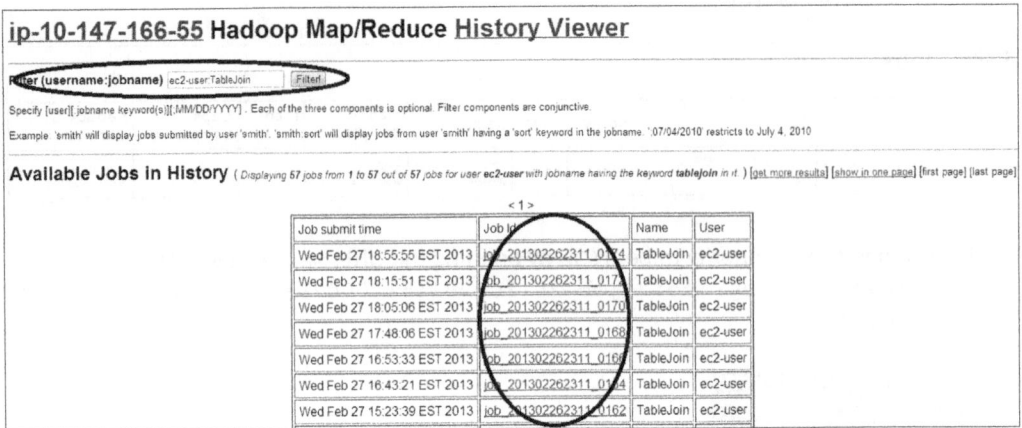

On the web UI, we can filter jobs based on the username and job name in the format **username:jobname** as shown in the screenshot. `username` should be the username that runs a certain job, and `job` name should contain keywords of Hadoop jobs.

2. From the web UI, we will be able to get a list of jobs in the **Available Jobs in History** section. By clicking on the **Job Id** link of a job, we can get the details of the job as shown in the following screenshot:

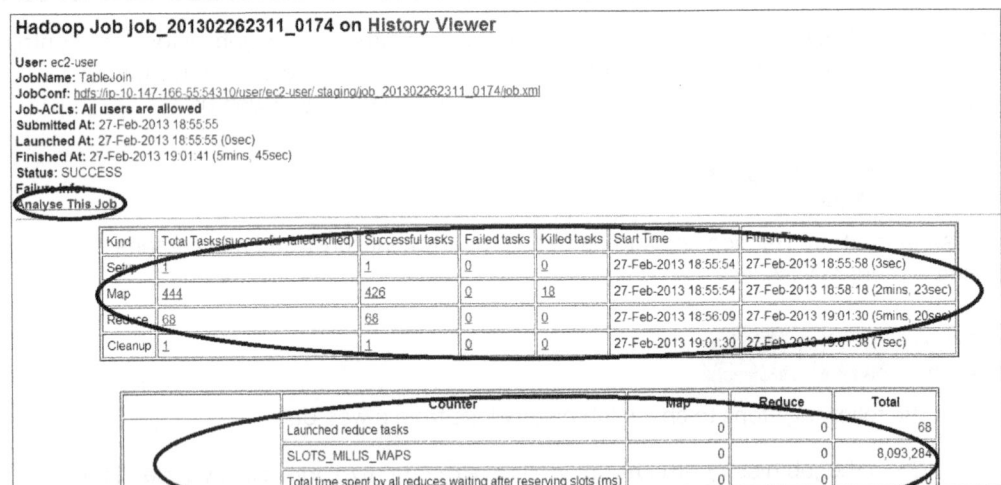

This web page shows the details of the job, including task information such as total, successful, failed, and killed tasks. The information also includes the start time and end time of four phases of a Hadoop job, including setup, map, reduce, and cleanup phases.

The web page also contains information of counters of the job as shown in the lower part of the screenshot.

3. In addition to the summary of the job information, the web UI provides an interface for us to analyze a job. By clicking on the link **Analyze This Job**, we will go to a web page similar to the following screenshot:

Hadoop Job job_201302262311_0174

User : ec2-user
JobName : TableJoin
JobConf : hdfs://ip-10-147-166-55:54310/user/ec2-user/.staging/job_201302262311_0174/job.xml
Submitted At : 27/02 18:55:55
Launched At : 27/02 18:55:55 (0sec)
Finished At : 27/02 19:01:41 (5mins, 45sec)
Status : SUCCESS

Time taken by best performing Map task task_201302262311_0174_m_000416 : 5sec

Average time taken by Map tasks: 18sec

Worse performing map tasks

Task Id	Time taken
task_201302262311_0174_m_000020	35sec
task_201302262311_0174_m_000022	35sec
task_201302262311_0174_m_000182	34sec
task_201302262311_0174_m_000179	33sec
task_201302262311_0174_m_000177	33sec
task_201302262311_0174_m_000176	32sec
task_201302262311_0174_m_000206	32sec
task_201302262311_0174_m_000372	31sec
task_201302262311_0174_m_000084	30sec
task_201302262311_0174_m_000113	30sec

The last Map task task_201302262311_0174_m_000359 finished at (relative to the Job launch time): 27/02 18:58:09 (2mins, 13sec)

The web page contains information of simple time analytics for each task, for example the best performing tasks that take the shortest time, the worst performing tasks, and the average time taken by all the tasks.

4. To further check the information of a task, we can click on the link for the task, and we will get a web page similar to the following screenshot:

task_201302262311_0174_m_000020 attempts for job_201302262311_0174

Task Id	Start Time	Finish Time	Host	Error	Task Logs	Counters
attempt_201302262311_0174_m_000020_0	27/02 18:56:17	27/02 18:56:52 (35sec)	/default-rack/ip-10-151-111-22		Last 4KB Last 8KB All	16

Input Split Locations

/default-rack/ip-10-151-21-199
/default-rack/ip-10-151-111-22

5. We can get the counters of a task by clicking on the `Counters` field of the task as shown in the preceding screenshot, or we can get the same web page by opening URL `http://master:50030/taskstats.jsp?tipid=task_201302281211_0 001_m_000000`.

 In this URL, `task_201302281211_0001_m_000000` is the task ID we want to get counters for.

We will be able to get task counters as shown in the following screenshot:

Counters for task_201302281211_0001_m_000000

File Input Format Counters
  Bytes Read   0

File Output Format Counters
  Bytes Written   810,572,991

FileSystemCounters
  HDFS_BYTES_READ   110
  FILE_BYTES_WRITTEN   24,143
  HDFS_BYTES_WRITTEN   810,572,999

org.apache.hadoop.examples.RandomTextWriter$Counters
  BYTES_WRITTEN   789,615,696
  RECORDS_WRITTEN   1,205,293

Map-Reduce Framework
  Map input records   1
  Physical memory (bytes) snapshot   82,300,928
  Spilled Records   0
  CPU time spent (ms)   22,920
  Total committed heap usage (bytes)   59,506,688
  Virtual memory (bytes) snapshot   1,933,426,688
  Map input bytes   0
  Map output records   1,205,293
  SPLIT_RAW_BYTES   110

6. In addition to all these web services, the web UI provides a graphical display of the progress of Hadoop jobs and each phase as shown in the following screenshot:

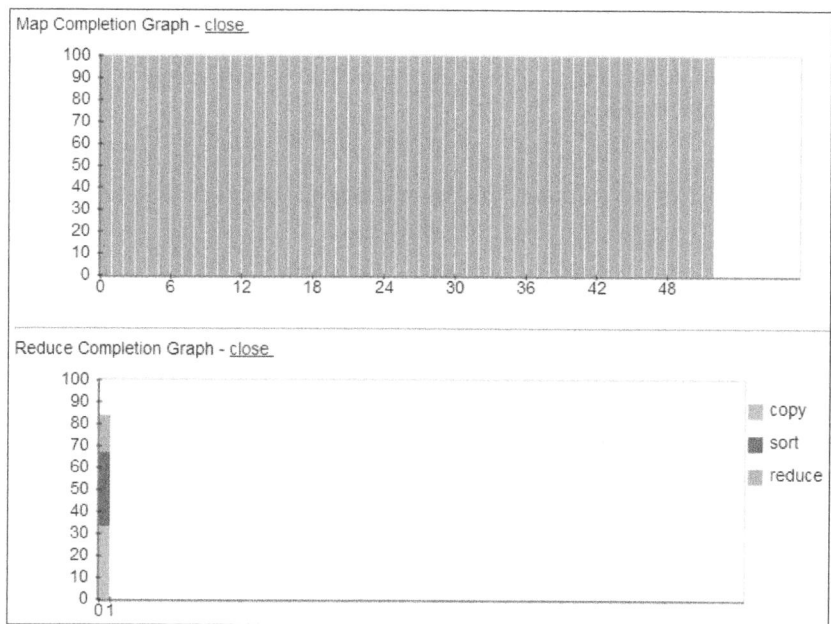

This screenshot shows the progress of each map and reduce task. The reduce task is composed of three phases: the shuffle phase, the sort phase, and the reduce phase, with each phase composing of 1/3 of the total reduce task.

How it works...

The meaning of the job history URL, `master:50030/jobhistoryhome.jsp`, can be explained as in the following table:

Field	Description
master	Hostname of machine that runs the JobTracker daemon.
50030	The port number of the JobTracker embedded web server.
jobhistoryhome.jsp	The .jsp file name that provides the job history service.

The web UI can be automatically updated every five seconds; this interval can be modified by changing the `mapreduce.client.completion.pollinterval` property in the `$HADOOP_HOME/conf/mapred-site.xml` file similar to the following:

```
<property>
    <name>mapreduce.client.completion.pollinterval</name>
    <value>5000</value>
</property>
```

The following table shows the summary of URLs we can use to check the status of jobs, tasks, and attempts:

URL	Description
`master:50030/jobtracker.jsp`	JobTracker.
`master:50030/jobhistoryhome.jsp`	Job history.
`master:50030/jobtasks.jsp?jobid=<jobID>&type=map&pagenum=1`	List of all map tasks.
`master:50030/jobtasks.jsp?jobid=<jobID>&type=reduce&pagenum=1`	List of all reduce tasks.
`master:50030/taskdetails.jsp?tipid=<taskID>`	Task attempt details.
`master:50030/taskstats.jsp?attemptid=<attempID>`	Attempt counters.

The following table lists the naming examples for `jobID`, `taskID`, and `attemptID`:

ID	Example
`jobID`	`job_201302281451_0001`
`taskID`	`task_201302281451_0001_m_000000`
`attemptID`	`attempt_201302281451_0001_m_000000_0`

See also

▶ The *Validating Hadoop installation* recipe in *Chapter 3, Configuring a Hadoop Cluster*

▶ The *Managing MapReduce jobs* recipe

Importing data to HDFS

If our Big Data is on the local filesystem, we need to move it to HDFS. In this section, we will list steps to move data from the local filesystem to the HDFS filesystem.

Getting ready

We assume that our Hadoop cluster has been properly configured and all the Hadoop daemons are running without any issues. And we assume that the data on the local system is in the directory /data.

How to do it...

Perform the following steps to import data to HDFS:

1. Use the following command to create a data directory on HDFS:

   ```
   hadoop fs -mkdir data
   ```

   This command will create a directory /user/hduser/data in the HDFS filesystem.

2. Copy the data file from the local directory to HDFS using the following command:

   ```
   hadoop fs -cp file:///data/datafile /user/hduser/data
   ```

   Alternatively, we can use the command hadoop fs -put /data/datafile /user/hduser/data.

3. Verify the data file on HDFS with the following command:

   ```
   hadoop fs -ls /user/hduser/data
   ```

4. Move the data file from the local directory to HDFS with the following command:

   ```
   hadoop fs -mv file:///data/datafile /user/hduser/data
   ```

    The local copy will be deleted if you use this command.

5. Use the distributed copy to copy the large data file to HDFS:

   ```
   hadoop distcp file:///data/datafile /user/hduser/data
   ```

   This command will initiate a MapReduce job with a number of mappers to run the copy task in parallel.

How it works...

We can get the usage of the `fs` command with the following:

```
hadoop fs
```

We will get an output similar to the following:

```
Usage: java FsShell
           [-ls <path>]
           [-lsr <path>]
           [-du <path>]
           [-dus <path>]
           [-count[-q] <path>]
           [-mv <src> <dst>]
           [-cp <src> <dst>]
           [-rm [-skipTrash] <path>]
           [-rmr [-skipTrash] <path>]
           [-expunge]
           [-put <localsrc> ... <dst>]
           [-copyFromLocal <localsrc> ... <dst>]
           [-moveFromLocal <localsrc> ... <dst>]
           [-get [-ignoreCrc] [-crc] <src> <localdst>]
           [-getmerge <src> <localdst> [addnl]]
           [-cat <src>]
           [-text <src>]
           [-copyToLocal [-ignoreCrc] [-crc] <src> <localdst>]
           [-moveToLocal [-crc] <src> <localdst>]
           [-mkdir <path>]
           [-setrep [-R] [-w] <rep> <path/file>]
           [-touchz <path>]
           [-test -[ezd] <path>]
           [-stat [format] <path>]
           [-tail [-f] <file>]
           [-chmod [-R] <MODE[,MODE]... | OCTALMODE> PATH...]
           [-chown [-R] [OWNER][:[GROUP]] PATH...]
           [-chgrp [-R] GROUP PATH...]
           [-help [cmd]]
```

The `<src>` and `<dst>` parameters for these data import commands use different default filesystem schema if no one has been explicitly specified in the command.

The default `<src>` filesystem schema for `-cp` and `-mv` is `hdfs:///`, which is configured with the `fs.default.name` property in the file `$HADOOP_HOME/conf/core-site.xml`, while the default `<src>` filesystem schema for `-put`, `-copyFromLocal`, and `-moveFromLocal` is `file:///`.

The default `<dst>` filesystem schema for all these commands is `hdfs:///`.

There's more...

To copy multiple files from the local directory to HDFS, we can use the following command:

```
hadoop fs -copyFromLocal src1 src2 data
```

This command will copy two files `src1` and `src2` from the local directory to the `data` directory on HDFS.

Similarly, we can move files from the local directory to HDFS. Its only difference from the previous command is that the local files will be deleted.

```
hadoop fs -moveFromLocal src1 src2 data
```

This command will move two files, `src1` and `src2`, from the local directory to HDFS.

Although the distributed copy can be faster than the simple data importing commands, it can incur a large load to the node that the data resides on because of the possibility of high data transfer requests. `distcp` will be more useful when copying data from one HDFS location to another. For example:

```
hadoop distcp hdfs:///user/hduser/file hdfs:///user/hduser/file-copy
```

See also

- ▸ The *Managing the HDFS cluster* recipe
- ▸ The *Manipulating files on HDFS* recipe

Manipulating files on HDFS

Besides commands to copy files from the local directory, HDFS provides commands to operate on files. In this section, we will show you how to operate files, such as downloading files from HDFS, checking the content of files, and removing files from HDFS.

Getting ready

We assume that our Hadoop cluster has been properly configured and all the daemons are running without any issues.

How to do it...

Perform the following steps to check the status of files and the directory on HDFS:

1. List files of the user's home directory on HDFS using the following command:

   ```
   hadoop fs -ls .
   ```

   For example, this command will give the following output on my machine:

   ```
   Found 7 items
   drwx------ - hduser supergroup    0 2013-02-21 22:17 /user/hduser/.
   staging
   -rw-r--r-- 2 hduser supergroup 646 2013-02-21 22:28 /user/hduser/
   file1
   -rw-r--r-- 2 hduser supergroup 848 2013-02-21 22:28 /user/hduser/
   file2
   ...
   ```

    To recursively list files in the home directory, we can use the command `hadoop fs -lsr ...`

2. Check the space usage of files and folders in the home directory with the following command:

   ```
   hadoop fs -du .
   ```

   We will get an output similar to the following:

   ```
   Found 7 items
   648521        hdfs://master:54310/user/hduser/.staging
   646           hdfs://master:54310/user/hduser/file1
   ```

```
3671517          hdfs://master:54310/user/hduser/file2
...
```

The first column shows the size of the file in bytes and the second column shows the location of files on HDFS.

Sometimes, we can get a summarized usage of a directory with the command `hadoop fs -dus` . It will show us the total space usage of the directory rather than the sizes of individual files and folders in the directory. For example, we can get a one-line output similar to the following:

```
hdfs://master:54310/user/hduser     109810605367
```

3. Check the content of a file with the following command:

```
hadoop fs -cat file1
```

This command is handy to check the content of small files. But when the file is large, it is not recommended. Instead, we can use the command `hadoop fs -tail file1` to check the content of the last few lines.

Alternatively, we can use the command `hadoop fs -text file1` to show the content of `file1` in text format.

4. Use the following commands to test if `file1` exists, is empty, or is a directory:

```
hadoop fs -test -e file1
hadoop fs -test -z file1
hadoop fs -test -d file1
```

5. Check the status of `file1` using the following command:

```
hadoop fs -stat file1
```

Perform the following steps to manipulate files and directories on HDFS:

1. Empty the trash using the following command:

```
hadoop fs -expunge
```

2. Merge files in a directory `dir` and download it as one big file:

```
hadoop fs -getmerge dir file1
```

This command is similar to the `cat` command in Linux. It is very useful when we want to get the MapReduce output as one file rather than several smaller partitioned files.

For example, the command can merge files `dir/part-00000`, `dir/part-00001`, and so on to `file1` to the local filesystem.

3. Delete `file1` under the current directory using the following command:

```
hadoop fs -rm file1
```

Note that this command will not delete a directory. To delete a directory, we can use the command `hadoop fs -rmr dir`. It is very similar to the Linux command `rm -r`, which will recursively delete everything in the directory `dir` and the directory itself. So use it with caution.

4. Download `file1` from HDFS using the following command:

```
hadoop fs -get file1
```

The `file1` file under the directory `/user/hduser` will be downloaded to the current directory on the local filesystem.

5. Change the group membership of a regular file with the following command:

```
hadoop fs -chgrp hadoop file1
```

In this command, we are assuming group `hadoop` exists.

Also, we can use the command `hadoop fs -chgrp -R hadoop dir` to change the group membership of a directory `dir` recursively.

6. Change the ownership of a regular file with the following command:

```
hadoop fs -chown hduser file1
```

Similarly, we can use the command `hadoop fs -chown hdadmin -R dir` to change the ownership of a directory `dir` recursively.

7. Change the mode of a file with the following command:

```
hadoop fs -chmod 600 file1
```

 The mode of files and directories under HDFS follows a similar rule as the mode under Linux.

8. Set the replication factor of `file1` to be 3 using the following command:

```
hadoop fs -setrep -w 3 file1
```

9. Create an empty file using the following command:

```
hadoop fs -touchz 0file
```

How it works...

We can get the usage of the `fs` command with the following command:

```
hadoop fs
```

We will get an output similar to the following:

```
Usage: java FsShell
           [-ls <path>]
           [-lsr <path>]
           [-du <path>]
           [-dus <path>]
           [-count[-q] <path>]
           [-mv <src> <dst>]
           [-cp <src> <dst>]
           [-rm [-skipTrash] <path>]
           [-rmr [-skipTrash] <path>]
           [-expunge]
           [-put <localsrc> ... <dst>]
           [-copyFromLocal <localsrc> ... <dst>]
           [-moveFromLocal <localsrc> ... <dst>]
           [-get [-ignoreCrc] [-crc] <src> <localdst>]
           [-getmerge <src> <localdst> [addnl]]
           [-cat <src>]
           [-text <src>]
           [-copyToLocal [-ignoreCrc] [-crc] <src> <localdst>]
           [-moveToLocal [-crc] <src> <localdst>]
           [-mkdir <path>]
           [-setrep [-R] [-w] <rep> <path/file>]
           [-touchz <path>]
           [-test -[ezd] <path>]
           [-stat [format] <path>]
           [-tail [-f] <file>]
           [-chmod [-R] <MODE[,MODE]... | OCTALMODE> PATH...]
           [-chown [-R] [OWNER][:[GROUP]] PATH...]
           [-chgrp [-R] GROUP PATH...]
           [-help [cmd]]
```

To get help for each individual command, we can use the -help option. For example, we can get the help of the list command with the following:

```
hadoop fs -help ls
```

This command will give us the following output:

```
-ls <path>:      List the contents that match the specified file pattern.
If

                 path is not specified, the contents of /
user/<currentUser>
                 will be listed. Directory entries are of the form
                        dirName (full path) <dir>
                 and file entries are of the form
                        fileName(full path) <r n> size
                 where n is the number of replicas specified for the file
                 and size is the size of the file, in bytes.
```

Configuring the HDFS quota

In a multiuser environment, **quota** can enforce the fair share of computing resources. HDFS supports quota for users and directories. In this recipe, we will list steps to configure the HDFS quota.

Getting ready

We assume that the Hadoop cluster has been configured properly and all the daemons are running without any issues.

How to do it...

Perform the following steps to manage an HDFS quota:

1. Set the name quota on the home directory with the following command:

    ```
    hadoop dfsadmin -setQuota 20 /usr/hduser
    ```

    This command will set name quota on the home directory to 20, which means at most 20 files, including directories, can be created under the home directory.

    If we reach the quota, an error message similar to the following will be given:

    ```
    put: org.apache.hadoop.hdfs.protocol.NSQuotaExceededException: The
    NameSpace quota (directories and files) of directory /user/hduser
    is exceeded: quota=20 file count=141
    ```

2. Set the space quota of the current user's home directory to be `100000000` with the following command:

    ```
    hadoop dfsadmin -setSpaceQuota 100000000 /user/hduser
    ```

If the space usage under the directory /user/hduser exceeds the specified quota, we will get an error message similar to the following:

```
put: org.apache.hadoop.hdfs.protocol.DSQuotaExceededException:
The DiskSpace quota of /user/hduser is exceeded: quota=100000000
diskspace consumed=204.5g
```

3. Check the quota status with the following command:

```
hadoop fs -count -q /user/hduser
```

We will get an output similar to the following before setting the quota:

```
none inf  none inf 13   127   109810605367 hdfs://master:54310/user/
hduser
```

And we will get the following quota has been set:

```
100  -40  100000000 -219525889438  13  127  1098106  05367 hdfs://
master:54310/user/hduser
```

The meaning of output columns is DIR_COUNT FILE_COUNT CONTENT_SIZE FILE_NAME or QUOTA REMAINING_QUATA SPACE_QUOTA REMAINING_SPACE_QUOTA DIR_COUNT FILE_COUNT CONTENT_SIZE FILE_NAME.

4. Clear the name quota with the following command:

```
hadoop dfsadmin -clrQuota /user/hduser
```

5. Clear the space quota with the following command:

```
hadoop dfsadmin -clrSpaceQuota /user/hduser
```

How it works...

We can get the usage of the hadoop fs command with the following command:

```
hadoop dfsadmin
```

We will get an output similar to the following:

```
Usage: java DFSAdmin
          [-report]
          [-safemode enter | leave | get | wait]
          [-saveNamespace]
          [-refreshNodes]
          [-finalizeUpgrade]
          [-upgradeProgress status | details | force]
          [-metasave filename]
```

```
[-refreshServiceAcl]

[-refreshUserToGroupsMappings]

[-refreshSuperUserGroupsConfiguration]

[-setQuota <quota> <dirname>...<dirname>]

[-clrQuota <dirname>...<dirname>]

[-setSpaceQuota <quota> <dirname>...<dirname>]

[-clrSpaceQuota <dirname>...<dirname>]

[-setBalancerBandwidth <bandwidth in bytes per second>]

[-help [cmd]]
```

The generic usage of the `-count` command is:

```
hadoop fs -count -q <path>
```

In this command `-q` specifies the directory to query.

Configuring CapacityScheduler

Hadoop **CapacityScheduler** is a pluggable MapReduce **job scheduler**. The goal is to maximize the Hadoop cluster utilization by sharing the cluster among multiple users. CapacityScheduler uses queues to guarantee the minimum share of each user. It has features of being secure, elastic, operable, and supporting job priority. In this recipe, we will outline steps to configure CapacityScheduler for a Hadoop cluster.

Getting ready

We assume that our Hadoop cluster has been properly configured and all the daemons are running without any issues.

Log in to the master node from the cluster administrator machine using the following command:

```
ssh hduser@master
```

How to do it...

Configure CapacityScheduler with the following steps:

1. Configure Hadoop to use CapacityScheduler by adding the following lines into the file $HADOOP_HOME/conf/mapred-site.xml:

```
<property>
    <name>mapred.jobtracker.taskScheduler</name>
```

```
    <value>org.apache.hadoop.mapred.CapacityTaskScheduler</value>
    </property>
```

2. Define a new queue, hdqueue, by adding the following lines into the file
   $HADOOP_HOME/conf/mapred-site.xml:

```
<property>
    <name>mapred.queue.names</name>
 <value>default,hdqueue</value>
    </property>
```

 By default, a Hadoop cluster has only one default queue.

3. Configure CapacityScheduler queues by adding the following lines into the file
   $HADOOP_HOME/conf/capacity-scheduler.xml:

```
<property>
    <name>mapred.capacity-scheduler.queue.hdqueue.capacity</name>
    <value>20</value>
</property>

<property>
    <name>mapred.capacity-scheduler.queue.default.capacity</name>
    <value>80</value>
</property>

<property>
    <name>mapred.capacity-scheduler.queue.hdqueue.minimum-user-
limit-percent</name>
    <value>20</value>
</property>

<property>
    <name>mapred.capacity-scheduler.maximum-system-jobs</name>
    <value>10</value>
</property>

<property>
    <name>mapred.capacity-scheduler.queue.hdqueue.maximum-
initialized-active-tasks</name>
    <value>500</value>
</property>

<property>
```

```
   <name>mapred.capacity-scheduler.queue.hdqueue.maximum-
initialized-active-tasks-per-user</name>
   <value>100</value>
</property>

<property>
   <name>mapred.capacity-scheduler.queue.hdqueue.supports-
priority</name>
   <value>true</value>
</property>
```

4. Restart the MapReduce cluster with the following commands:

   stop-mapred.sh

   start-mapred.sh

5. From the JobTracker web UI, we can get a queue scheduling information web page similar to the following screenshot:

<table>
<tr><th colspan="3">Scheduling Information</th></tr>
<tr><th>Queue Name</th><th>State</th><th>Scheduling Information</th></tr>
<tr>
<td>default</td>
<td>running</td>
<td>
Queue configuration
Capacity Percentage: 80.0%
User Limit: 100%
Priority Supported: NO

Map tasks
Capacity: 8 slots
Used capacity: 0 (0.0% of Capacity)
Running tasks: 0

Reduce tasks
Capacity: 8 slots
Used capacity: 0 (0.0% of Capacity)
Running tasks: 0

Job info
Number of Waiting Jobs: 0
Number of Initializing Jobs: 0
Number of users who have submitted jobs: 0
</td>
</tr>
<tr>
<td>hdqueue</td>
<td>running</td>
<td>
Queue configuration
Capacity Percentage: 20.0%
User Limit: 15%
Priority Supported: YES

Map tasks
Capacity: 2 slots
Used capacity: 0 (0.0% of Capacity)
Running tasks: 0

Reduce tasks
Capacity: 2 slots
Used capacity: 0 (0.0% of Capacity)
Running tasks: 0

Job info
Number of Waiting Jobs: 0
Number of Initializing Jobs: 0
Number of users who have submitted jobs: 0
</td>
</tr>
</table>

Alternatively, we can use the command `hadoop queue -list` to get the same information.

6. Get the schedule details of each queue by opening the URL, `master:50030/ scheduler`, and we can get a web page similar to the following:

master **Job Scheduler Administration**

Queues

Queue	Running Jobs	Pending Jobs	Capacity Percentage	Map Task Capacity	Map Task Used Capacity	Running Maps	Reduce Task Capacity	Reduce Task Used Capacity	Running Reduces
default	0	0	80.0%	8	0 (0.0% of Capacity)	0	8	0 (0.0% of Capacity)	0
hdqueue	1	0	20.0%	2	8 (400.0% of Capacity)	8	2	1 (50.0% of Capacity)	1

This screenshot shows the status of each queue in the cluster, including the numbers of running jobs, pending jobs, and so on.

7. Test the queue configuration by submitting an example `wordcount` job to the queue `hdqueue` using the following command:

```
hadoop jar $HADOOP_HOME/hadoop-examples-1.1.2.jar wordcount
-Dmapred.job.queue.name=hdqueue randtext wordcount.out
```

From the job information web UI, we can get the job scheduling information similar to the following:

```
Job Scheduling information: 8 running map tasks using 8 map slots.
0 additional slots reserved. 1 running reduce tasks using 1 reduce
slots. 0 additional slots reserved.
```

How it works...

CapacityScheduler is available as a JAR file under the `$HADOOP_HOME/lib directory`. For example, in our Hadoop distribution, the JAR file is `$HADOOP_HOME/lib/hadoop-capacity-scheduler-1.1.2.jar`.

The following table shows the description of queue configuration properties:

Property	Description
`mapred.capacity-scheduler.queue.hdqueue.capacity`	The percentage share of the total number of slots for the `hdqueue` queue.
`mapred.capacity-scheduler.queue.default.capacity`	The percentage share of the total number of slots for the default queue.
`mapred.capacity-scheduler.queue.hdqueue.minimum-user-limit-percent`	The percentage of minimum resources allocated for each user in the queue `hdqueue`.

Property	Description
`mapred.capacity-scheduler.maximum-system-jobs`	The maximum number of jobs that can be initialized concurrently by CapacityScheduler.
`mapred.capacity-scheduler.queue.hdqueue.maximum-initialized-active-tasks`	The maximum number of concurrently initialized tasks across all jobs in the queue `hdqueue`.
`mapred.capacity-scheduler.queue.hdqueue.maximum-initialized-active-tasks-per-user`	The maximum number of concurrently initialized tasks across all jobs in the queue `hdqueue` for each user.
`mapred.capacity-scheduler.queue.hdqueue.supports-priority`	Whether to support job priority for job scheduling or not.

There's more...

Hadoop supports access control on the queue using queue ACLs. Queue ACLs control the authorization of MapReduce job submission to a queue. More information about queue ACLs can be found at `http://hadoop.apache.org/docs/r1.1.2/cluster_setup.html#Configuring+the+Hadoop+Daemons`.

See also

- The *Managing MapReduce jobs* recipe
- The *Checking job history from the web UI* recipe
- The *Configuring Fair Scheduler* recipe
- The *Configuring job authorization with ACL* recipe of *Chapter 5, Hardening a Hadoop Cluster*
- Refer to `http://hadoop.apache.org/docs/r1.1.2/capacity_scheduler.html`

Configuring Fair Scheduler

Similar to CapacityScheduler, **Fair Scheduler** was designed to enforce fair shares of cluster resources in a multiuser environment. In this recipe, we will outline steps to configure Fair Scheduler for a Hadoop cluster.

Getting ready

We assume that our Hadoop cluster has been configured properly and all the daemons are running without any problems.

Log in to the master node from the Hadoop administrator machine using the following command:

```
ssh hduser@master
```

How to do it...

Perform the following steps to configure Hadoop Fair Scheduler:

1. Enable fair scheduling by changing the following property in the file `$HADOOP_HOME/conf/mapred-site.xml`:

    ```xml
    <property>
      <name>mapred.jobtracker.taskScheduler</name>
      <value>org.apache.hadoop.mapred.FairScheduler</value>
    </property>
    ```

2. Create the Fair Scheduler configuration file, `$HADOOP_HOME/conf/fair-scheduler.xml`, with content similar to the following:

    ```xml
    <?xml version="1.0"?>

    <allocations>
    <pool name="hduser">
        <minMaps>5</minMaps>
        <minReduces>5</minReduces>
        <maxMaps>90</maxMaps>
        <maxReduces>20</maxReduces>
        <weight>2.0</weight>
      </pool>
      <user name="hduser">
        <maxRunningJobs>1</maxRunningJobs>
      </user>
      <userMaxJobsDefault>3</userMaxJobsDefault>
    </allocations>
    ```

3. Restart the MapReduce cluster with the following commands:

    ```
    stop-mapred.sh
    start-mapred.sh
    ```

4. Verify the setting of Fair Scheduler by opening the URL `http://master:50030/scheduler`.

    The web page will be similar to the following screenshot:

master Fair Scheduler Administration

Pools

Pool	Running Jobs	Map Tasks				Reduce Tasks				Scheduling Mode
		Min Share	Max Share	Running	Fair Share	Min Share	Max Share	Running	Fair Share	
hduser	1	5	90	10	10.0	5	73	0	0.0	FAIR
default	0	0	-	0	0.0	0	-	0	0.0	FAIR

Running Jobs

Submitted	JobID	User	Name	Pool	Priority	Map Tasks			Reduce Tasks		
						Finished	Running	Fair Share	Finished	Running	Fair Share
Mar 01, 16:16	job_201302281451_0017	ec2-user	TableJoin	hduser	NORMAL	0 / 86	10	10.0	0 / 1	0	0.0

How it works...

The Hadoop Fair Scheduler schedules jobs in such a way that all jobs can get an equal share of computing resources. Jobs are organized with scheduling pools. A pool can be configured for each Hadoop user. If the pool for a user is not configured, the default pool will be used. A pool specifies the amount of resources a user can share on the cluster, for example the number of map slots, reduce slots, the total number of running jobs, and so on.

`minMaps` and `minReduces` are used to ensure the minimum share of computing slots on the cluster for a pool. The minimum share guarantee can be useful when the required number of computing slots is larger than the number of configured slots. In case the minimum share of a pool is not met, JobTracker will kill tasks on other pools and assign the slots to the starving pool. In such cases, the JobTracker will restart the killed tasks on other nodes and thus, the job will take a longer time to finish.

Besides computing slots, the Fair Scheduler can limit the number of concurrently running jobs and tasks on a pool. So, if a user submits more jobs than the configured limit, some jobs have to in-queue until other jobs finish. In such a case, higher priority jobs will be scheduled by the Fair Scheduler to run earlier than lower priority jobs. If all jobs in the waiting queue have the same priority, the Fair Scheduler can be configured to schedule these jobs with either Fair Scheduler or FIFO Scheduler.

The following table shows the properties supported by fair scheduler:

Property	Value	Description
minMaps	Integer	Minimum map slots for a pool.
minReduces	Integer	Maximum map slots for a pool.
minReduces	Integer	Minimum reduce slots for a pool.
minReduces	Integer	Maximum reduce slots for a pool.
schedulingMode	Fair/FIFO	Pool internal scheduling mode, fair or fifo.
maxRunningJobs	Integer	Maximum number of concurrently running jobs for a pool. Default value is unlimited.
weight	Float	Value to control non-proportional share of a cluster resource. The default value is 1.0.
minSharePreemption Timeout	Integer	Seconds to wait before killing other pool's tasks if a pool's share is under the minimum share.
maxRunningJobs	Integer	Maximum number of concurrent running jobs for a user. Default is unlimited.
poolMaxJobsDefault	Integer	Default maximum number of concurrently running jobs for a pool.
userMaxJobsDefault	Integer	Default maximum number of concurrently running jobs for a user.
defaultMinShare PreemptionTimeout	Integer	Default seconds to wait before killing other pools' tasks when a pool's share is under minimum share.
fairSharePreemption Timeout	Integer	Pre-emption time when a job's resource is below half of the fair share.
defaultPool SchedulingMode	Fair/FIFO	Default in-pool scheduling mode.

See also

- The *Configuring CapacityScheduler* recipe
- Refer to http://hadoop.apache.org/docs/r1.1.2/fair_scheduler.html

Configuring Hadoop daemon logging

System **logging** plays an important role in dealing with performance and security problems. In addition, the logging information can be used analytically to tune the performance of a Hadoop cluster. In this recipe, we will show you how to configure Hadoop logging.

Getting ready

We assume that our Hadoop cluster has been properly configured.

How to do it...

Perform the following steps to configure Hadoop logging:

1. Log in to the master node with the following command from the Hadoop administrator machine:

   ```
   ssh hduser@master
   ```

2. Check the current logging level of JobTracker with the following command:

   ```
   hadoop daemonlog -getlevel master:50030 org.apache.hadoop.mapred.
   JobTracker
   ```

   We will get an output similar to the following:

   ```
   Connecting to http://master:50030/logLevel?log=org.apache.hadoop.
   mapred.JobTracker

   Submitted Log Name: org.apache.hadoop.mapred.JobTracker

   Log Class: org.apache.commons.logging.impl.Log4JLogger

   Effective level: INFO
   ```

3. Tell Hadoop to only log error events for JobTracker using the following command:

   ```
   hadoop daemonlog -setlevel master:50030 org.apache.hadoop.mapred.
   JobTracker ERROR
   ```

   We will get an output similar to the following:

   ```
   Connecting to http://master:50030/logLevel?log=org.apache.hadoop.
   mapred.JobTracker&level=ERROR

   Submitted Log Name: org.apache.hadoop.mapred.JobTracker

   Log Class: org.apache.commons.logging.impl.Log4JLogger

   Submitted Level: ERROR
   ```

```
Setting Level to ERROR ...
Effective level: ERROR
```

Now, the logging status of the JobTracker daemon will be similar to the following:

```
Connecting to http://master:50030/logLevel?log=org.apache.hadoop.
mapred.JobTracker
Submitted Log Name: org.apache.hadoop.mapred.JobTracker
Log Class: org.apache.commons.logging.impl.Log4JLogger
Effective level: ERROR
```

4. Get the log levels for TaskTracker, NameNode, and DataNode with the following commands:

```
hadoop daemonlog -getlevel master:50030 org.apache.hadoop.mapred.
TaskTracker hadoop daemonlog -getlevel master:50070 org.apache.
hadoop.dfs.NameNode
hadoop daemonlog -getlevel master:50070 org.apache.hadoop.dfs.
DataNode
```

We will get the following output:

```
Connecting to http://master:50030/logLevel?log=org.apache.hadoop.
mapred.TaskTracker
Submitted Log Name: org.apache.hadoop.mapred.TaskTracker
Log Class: org.apache.commons.logging.impl.Log4JLogger
Effective level: WARN


Connecting to http://master:50070/logLevel?log=org.apache.hadoop.
dfs.NameNode
Submitted Log Name: org.apache.hadoop.dfs.NameNode
Log Class: org.apache.commons.logging.impl.Log4JLogger
Effective level: INFO


Connecting to http://master:50070/logLevel?log=org.apache.hadoop.
dfs.DataNode
Submitted Log Name: org.apache.hadoop.dfs.DataNode
Log Class: org.apache.commons.logging.impl.Log4JLogger
Effective level: INFO
```

How it works...

By default , Hadoop sends log messages to **Log4j**, which is configured in the file `$HADOOP_HOME/conf/log4j.properties`. This file defines both what to log and where to log. For applications, the default root logger is `INFO, console`, which logs all messages at level INFO and above the console's `stderr`. Log files are named `$HADOOP_LOG_DIR/hadoop-$HADOOP_IDENT_STRING-<hostname>.log`.

Hadoop supports a number of log levels for different purposes. The log level should be tuned based on the purpose of logging. For example, if we are debugging a daemon, we can set its logging level to be `DEBUG` rather than something else. Using a verbose log level can give us more information, while on the other hand will incur overhead to the cluster.

The following table shows all the logging levels provided by Log4j:

Log level	Description
ALL	The lowest logging level, all loggings will be turned on.
DEBUG	Logging events useful for debugging applications.
ERROR	Logging error events, but applications can continue to run.
FATAL	Logging very severe error events that will abort applications.
INFO	Logging informational messages that indicate the progress of applications.
OFF	Logging will be turned off.
TRACE	Logging more finger-grained events for application debugging.
TRACE_INT	Logging in TRACE level on integer values.
WARN	Logging potentially harmful events.

We can get the usage of `daemonlog` with the following command:

```
hadoop daemonlog
```

The usage message will be similar to the following:

```
USAGES:
java org.apache.hadoop.log.LogLevel -getlevel <host:port> <name>
java org.apache.hadoop.log.LogLevel -setlevel <host:port> <name> <level>
```

There's more...

Other than configuring Hadoop logging on the fly from command line, we can configure it using configuration files. The most important file that we need to configure is `$HADOOP/conf/hadoop-env.sh`.

Sometimes, audit logging is desirable for corporate auditing purposes. Hadoop provides audit logging through Log4j using the `INFO` logging level. We will show you how to configure Hadoop audit logging in the next recipe.

Configuring Hadoop logging with hadoop-env.sh

Open the file `$HADOOP_HOME/conf/hadoop-env.sh` with a text editor and change the following line:

```
# export HADOOP_LOG_DIR=${HADOOP_HOME}/logs
```

We change the preceding command to the following:

```
export HADOOP_LOG_DIR=${HADOOP_HOME}/logs
```

Configure the logging directory to `/var/log/hadoop` by changing the following line:

```
export HADOOP_LOG_DIR=/var/log/hadoop
```

Additionally, the following table shows other environment variables we can configure for Hadoop logging:

Variable name	Description
HADOOP_LOG_DIR	Directory for log files.
HADOOP_PID_DIR	Directory to store the PID for the servers.
HADOOP_ROOT_LOGGER	Logging configuration for `hadoop.root.logger`. default, `"INFO,console"`
HADOOP_SECURITY_LOGGER	Logging configuration for `hadoop.security.logger`. default, `"INFO,NullAppender"`
HDFS_AUDIT_LOGGER	Logging configuration for `hdfs.audit.logger`. default, `"INFO,NullAppender"`

The cluster needs to be restarted for the configuration to take effect.

Configuring Hadoop security logging

Security logging can help Hadoop cluster administrators to identify security problems. It is enabled by default.

The security logging configuration is located in the file `$HADOOP_HOME/conf/log4j. properties`. By default, the security logging information is appended to the same file as NameNode logging. We can check the security logs with the following command:

```
grep security $HADOOP_HOME/logs/hadoop-hduser-namenode-master.log
```

The output is similar to the following:

```
2013-02-28 13:36:01,008 ERROR org.apache.hadoop.security.
UserGroupInformation: PriviledgedActionException as:hduser cause:org.
apache.hadoop.hdfs.server.namenode.SafeModeException: Cannot create file/
user/hduser/test. Name node is in safe mode.
```

The error message tells that the NameNode is in safe mode, so the file `/user/hduser/test` cannot be created. Similar information can give us a very useful hint to figure out operation errors.

Hadoop logging file naming conventions

Hadoop logfiles are kept under the directory `$HADOOP_HOME/logs`. The tree structure of this directory on the master node will be similar to the following:

```
logs
├── hadoop-hduser-namenode-master.log
├── hadoop-hduser-namenode-master.out
├── hadoop-hduser-jobtracker-master.log
├── hadoop-hduser-jobtracker-master.out
├── hadoop-hduser-secondarynamenode-master.log
├── hadoop-hduser-secondarynamenode-master.out
├── history
│   ├── done
│   ├── job_201302262311_0180_1362011591521_hduser_TableJoin
│   └── job_201302262311_0180_conf.xml
└── job_201302281211_0006_conf.xml


6 directories, 9 files
```

On a slave node, the `$HADOOP_HOME/logs` folder will have contents similar to the following:

```
logs
├── hadoop-hduser-datanode-slave1.log
├── hadoop-hduser-datanode-slave1.out
├── hadoop-hduser-tasktracker-slave1.log
├── hadoop-hduser-tasktracker-slave1.out
└── userlogs
    └── job_201302281211_0007
```

```
        ├── attempt_201302281211_0007_m_000003_0 -> /tmp/hadoop-hduser/
mapred/local/userlogs/job_201302281211_0007/attempt_201302281211_0007
_m_000003_0

        ├── attempt_201302281211_0007_m_000007_0 -> /tmp/hadoop-hduser/
mapred/local/userlogs/job_201302281211_0007/attempt_201302281211_0007
_m_000007_0

        └── job-acls.xml
```

4 directories, 5 files

The folder contains one `.log` file and one `.out` file for each Hadoop daemon, for example, NameNode, SecondaryNameNode, and JobTracker on the master node and TaskTracker and DataNode on a slave node. The `.out` file is used when a daemon is being started. Its content will be emptied after the daemon has started successfully. The `.log` files contain all the log messages for a daemon, including startup logging messages.

On the master node, the logs directory contain a `history` folder that contains logs of the MapReduce job history. Similarly, on a slave node, the `logs` directory contains a `userlogs` directory, which maintains the history information of the tasks that ran on the node.

In Hadoop, the names of logging files use the following format:

`hadoop-<username>-<daemonname>-<hostname>.log`

See also

▸ The *Configuring Hadoop audit logging* recipe

▸ Refer to `http://wiki.apache.org/hadoop/HowToConfigure`

Configuring Hadoop audit logging

Audit logging might be required for data processing systems such as Hadoop. In Hadoop, audit logging has been implemented using the Log4j Java logging library at the `INFO` logging level. By default, Hadoop audit logging is disabled. This recipe will guide you through the steps to configure Hadoop audit logging.

Getting ready

We assume that our Hadoop cluster has been configured properly.

Log in to the master node from the administrator machine using the following command:

`ssh hduser@master`

How to do it...

Perform the following steps to configure Hadoop audit logging:

1. Enable audit logging by changing the following line in the `$HADOOP_HOME/conf/log4j.properties` file from:

   ```
   log4j.logger.org.apache.hadoop.hdfs.server.namenode.FSNamesystem.audit=WARN
   ```

   to the following:

   ```
   log4j.logger.org.apache.hadoop.hdfs.server.namenode.FSNamesystem.audit=INFO
   ```

2. Try making a directory on HDFS with the following command:

   ```
   hadoop fs -mkdir audittest
   ```

3. Check the audit log messages in the NameNode log file with the following command:

   ```
   grep org.apache.hadoop.hdfs.server.namenode.FSNamesystem.audit
   $HADOOP_HOME/logs/hadoop-hduser-namenode-master.log
   ```

   We will get an output similar to the following:

   ```
   2013-02-28 13:38:04,235 INFO org.apache.hadoop.hdfs.server.
   namenode.FSNamesystem.audit: ugi=hduser     ip=/10.0.0.1
   cmd=mkdirs    src=/user/hduser/audittest  dst=null
   perm=hduser:supergroup:rwxr-xr-x
   ```

   The Hadoop NameNode is responsible for managing audit logging messages, which are forwarded to the NameNode logging facility. So what we have seen so far is that the audit logging message has been mixed with the normal logging message.

4. We can separate the audit logging messages from the NameNode logging messages by configuring the file `$HADOOP_HOME/conf/log4j.properties` with the following content:

   ```
   # Log at INFO level, SYSLOG appenders
   log4j.logger.org.apache.hadoop.hdfs.server.namenode.FSNamesystem.audit=INFO


   # Disable forwarding the audit logging message to the NameNode logger.
   log4j.additivity.org.apache.hadoop.hdfs.server.namenode.FSNamesystem.audit=false
   ```

```
###############################
# Configure logging appender
###############################
#
# Daily Rolling File Appender (DRFA)
log4j.appender.DRFAAUDIT=org.apache.log4j.DailyRollingFileAppender
log4j.appender.DRFAAUDIT.File=$HADOOP_HOME/logs/audit.log
log4j.appender.DRFAAUDIT.DatePattern=.yyyy-MM-dd
log4j.appender.DRFAAUDIT.layout=org.apache.log4j.PatternLayout
log4j.appender.DRFAAUDIT.layout.ConversionPattern=%d{ISO8601} %p
%c: %m%n
```

How it works...

Hadoop logs auditing messages of operations, such as creating, changing, or deleting files into a configured log file. By default, audit logging is set to WARN, which disables audit logging. To enable it, the logging level needs be changed to INFO.

When a Hadoop cluster has many jobs to run, the log file can become large very quickly. Log file rotation is a function that periodically rotates a log file to a different name, for example, by appending the date to the filename, so that the original logfile name can be used as an empty file.

See also

▶ The *Configuring Hadoop daemon logging* recipe

Upgrading Hadoop

A Hadoop cluster needs to be upgraded when new versions with bug fixes or new features are released. In this recipe, we will outline steps to upgrade a Hadoop cluster to a newer version.

Getting ready

Download the desired Hadoop release from an Apache mirror site: http://www.apache.org/dyn/closer.cgi/hadoop/common/. In this book, we assume to upgrade Hadoop from version 1.1.2 to version 1.2.0, which is still in the beta state when writing this book.

We assume that there are no running or pending MapReduce jobs in the cluster.

In the process of upgrading a Hadoop cluster, we want to minimize the damage to the data stored on HDFS, and this procedure is the cause of most of the upgrade problems. The data damages can be caused by either human operation or software and hardware failures. So, a backup of the data might be necessary. But the sheer size of the data on HDFS can be a headache for most of the upgrade experience.

A more practical way is to only back up the HDFS filesystem metadata on the master node, while leaving the data blocks intact. If some data blocks are lost after upgrade, Hadoop can automatically recover it from other backup replications.

Log in to the master node from the administrator machine with the following command:

```
ssh hduser@master
```

How to do it...

Perform the following steps to upgrade a Hadoop cluster:

1. Stop the cluster with the following command:

   ```
   stop-all.sh
   ```

2. Back up block locations of the data on HDFS with the `fsck` command:

   ```
   hadoop fsck / -files -blocks -locations > dfs.block.locations.
   fsck.backup
   ```

   The resulting file, `dfs.block.locations.fsck.backup`, will contain the locations of each data block on the HDFS filesystem.

3. Save the list of all files on the HDFS filesystem with the following command:

   ```
   hadoop dfs -lsr / > dfs.namespace.lsr.backup
   ```

4. Save the description of each DataNode in the HDFS cluster with the following command:

   ```
   hadoop dfsadmin -report > dfs.datanodes.report.backup
   ```

5. Copy the checkpoint files to a backup directory with the following commands:

   ```
   sudo cp dfs.name.dir/edits /backup
   sudo cp dfs.name.dir/image/fsimage /backup
   ```

6. Verify that no DataNode daemon is running with the following command:

```
for node in 'cat $HADOOP_HOME/conf/slaves'
  do
  echo 'Checking node ' $node
  ssh $node -C "jps"
done
```

7. If any DataNode process is still running, kill the process with the following command:

```
ssh $node -C "jps | grep 'DataNode' | cut -d'\t' -f 1 | xargs kill -9 "
```

 A still running DataNode can fail an update if it is not killed because the old version DataNode might register with the newer version NameNode, causing compatibility problems.

8. Decompress the Hadoop archive file with the following commands:

```
sudo mv hadoop-1.2.0.tar.gz /usr/local/
sudo tar xvf hadoop-1.2.0.tar.gz
```

9. Copy the configuration files from the old configuration directory to the new one using the following command:

```
sudo cp $HADOOP_HOME/conf/* /usr/local/hadoop-1.2.0/conf/*
```

You can make changes to the configuration files if necessary.

10. Update the Hadoop symbolic link to the Hadoop version with the following command:

```
sudo rm -rf /usr/local/hadoop
sudo ln -s /usr/local/hadoop-1.2.0 /usr/local/hadoop
```

11. Upgrade in the slave nodes with the following commands:

```
for host in 'cat $HADOOP_HOME/conf/slaves'
  do
  echo 'Configuring hadoop on slave node ' $host
  sudo scp -r /usr/local/hadoop-1.2.0 hduser@$host:/usr/local/
  echo 'Making symbolic link for Hadoop home directory on host ' $host
  sudo ssh hduser@$host -C "ln -s /usr/local/hadoop-1.2.0 /usr/local/hadoop"
done
```

12. Upgrade the NameNode with the following command:

```
hadoop namenode -upgrade
```

This command will convert the checkpoint to the new version format. We need to wait to let it finish.

13. Start the HDFS cluster using the following commands:

```
start-dfs.sh
```

14. Get the list of all files on HDFS and compare its difference with the backed up one using the following commands:

```
hadoop dfs -lsr / > dfs.namespace.lsr.new
```

```
diff dfs.namespace.lsr.new dfs.namespace.lsr.backup
```

The two files should have the same content if there is no error in the upgrade.

15. Get a new report of each DataNode in the cluster and compare the file with the backed up one using the following command:

```
hadoop dfsadmin -report > dfs.datanodes.report.new
```

```
diff dfs.datanodes.report.1.log dfs.datanodes.report.backup
```

The two files should have the same content if there is no error.

16. Get the locations of all data blocks and compare the output with the previous backup using the following commands:

```
hadoop fsck / -files -blocks -locations > dfs.block.locations.
fsck.new
```

```
diff dfs.locations.fsck.backup dfs.locations.fsck.new
```

The result of this command should tell us that the data block locations should be the same.

17. Start the MapReduce cluster using the following command:

```
start-mapred.sh
```

Now, we can check the status of the cluster either by running a sample MapReduce job such as `teragen` and `terasort`, or by using the web user interface.

How it works...

We can use the following command to get the usage of HDFS upgrade commands:

```
hadoop dfsadmin
```

We will get an output similar to the following:

```
Usage: java DFSAdmin
          [-report]
          [-safemode enter | leave | get | wait]
          [-saveNamespace]
          [-refreshNodes]
          [-finalizeUpgrade]
          [-upgradeProgress status | details | force]
          [-metasave filename]
          [-refreshServiceAcl]
          [-refreshUserToGroupsMappings]
          [-refreshSuperUserGroupsConfiguration]
          [-setQuota <quota> <dirname>...<dirname>]
          [-clrQuota <dirname>...<dirname>]
          [-setSpaceQuota <quota> <dirname>...<dirname>]
          [-clrSpaceQuota <dirname>...<dirname>]
          [-setBalancerBandwidth <bandwidth in bytes per second>]
          [-help [cmd]]
```

The following table lists the meanings of the command options:

Option	Description
-report	Reports filesystem information and statistics.
-saveNamespace	Saves a snapshot of the filesystem metadata into configured directories.
-finalizeUpgrade	Finalizes the upgrade of HDFS; this command will cause the DataNode to delete the previous version working directories.
-metasave	Saves the metadata of the HDFS cluster.

See also

▶ The *Configuring Hadoop in pseudo-distributed mode* recipe of *Chapter 3, Configuring a Hadoop Cluster*

▶ The *Configuring Hadoop in fully-distributed mode* recipe of *Chapter 3, Configuring a Hadoop Cluster*

▶ The *Validating Hadoop installation* recipe of *Chapter 3, Configuring a Hadoop Cluster*

5
Hardening a
Hadoop Cluster

In this chapter, we will cover:

- ▸ Configuring service-level authentication
- ▸ Configuring job authorization with ACL
- ▸ Securing a Hadoop cluster with Kerberos
- ▸ Configuring web UI authentication
- ▸ Recovering from NameNode failure
- ▸ Configuring NameNode high availability
- ▸ Configuring HDFS federation

Introduction

The security of a Hadoop cluster is critical for its availability. Hardening a Hadoop cluster includes configuring access control over resources, such as jobs, queues, and various administrative services. We will introduce NameNode **High Availability** (**HA**) for the problem of single node failure. In the end, we will introduce Hadoop federation, which federates multiple machines to expand the capacity of a cluster.

Configuring service-level authentication

The purpose of **service-level authentication** (**SLA**) is to ensure that Hadoop users have the proper permission to access certain services. One use case of this configuration is to control a list of allowed users who can use the cluster. This is enforced with **Access Control List** (**ACL**) in Hadoop. In this recipe, we will list steps to configure SLA.

Getting ready

Before getting started, we assume that our Hadoop cluster has been properly configured and all the daemons are running without any issues.

Log in to the master node from the administrator machine with the following command:

```
ssh hduser@master
```

How to do it...

Use the following steps to configure Hadoop SLA:

1. Enable SLA by opening the `$HADOOP_HOME/conf/core-site.xml` file and add or change the `hadoop.property.authorization` value to be `true`, as shown in the following snippet:

    ```
    <property>
      <name>hadoop.property.authorization</name>
      <value>true</name>
    </property>
    ```

     SLA of a Hadoop cluster is disabled by default.

2. Allow only specific users to submit jobs to the Hadoop cluster by adding or changing the following property in the `$HADOOP_HOME/conf/hadoop-policy.xml` file:

    ```
    <property>
      <name>security.job.submission.protocol.acl</name>
      <value>hduser hadoop</name>
    </property>
    ```

     This configuration only allows user `hduser` and group `hadoop` to submit jobs to the Hadoop cluster.

3. Allow only specific users and groups to talk to HDFS by opening the `$HADOOP_HOME/conf/hadoop-policy.xml` file and add the following property:

    ```
    <property>
      <name>security.client.protocol.acl</name>
      <value>hduser,hdadmin hadoop</name>
    </property>
    ```

This configuration only allows users `hduser` and `hdadmin`, and group `hadoop` to access HDFS

4. Allow only specific DataNodes to communicate with the NameNode by changing the `security.datanode.protocol.acl` property in the `$HADOOP_HOME/conf/hadoop-policy.xml` file similar to the following code:

```
<property>
  <name>security.datanode.protocol.acl</name>
  <value>datanode</name>
</property>
```

 This configuration only allows the DataNode instances running as users belonging to the group `datanode` to communicate with the NameNode in the cluster.

5. Force the NameNode to reload the ACL configurations with the following command:

```
hadoop dfsadmin -refreshServiceAcl
```

 This command will force the reloading of the HDFS related ACLs from the `policy` file.

6. Force the JobTracker to reload the service ACL configurations with the following command:

```
hadoop mradmin -refreshServiceAcl
```

How it works...

The value of properties such as `security.namenode.protocol.acl` is a comma-separated list of users and a comma-separated list of groups. The users list and the groups list are separated by space. For example, the generic format of the value should be similar to the following:

```
<value>user1,user2,user3 group1,group2</value>
```

There's more...

Besides the three properties we mentioned in this recipe, a number of other ACL properties are available in Hadoop. The following table shows the meaning of these properties:

Property	Service description
`security.client.protocol.acl`	Client's access to HDFS
`security.client.datanode.protocol.acl`	Client to DataNode for block recovery
`security.inter.datanode.protocol.acl`	DataNode to DataNode updating timestamps
`security.inter.tracker.protocol.acl`	TaskTracker to JobTracker
`security.job.submission.protocol.acl`	Client to JobTracker for job submission, querying, and so on
`security.task.umbilical.protocol.acl`	For map and reduce tasks talk to TaskTracker
`security.refresh.policy.protocol.acl`	dfsadmin and mradmin to refresh ACL policies

The default value of these properties is *, which means all entities can access the service or, in other words, SLA is disabled.

See also

▶ The *Configuring job authorization with ACL* recipe in Chapter 5, *Hardening a Hadoop Cluster*

▶ `http://hadoop.apache.org/docs/r1.1.2/service_level_auth.html#En able+Service+Level+Authorization`

Configuring job authorization with ACL

Hadoop provides two levels of **job authorization**: job level and queue level. When job authorization is enabled, the JobTracker will authenticate users who submit jobs to the cluster. Users' operations on jobs and queues will also be authenticated by the JobTracker. In this recipe, we will show steps to configure job authorization with ACLs.

Getting ready

We assume that our Hadoop cluster has been properly configured without any problems.

Log in to the master node from the administrator machine with the following command:

```
ssh hduser@master
```

How to do it...

Use the following steps to configure job authorization with ACLs:

1. Enable job ACL authorization by adding the following property to the $HADOOP_HOME/conf/mapred-site.xml file:

```
<property>
  <name>mapred.acls.enabled</name>
  <value>true</name>
</property>
```

 This property will enable both the queue ACL and the job ACL.

2. Configure job authorization to only allow specific users and groups to submit jobs by adding the following property to the $HADOOP_HOME/conf/mapred-queue-acls.xml file:

```
<property>
  <name>mapred.queue.hdqueue.acl-submit-job</name>
  <value>hduser hadoop</name>
</property>
```

 This configuration will only allow user hduser and group hadoop to submit jobs to the queue hdqueue.

3. Configure job authorization to allow specific users and groups to manage jobs in a named queue by adding the following property to the $HADOOP_HOME/conf/mapred-queue-acls.xml file:

```
<property>
  <name>mapred.queue.hdqueue.acl-administer-job</name>
  <value>hduser hadoop</name>
</property>
```

 This configuration will only allow user hduser and group hadoop to administrate jobs to queue hdqueue.

4. Check the status of queue ACLs with the following command:

```
hadoop queue -showacls
```

The output will be similar to the following:

```
Queue acls for user :   hduser

Queue   Operations

=====================

default   submit-job,administer-jobs

hdqueue   submit-job,administer-jobs
```

5. Configure job authorization to allow only specific users and groups to view the status of a job by adding the following property to the $HADOOP_HOME/conf/mapred-queue-acls.xml file:

```
<property>
    <name>mapreduce.job.acl-view-job</name>
    <value>hduser hadoop</name>
</property>
```

 Different to queue level ACL, job level ACL specifies access control for any submitted jobs, regardless of the queue a job has been submitted to.

6. Configure job authorization to allow only specific users and groups to modify a job by adding the following property to the $HADOOP_HOME/conf/mapred-queue-acls.xml file:

```
<property>
    <name>mapreduce.job.acl-modify-job</name>
    <value>hduser hadoop</name>
</property>
```

7. Force the NameNode and the JobTracker to reload the ACL configurations with the following commands:

```
hadoop dfsadmin -refreshServiceAcl
hadoop mradmin -refreshServiceAcl
```

How it works...

Similar to the SLA properties in the previous recipe, the value of properties such as `mapred.queue.hdqueue.acl-submit-job` is a comma-separated list of users and a comma-separated list of groups. The user list and group list are separated by a space. For example, the generic format of the value should be similar to the following:

```
<value>user1,user2,user3 group1,group2</value>
```

The job owner, the super user, and the cluster administrators to which the job was submitted, will always have the right to view and modify a job.

Job view ACLs control the access of job status information, including counters, diagnostic information, logs, job configuration, and so on.

Job modification ACLs can overlap with queue-level ACLs. When this happens, a user's operation will be granted if the user has been listed in either of these ACLs.

See also

- The *Configuring service-level authentication* recipe in *Chapter 5, Hardening a Hadoop Cluster*
- `http://hadoop.apache.org/docs/r1.1.2/mapred_tutorial.html#Job+Authorization`
- `http://hadoop.apache.org/docs/r1.1.2/cluster_setup.html`

Securing a Hadoop cluster with Kerberos

Recent Hadoop releases have added the security feature by integrating **Kerberos** into Hadoop. Kerberos is a network authentication protocol that provides strong authentication for client/server applications. Hadoop uses Kerberos to secure data from unexpected and unauthorized accesses. It achieves this by authenticating on the underlying **Remote Procedure Calls** (**RPC**). In this recipe, we will outline steps to configure Kerberos authentication for a Hadoop cluster.

Getting ready

Kerberos was created by MIT. It was designed to provide strong authentication for client/server applications by using secret key cryptography. The Kerberos protocol requires that a client provide its identity to the server and vice versa. When their identities are proved by Kerberos, all of their following communication will be encrypted.

Before getting started, we assume that our Hadoop has been properly configured without any problems, and all the Hadoop daemons are running without any issues. On our CentOS machine, use the following command to install the Kerberos packages:

```
sudo yum install krb5-libs, krb5-server, krb5-workstation
```

After this, the `kadmin` and `kinit` commands should be accessible from the command line.

If you are also using CentOS or other Red Hat-compatible operating systems, we need to install Java Cryptography Extension (JCE) Unlimited Strength Jurisdiction Policy Files, by downloading it from the following link:

```
http://www.oracle.com/technetwork/java/javase/downloads/index.html
```

At the bottom of the web page, you should see options similar to the following:

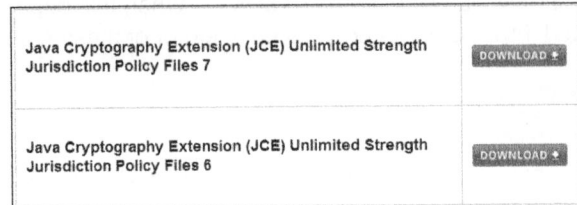

Click on the download link at the right-hand side of the screen based on your Java version, which we can get with the `java -version` command.

How to do it...

Use the following steps to configure Kerberos for a Hadoop cluster:

1. Start the Kerberos admin shell:

    kadmin

     If your account does not have root access, you need to use the `kadmin.local` command!

2. Create the `hduser` principal with the following command in the `kadmin` shell:

    addprinc -randkey hduser/master.hdcluster.com@HDREALM

3. Create the HTTP principal for SPNEGO with the following command in the `kadmin` shell:

    addprinc -randkey HTTP/master.hdcluster.com@HDREALM

4. Create the `keytab` file that contains the `hduser` instances and HTTP principal with the following command:

    xst -norandkey -k hduser.keytab hduser/master.hdcluster.com HTTP/master.hdcluster.com

5. Show available `keytab` file entries with the following command:

    klist -e -k -t hduser.keytab

The output will be similar to the following:

```
Keytab name: WRFILE:hduser.keytab

slot KVNO Principal

---- ---- -----------------------------------------------------------
-------

1    7       HTTP/master.hdcluster.com@HDREALM (DES cbc mode with
CRC-32)

2    7       HTTP/master.hdcluster.com@HDREALM (Triple DES cbc mode
with HMAC/sha1)

3    7       hduser/master.hdcluster.com@HDREALM (DES cbc mode with
CRC-32)

4    7       hduser/master.hdcluster.com@HDREALM (Triple DES cbc mode
with HMAC/sha1)
```

6. Move the `keytab` files to the Hadoop configuration directory with the following:

   `cp *.keytab $HADOOP_HOME/conf`

7. Change the owner of the `hduser keytab` file with the following:

   `sudo chown hduser:hadoop $HADOOP_HOME/conf/hduser.keytab`

8. Change the permission of the `keytab` files with:

   `sudo chmod 400 $HADOOP_HOME/conf/*.keytab`

 Only the owner is allowed to read the `keytab` files.

9. Copy all the `kaytab` files to the slave nodes with:

   ```
   for node in `cat $HADOOP_HOME/conf/slaves`; do
     echo 'Copying keytab files to ' $host
     scp $HADOOP_HOME/conf/*.keytab $host:$HADOOP_HOME/conf/
   done
   ```

10. Stop the cluster with the following command:

    `stop-all.sh`

11. Open the `$HADOOP_HOME/conf/core-site.xml` file with your favorite text editor and add the following lines to the file:

    ```
    <property>
      <name>hadoop.security.authorization</name>
      <value>true</value>
    </property>
    ```

```
<property>
  <name>hadoop.security.authentication</name>
  <value>kerberos</value>
</property>

<property>
  <name>hadoop.security.use-weak-http-crypto</name>
  <value>false</value>
</property>
```

12. Open the `$HADOOP_HOME/conf/hdfs-site.xml` file with your favorite text editor and add the following lines into the file:

```
<property>
  <name>dfs.block.access.token.enable</name>
  <value>true</value>
</property>

<property>
  <name>dfs.http.address</name>
  <value>master:50070</value>
</property>

<property>
  <name>dfs.namenode.keytab.file</name>
  <value>$HADOOP_HOME/conf/hduser.keytab</value>
</property>

<property>
  <name>dfs.namenode.kerberos.principal</name>
  <value>hduser/master.hdcluster.com@HDREALM</value>
</property>

<property>
  <name>dfs.namenode.kerberos.internal.spnego.principal</name>
  <value>HTTP/master.hdcluster.com@HDREALM</value>
</property>

<property>
  <name>dfs.secondary.namenode.keytab.file</name>
  <value>$HADOOP_HOME/conf/hduser.keytab</value>
</property>

<property>
  <name>dfs.secondary.namenode.kerberos.principal</name>
  <value>hduser/master.hdcluster.com@HDREALM</value>
</property>
```

```
<property>
  <name>dfs.secondary.namenode.kerberos.internal.spnego.
principal</name>
  <value>HTTP/master.hdcluster.com@HDREALM</value>
</property>

<property>
  <name>dfs.secondary.http.address</name>
  <value>master.hdcluster.com:50090</value>
</property>


<property>
  <name>dfs.datanode.data.dir.perm</name>
  <value>700</value>
</property>

<property>
  <name>dfs.datanode.address</name>
  <value>0.0.0.0:1004</value>
</property>

<property>
  <name>dfs.datanode.http.address</name>
  <value>0.0.0.0:1006</value>
</property>

<property>
  <name>dfs.datanode.keytab.file</name>
  <value>$HADOOP_HOME/conf/hduser.keytab</value>
</property>

<property>
  <name>dfs.datanode.kerberos.principal</name>
  <value>hduser/master.hdcluster.com@HDREALM</value>
</property>
```

13. Enable webHDFS by adding the following property to the `$HADOOP_HOME/conf/hdfs-site.xml` file:

```
<property>
  <name>dfs.webhdfs.enabled</name>
  <value>true</value>
</property>
```

14. Configure Kerberos web authentication by adding the following two properties to the `$HADOOP_HOME/conf/hdfs-site.xml` file:

```
<property>
    <name>dfs.web.authentication.kerberos.principal</name>
    <value>HTTP/master.hdcluster.com@HDREALM</value>
</property>

<property>
    <name>dfs.web.authentication.kerberos.keytab</name>
    <value>$HADOOP_HOME/conf/HTTP.keytab</value>
</property>
```

15. Start the cluster with the following command:

```
start-all.sh
```

We will get log messages similar to the following:

```
13/02/25 10:19:02 INFO security.UserGroupInformation:
Login successful for user hduser/master.hdcluster.com@HDREALM
using keytab file /usr/local/hadoop/hduser.keytab
13/02/25 10:19:07 INFO http.HttpServer: Added global filtersafety
(class=org.apache.hadoop.http.HttpServer$QuotingInputFilter)
13/02/25 10:19:12 INFO http.HttpServer: Adding Kerberos (SPNEGO)
filter to getDelegationToken
13/02/25 10:19:15 INFO http.HttpServer: Adding Kerberos (SPNEGO)
filter to renewDelegationToken
13/02/25 10:19:22 INFO http.HttpServer: Adding Kerberos (SPNEGO)
filter to cancelDelegationToken
13/02/25 10:19:32 INFO http.HttpServer: Adding Kerberos (SPNEGO)
filter to fsck
13/02/25 10:19:36 INFO http.HttpServer: Adding Kerberos (SPNEGO)
filter to getimage
```

16. Test the Kerberos configuration by copying a simple text file into HDFS with the following command:

```
hadoop fs -put $HADOOP_HOME/conf/slaves .
```

17. Set the *sticky* bit on HDFS directory to prevent the directories or files from being deleted by unauthorized users with the following command:

```
sudo -u hdfs hadoop fs -chmod 1777 /tmp
```

18. Verify the sticky bit setting with the following command:

```
hadoop fs -ls /
```

The output should be similar to:

```
Found 2 items
drwxrwxrwt - hduser supergroup 0 2013-03-10 15:55 /tmp
drwxr-xr-x - hduser supergroup 0 2013-03-10 14:01 /user
```

19. Configure MapReduce Kerberos authentication by adding the following lines into the `$HADOOP_HOME/conf/mapred-site.xml` file:

```
<property>
  <name>mapreduce.jobtracker.kerberos.principal</name>
  <value>hduser/master.hdcluster.com@HDREALM</value>
</property>

<property>
  <name>mapreduce.jobtracker.keytab.file</name>
  <value>$HADOOP_HOME/conf/hduser.keytab</value>
</property>


<property>
  <name>mapreduce.tasktracker.kerberos.principal</name>
  <value>$HADOOP_HOME/conf/hduser.keytab</value>
</property>

<property>
  <name>mapreduce.tasktracker.keytab.file</name>
  <value>$HADOOP_HOME/conf/hduser.keytab</value>
</property>

<property>
  <name>mapred.task.tracker.task-controller</name>
  <value>org.apache.hadoop.mapred.LinuxTaskController</value>
</property>

<property>
  <name>mapreduce.tasktracker.group</name>
  <value>hadoop</value>
</property>
```

20. Create a `$HADOOP_HOME/conf/taskcontrol.cfg` file with the following content:

```
mapred.local.dir=${hadoop.tmp.dir}/mapred/local
hadoop.log.dir=$HADOOP_HOME/logs
mapreduce.tasktracker.group=hduser
banned.users=
min.user.id=2000
```

21. Change the ownership and permission of the `$HADOOP_HOME/conf/taskcontroller.cfg` file:

```
sudo chown root:mapred $HADOOP_HOME/conf/task-controller.cfg
sudo chmod 4754 $HADOOP_HOME/conf/task-controller.cfg
```

 The modified permission should be similar to the following:
```
-rwsr-xr-- 1 hduser superuser 91886 2013-03-10 13:44
task-controller.cfg
```

22. Start the MapReduce cluster with the following command:

```
start-mapred.sh
```

 We should be able to get logging message similar to the following:
```
13/02/26 12:25:02 INFO security.UserGroupInformation:
Login successful for user hduser/master.hdcluster.com@
HDREALM using keytab file $HADOOP_HOME/conf/hduser.
keytab.
```

23. Test the Kerberos configuration by running an example MapReduce job with the following command:

```
hadoop jar $HADOOP_HOME/hadoop-example*.jar pi 20 1000000
```

See also

- The *Configuring web UI authentication* recipe in *Chapter 5, Hardening a Hadoop Cluster*
- `http://en.wikipedia.org/wiki/SPNEGO`
- `https://ccp.cloudera.com/display/CDHDOC/Configuring+Hadoop+Security+in+CDH3+(SPNEGO)`
- Get more information about Kerberos from `http://web.mit.edu/kerberos/`

Configuring web UI authentication

By default, Hadoop users and administrators can access the web UIs of the Hadoop daemons without requiring any authentication. Hadoop daemon web UIs can be configured to authenticate users with Kerberos. In this recipe, we will outline steps to configure user authentication for accessing the web UI.

Getting ready

We assume that our Hadoop has been properly configured and all the daemons are running without any issues. We also assume that Kerberos authentication has been configured properly.

In this recipe, we assume all the property configurations will make changes on the `$HADOOP_HOME/conf/core-site.xml` file.

How to do it...

Use the following steps to configure web UI authentication:

1. Stop the cluster with the following command:

    stop-all.sh

2. Add or change the following property:

    ```
    <property>
      <name>hadoop.http.filter.initializers</name>
    <value>org.apache.hadoop.security.
    AuthenticationFilterInitializer</value>
    </property>
    ```

3. Change the HTTP authentication type by adding the following code:

    ```
    <property>
      <name>hadoop.http.authentication.type</name>
      <value>kerberos</value>
    </property>
    ```

 Other HTTP authentication types include simple and user customized, which are selected by specifying the `AUTHENTICATION_HANDLER_CLASSNAME` value. The default authentication type is simple.

4. Configure the authentication token's valid time length by changing the `hadoop.http.authentication.token.validity` property to the following:

    ```
    <property>
      <name>hadoop.http.authentication.token.validity</name>
      <value>10000</value>
    </property>
    ```

 The unit of the value is seconds. The default value for this property is `36000`.

5. Configure the location of the `signature.secret` file, which will be used to sign the authentication tokens, by changing the `hadoop.http.authentication.signature.secret.file` property similar to the following:

```
<property>
    <name>hadoop.http.authentication.signature.secret.file</name>
    <value>$HADOOP_HOME/conf/http-auth.secret</value>
</property>
```

 If this property is not set, a random `secret` file will be generated at startup time. The default file used to keep the secret will be `${user.name}/hadoop-auth-signature-secret`.

6. Configure the domain name for HTTP cookies, which stores authentication tokens, by changing the `hadoop.http.authentication.cookie.domain` property similar to the following:

```
<property>
    <name>hadoop.http.authentication.cookie.domain</name>
    <value>hdcluster.com</value>
</property>
```

 Warning!

This property is required for HTTP authentication to work properly.

7. Configure the Kerberos principal for HTTP endpoint by changing the `hadoop.http.authentication.kerberos.principal` property similar to the following:

```
<property>
    <name>hadoop.http.authentication.kerberos.principal</name>
    <value>HTTP/master.hdcluster.com@HDREALM</value>
</property>
```

8. Configure the location of the `keytab` file for the Kerberos principal for HTTP endpoints by changing the `hadoop.http.authentication.kerberos.keytab` property similar to the following:

```
<property>
    <name>hadoop.http.authentication.kerberos.keytab</name>
    <value>${user.home}/kerberos.hadoop.keytab</value>
</property>
```

9. Sync the configurations to the slave nodes with the following command:

```
for host in `cat $HADOOP_HOME/conf/slaves`; do
    echo "Copying Hadoop configration files to host: ' $host
    scp $HADOOP_HOME/conf/core-site.xml $host:$HADOOP_HOME/conf
done
```

10. Start the Hadoop cluster with the following command:

```
start-all.sh
```

11. Validate the configuration by opening URL `master:50030/jobtracker.jsp`.

12. Alternatively, we can test our configuration with the following `curl` command:

```
curl -v -u hduser --negotiate http://master:50030/jobtracker.jsp
```

How it works...

Web UI authentication is implemented with the HTTP SPNEGO protocol. **SPNEGO** stands for **Simple and Protected Negotiation** mechanism. It is a GSSAPI mechanism used to negotiate one of a number of possible real mechanisms. SPNEGO is used when a client application wants to authenticate to a remote server, but neither end is sure which authentication protocols the other supports.

The pseudo mechanism uses a protocol to determine what common GSSAPI mechanisms are available, selects one, and then dispatches all further security operations to it. This can help organizations deploy new security mechanisms in a phased manner.

For more information about SPNEGO, please refer to its wiki page at `http://en.wikipedia.org/wiki/SPNEGO`.

There's more...

Other authentication methods include the simple authentication. If this authentication method is used, we must specify the username in the first browser interaction using the `user.name` parameter in the URL. For example, we need to open JobTracker URL: `http://master:50030/jobtracker.jsp?user.name=hduser`.

If simple authentication is used as the authentication type, anonymous user web UI requests can be configured by changing the following property:

```
<property>
  <name>hadoop.http.authentication.simple.anonymous.allowed</name>
  <value>true</value>
</property>
```

See also

▶ The *Securing a Hadoop cluster with Kerberos* recipe in *Chapter 5, Hardening a Hadoop Cluster*

▶ `http://hadoop.apache.org/docs/stable/HttpAuthentication.html`

Recovering from NameNode failure

The NameNode in a Hadoop cluster keeps track of the metadata for the whole HDFS filesystem. Unfortunately, as of this book's writing, the NameNode in the current stable version of Hadoop is a single point of failure. If the metadata of the NameNode is corrupted, for example, due to hard drive failure, the whole cluster will become unavailable. So, it is important to safeguard the NameNode from these disastrous failures.

There are multiple ways we can increase the resilience of a HDFS cluster. In this recipe, we will show you how to configure a SecondaryNameNode as a backup NameNode and how to recover from NameNode failures.

Getting ready

We assume that our Hadoop cluster has been properly configured, and we have one machine, master1, as the NameNode and a second machine, master2, to run the SecondaryNameNode.

 Please be prepared that a NameNode failure can cause the cluster to halt. It might take some time to recover from the failure.

How to do it...

The first method we want to introduce is to configure the NameNode to write edit logs and the filesystem image into two locations—one is on the local directory for the NameNode machine and the other is on the SecondaryNameNode machine. These directories are specified with the HDFS property dfs.name.dir. We can use the following steps to configure this:

1. Log into master1 with the following command:

   ssh hduser@master1

2. Configure the following property in the $HADOOP_HOME/conf/hdfs-site.xml file:

```
<property>
    <name>dfs.name.dir</name>
    <value>/hadoop/dfs/name,/mnt/snn/name</value>
</property>
```

In this property, we configured two directories for the NameNode to write metadata to. The first directory `/hadoop/dfs/name` is a directory on `master1`, and the second directory `/mnt/ssn/name` is one NFS shared directory `/hadoop/dfs/name` on `master2`. In other words, we are configuring the two machines `master1` and `master2` to have the same directory layout for the NameNode.

For brevity purposes, we are not showing you the configuration of NFS in this recipe. More information about this topic can be obtained from `http://www.tldp.org/HOWTO/NFS-HOWTO/`

3. Configure the following property in the `$HADOOP_HOME/conf/core-site.xml` file:

```
<property>
    <name>fs.default.name </name>
    <value>master1:54310</value>
</property>
```

4. Copy the configuration to `master2` with the following command:

```
scp $HADOOP_HOME/conf/hdfs-site.xml master2:$HADOOP_HOME/conf/
scp $HADOOP_HOME/conf/slaves master2:$HADOOP_HOME/conf/
```

5. Copy the configuration file to all the slave nodes in the cluster with the following command:

```
for host in `cat $HADOOP_HOME/conf/slaves`; do
  echo 'Sync configuration files to ' $host
  scp $HADOOP_HOME/conf/core-site.xml $host:$HADOOP_HOME/conf
done
```

6. Start the Hadoop cluster in `master1` with the following command:

```
start-all.sh
```

In this configuration, we actually are not starting any daemons on the SecondaryNameNode machine `master2`. We just use this machine to store the metadata files for the NameNode on `master1`. Once the NameNode fails, we can quickly start the NameNode on `master2` with little effort.

Once the NameNode on `master1` fails, we can use the following steps to recover:

1. Log in to `master2` with the following command:

```
ssh hduser@master2
```

2. Stop the cluster with the following command:

```
ssh master1 -C "stop-all.sh"
```

3. Configure the `$HADOOP_HOME/conf/core-site.xml` file to use `master2` as the NameNode by adding the following property to it:

```
<property>
    <name>fs.default.name </name>
    <value>master2:54310</value>
</property>
```

4. Copy the configurations to all the slave nodes in the cluster with the following command:

```
for host in `cat $HADOOP_HOME/conf/slaves`; do
   echo 'Sync configuration files to ' $host
   scp $HADOOP_HOME/conf/core-site.xml $host:$HADOOP_HOME/conf
done
```

5. Start the Hadoop cluster with command:

```
start-all.sh
```

How it works...

Strictly speaking, the HDFS SecondaryNameNode daemon is not NameNode. It only acts as the role of periodically fetching the filesystem metadata image file and the edit logfiles to the directory specified with the property `fs.checkpoint.dir`. In case of NameNode failure, the backup files can be used to recover the HDFS filesystem.

There's more...

As we have mentioned previously, the failure of a NameNode is mainly caused by the corrupted metadata files. So the key for NameNode resilience is the recovery of metadata files. Here, we will introduce two more methods to do this—one is by writing metadata onto multiple hard drives, and the other is to recover from the checkpoint of a SecondaryNameNode.

NameNode resilience with multiple hard drives

We can use the following steps to configure the NameNode with multiple hard drives:

1. Install, format, and mount the hard drive onto the machine; suppose the mount point is /hadoop1/.

2. Create the Hadoop directory with the following command:

```
mkdir /hadoop1/dfs/name
```

3. Configure the following property in the `$HADOOP_HOME/conf/hdfs-site.xml` file:

```
<property>
    <name>dfs.name.dir</name>
    <value>/hadoop/dfs/name, /hadoop1/dfs/name</value>
</property>
```

 In this configuration, we added two directories. The first is the major directory for Hadoop. The second directory is a directory on a separate hard drive.

We can use the following steps to recover from the NameNode failure:

1. Stop the Hadoop cluster with the following command:

   stop-all.sh

2. Configure the following property in the `$HADOOP_HOME/conf/hdfs-site.xml` file:

```
<property>
    <name>dfs.name.dir</name>
    <value>/hadoop1/dfs/name</value>
</property>
```

3. Start the cluster with the following command:

   start-all.sh

Recovering NameNode from the checkpoint of a SecondaryNameNode

We can use the following steps to configure SecondaryNameNode, and recover from the NameNode failure:

1. Log in to `master1` with the following command:

   ssh hduser@master1

2. Add the following line into the `$HADOOP_HOME/conf/masters` file:

   master2

    By doing this, we configure it to run SecondaryNameNode on `master2`.

3. Configure the following property in the `$HADOOP_HOME/conf/hdfs-site.xml` file:

```
<property>
    <name>dfs.name.dir</name>
    <value>/hadoop/dfs/name</value>
</property>
```

4. Sync the configuration files to the slave nodes in the cluster with the following command:

```
for host in `cat $HADOOP_HOME/conf/slaves`; do
   echo 'Sync configuration files to ' $host
   scp $HADOOP_HOME/conf/hdfs-site.xml $host:$HADOOP_HOME/conf
done
```

5. Start the cluster with the following command:

```
start-all.sh
```

In case the NameNode fails, we can use the following steps to recover:

1. Stop the cluster with the following command:

```
stop-all.sh
```

2. Prepare a new machine for running the NameNode.

 The preparation should include properly configuring Hadoop. It is recommended that the new NameNode machine has the same configuration as the failed NameNode.

3. Format the NameNode with the following command:

```
hadoop fs -format
```

4. Configure the NameNode version number with the following command:

```
scp slave1:/hadoop/dfs/data/current/VERSION* /hadoop/dfs/name/
current/VERSION
```

5. Copy the checkpoint image from SecondaryNameNode with the following command:

```
scp master2:/hadoop/dfs/namesecondary/image/fsimage /hadoop/dfs/
name/fsimage
```

6. Copy the current edit logs from SecondaryNameNode with the following command:

```
scp master2:/hadoop/dfs/namesecondary/current/* /hadoop/dfs/name/
current
```

7. Convert the checkpoint to the new version format with the following command:

```
hadoop namenode -upgrade
```

8. Start the cluster with the following command:

```
start-all.sh
```

See also

▶ The *Managing HDFS Cluster* recipe in *Chapter 4, Managing a Hadoop Cluster*

▶ The *Managing DataNode daemons* recipe in *Chapter 4, Managing a Hadoop Cluster*

▶ https://issues.apache.org/jira/browse/HADOOP-2585

Configuring NameNode high availability

As of this book's writing, the NameNode of the Hadoop stable release is a single point of failure. In case of either accidental failures or regular maintenance, the cluster will become unavailable. This is a big problem for a production Hadoop cluster. In this recipe, we list the steps to configure NameNode HA.

In order for the standby NameNode to automatically recover from the active NameNode failure, the NameNode HA implementation requires that the edit logs of the standby NameNode to be always kept synchronized with the active NameNode. Hadoop HA offers two ways to do this. One is based on Quorum and the other is based on shared storage using NFS. In this recipe, we will only show you how to configure HA using Quorum.

Getting ready

Currently, Hadoop release 1.x.y (MRv1) doesn't support NameNode HA, so we are assuming that all the cluster nodes already have Hadoop Version 2.0.x (MRv2) installed.

 Be cautious that this Hadoop version is still in alpha status, so it is not recommended for production deployment. For more development status of MRv2, please refer to the official website at: http://hadoop.apache.org/docs/current/hadoop-yarn/hadoop-yarn-site/YARN.html.

We are assuming that we have two master nodes, with hostnames master1 and master2, to run the NameNode daemons.

How to do it...

Use the following steps to configure Hadoop NameNode HA:

1. Log in to one of the NameNode machines with the following command:

   ssh hduser@master1

2. Configure a logical name service by adding the following property to the `$HADOOP_CONF_DIR/hdfs-site.xml` file:

```
<property>
  <name>dfs.nameservices</name>
  <value>hdcluster</value>
</property>
```

 We are assuming all the subsequent configurations are making changes on the `$HADOOP_CONF_DIR/hdfs-site.xml` file.

3. Specify the NameNode IDs for the configured name service by adding the following property to the file:

```
<property>
  <name>dfs.ha.namenodes.hdcluster</name>
  <value>namenode1,namenode2</value>
</property>
```

 This property specifies the NameNode IDs with the property `dfs.ha.namenodes.<nameservices>`. For example, in the previous step, we have configured the name service `hdcluster`, so the property name here will be `dfs.ha.namenodes.hdcluster`. In this property, we specified `namenode1` and `namenode2` for the `logic` name service.

Current HA implementation only supports two NameNodes maximum.

4. Configure the RPC address for `namenode1` on the `master1` host by adding the following property:

```
<property>
  <name>dfs.namenode.rpc-address.hdcluster.namenode1</name>
  <value>master1:54310</value>
</property>
```

 The MRv1 RPC address specification for the NameNode is similar to the specification in MRv2. They both use the format `host:port`.

5. Configure the RPC address for `namenode2` on the `master2` host, by adding the following property:

```
<property>
  <name>dfs.namenode.rpc-address.hdcluster.namenode2</name>
  <value>master2:54310</value>
</property>
```

6. Configure the HTTP web UI address of the two NameNodes by adding the following lines to the file:

```
<property>
  <name>dfs.namenode.http-address.hdcluster.namenode1</name>
  <value>master1:50070</value>
</property>

<property>
  <name>dfs.namenode.http-address.hdcluster.namenode2</name>
  <value>master2:50070</value>
</property>
```

7. Configure the NameNode `shared edits` directory by adding the following property to the file:

```
<property>
  <name>dfs.namenode.shared.edits.dir</name> <value>qjournal://mas
ter1:8485;master1:8486;master2:8485/hdcluster</value>
</property>
```

This property configures three **journal node** addresses for Quorum to provide the shared edits storage. The shared edits logs will be written by the active NameNode and read by the standby NameNode.

8. Configure the Quorum `Journal Node` directory for storing edit logs in the local filesystem by adding the following property to the file:

```
<property>
  <name>dfs.journalnode.edits.dir</name>
  <value>/hadoop/journaledits/</value>
</property>
```

This property should be configured on each NameNode machine.

9. Configure the proxy provider for the NameNode HA by adding the following lines to the file:

```
<property>
  <name>dfs.client.failover.proxy.provider.hdcluster</name>
<value>org.apache.hadoop.hdfs.server.namenode.ha.ConfiguredFailove
rProxyProvider</value>
</property>
```

10. Configure the `fencing` method by adding the following property to the file:

```
<property>
  <name>dfs.ha.fencing.methods</name>
  <value>sshfence</value>
</property>
```

Currently, NameNode HA supports two fencing methods, one is `sshfence` and the other one is `shell`. `sshfence` uses SSH to log in to the active NameNode and kill the process, and the `shell` fencing uses regular shell commands to fence the active NameNode. In this recipe, we are assuming to use the `sshfence` method.

11. Configure the `private key` file for the `sshfence` method by adding the following property to the file:

```
<property>
  <name>dfs.ha.fencing.ssh.private-key-files</name>
  <value>$HOME/.ssh/id_rsa</value>
</property>
```

The value of this property should be a comma-separated list of private key files. In order for `sshfence` to work, we are configuring the private key files so that it can log in to the target node without providing a paraphrase.

12. Configure the SSH connection timeout, in milliseconds, by adding the following property to the file:

```
<property>
  <name>dfs.ha.fencing.ssh.connect-timeout</name>
  <value>50000</value>
</property>
```

13. Enable automatic failover by adding the following property to the file:

```
<property>
  <name>dfs.ha.automatic-failover.enabled</name>
  <value>true</value>
</property>
```

This configuration will enable automatic failover for all the name service IDs. If we want to enable automatic failover for a specific name service ID, for example `hdcluster`, we can configure the following property:

```
<property>
  <name>dfs.ha.automatic-failover.enabled.hdcluster</name>
  <value>true</value>
</property>
```

14. Configure the ZooKeeper services by adding the following property into the `$HADOOP_CONF_DIR/core-site.xml` file:

```
<property>
    <name>ha.zookeeper.quorum</name>
    <value>master1:2181,master2:2181</value>
</property>
```

15. Sync the configurations to all the nodes in the cluster with the following commands:

```
for host in cat $HADOOP_CONF_DIR/slaves; do
    echo 'Sync configuration files to ' $host
    scp $HADOOP_CONF_DIR/hdfs-site.xml $host:$HADOOP_CONF_DIR/
    scp $HADOOP_CONF_DIR/core-site.xml $host:$HADOOP_CONF_DIR/
done
```

16. Initialize the ZooKeeper with the following command:

```
hdfs zkfc -formatZK
```

 This command will create a **znode** in ZooKeeper where the automatic failover system will store the data.

17. Start the HDFS cluster with the following command:

```
start-dfs.sh
```

 This command will start a ZKFC daemon on each NameNode machine, and the active NameNode will be selected after the daemons start.
Alternatively, we can manually start the ZKFC daemon on each NameNode machine with the command `hadoop-daemon.sh start zkfc`.

We can use the following steps to test the NameNode HA configuration:

1. Check the status of the NameNode by visiting the NameNode web UI with the following URLs:

    `master1:50070`

    `master2:50070`

2. Assuming `master1` has the active NameNode, we can get the NameNode process ID on `master1` with the following command:

    `jps`

The command will give output similar to the following:

```
...

22459 NameNode

...
```

3. Kill the NameNode process with the following command on `master1`:

```
kill -9 22459
```

 If the standby NameNode becomes the active NameNode automatically and the Hadoop cluster is still working without any problems, the configuration is successful.

How it works...

Hadoop NameNode HA was introduced since Versions 0.23.x or 2.0.x branch (MRv2). The goal is to guarantee the availability of the cluster. It addresses the problem by using two NameNodes in the cluster, an active NameNode, and a standby NameNode. The active NameNode will provide the same service as the NameNode in MRv1. Different from the SecondaryNameNode, which simply copies the NameNode images and edit logs to a backup directory, the standby NameNode is a hot standby node for the active NameNode. In case the active NameNode fails, the standby NameNode will become the active node in minimum time.

There's more...

In the NameNode HA implementation, ZooKeeper is playing an important role. The security of ZooKeeper can be a necessary concern. We can use the following steps to configure a secured ZooKeeper:

1. Log in to the `master1` machine with the `ssh` command.

2. Add the following property to the `$HADOOP_CONF_DIR/core-site.xml` file:

```xml
<property>
  <name>ha.zookeeper.auth</name>
  <value>@$HADOOP_CONF_DIR/zkauth.txt</value>
</property>
```

 This property configures the file used for ZooKeeper authentication. The special symbol @ specifies that the configuration is pointing to a file rather than inline. The content of this file should be similar to `digest:zkuser:password`, where `zkuser` is a user for ZooKeeper and `password` is the password for `zkuser`.

3. Add the following property into the $HADOOP_CONF_DIR/core-site.xml file for ZooKeeper access control:

```
<property>
  <name>ha.zookeeper.acl</name>
  <value>@$HADOOP_CONF_DIR/zkacl.txt</value>
</property>
```

 Similar to the ha.zookeeper.auth property, the @ character in the value specifies that configuration is a file on disk.

4. Generate ZooKeeper ACL corresponding to the authentication with the following command:

```
java -cp $ZK_HOME/lib/*:$ZK_HOME/zookeeper-*.jar org.apache.
zookeeper.server.auth.DigestAuthenticationProvider zkuser:password
```

We will get output similar to the following:

```
zkuser:password->zkuser:a4XNgljR6VhODbC7jysuQ4gBt98=
```

5. Add the encrypted password to the $HADOOP_CONF_DIR/zkacl.txt file:

```
digest:zkuser:a4XNgljR6VhODbC7jysuQ4gBt98=
```

6. Sync the configuration to master2 with the following commands:

```
scp $HADOOP_CONF_DIR/zkacl.txt master2:$HADOOP_CONF_DIR/
scp $HADOOP_CONF_DIR/zkauth.txt master2:$HADOOP_CONF_DIR/
```

7. Format the ZooKeeper with the following command:

```
hdfs zkfc -formatZK
```

8. Test the configuration with the following command:

```
zkCli.sh
```

We will have output similar to the following:

```
[zk: master1:2181(CONNECTED) 1] getAcl /hadoop-ha'digest, zkuser:
a4XNgljR6VhODbC7jysuQ4gBt98=
: cdrwa
```

9. Restart the cluster with the following command:

```
start-dfs.sh
```

See also

▸ The *Configuring HDFS federation* recipe in *Chapter 5, Hardening a Hadoop Cluster*

▸ `http://hadoop.apache.org/docs/current/hadoop-yarn/hadoop-yarn-site/HDFSHighAvailabilityWithNFS.html`

Configuring HDFS federation

Hadoop NameNode keeps the metadata in the main memory. When the HDFS namespace becomes large, the main memory can become a bottleneck of the cluster. HDFS federation was introduced in Hadoop for MRv2. It increases the NameNode capacity and throughput by leveraging the capacity of multiple independent NameNodes, with each NameNode hosting or managing part of the HDFS namespace.

Getting ready

Currently, only Hadoop MRv2 supports NameNode federation, so we are assuming that Hadoop MRv2 has been properly configured on all the cluster machines.

We are assuming that all the configurations are making changes to the `$HADOOP_CONF_DIR/hdfs-site.xml` file.

How to do it...

Use the following steps to configure HDFS federation:

1. Log in to `master1` with the following command:

   ssh hduser@master1

2. Specify a list of NameNode service IDs by adding the following lines into the file:

   ```
   <property>
     <name>dfs.nameservices</name>
     <value>namenode1,namenode2</value>
   </property>
   ```

The value of this property is a comma-separated list of NameNode service IDs. For example, in this step, the value specifies two NameNode services: `namenode1` and `namenode2`.

3. Configure the NameNode RPC and HTTP URI for `namenode1` by adding the following into the file:

```
<property>
    <name>dfs.namenode.rpc-address.namenode1</name>
    <value>master1:54310</value>
</property>

<property>
    <name>dfs.namenode.http-address.namenode1</name>
    <value>master1:50070</value>
</property>

<property>
    <name>dfs.namenode.secondaryhttp-address.namenode1</name>
    <value>master1:50071</value>
</property>
```

 The previous configurations assume that the NameNode daemons and NameNode HTTP and secondary HTTP daemons locate on the host `master1`.

4. Specify the NameNode RPC and HTTP URI for `namenode2` by adding the following into the file:

```
<property>
    <name>dfs.namenode.rpc-address.namenode2</name>
    <value> master2:54310</value>
</property>
<property>
    <name>dfs.namenode.http-address.namenode2</name>
    <value> master2:50070</value>
</property>
<property>
    <name>dfs.namenode.secondaryhttp-address.namenode2</name>
    <value>master2:50071</value>
</property>
```

5. Sync the configuration to all the nodes in the cluster with the following commands:

```
for host in cat $HADOOP_CONF_DIR/slaves; do
   echo 'Sync configuration files to ' $host
   scp $HADOOP_CONF_DIR/hdfs-site.xml $host:$HADOOP_CONF_DIR/
done
```

6. Format `namenode1` on `master1` with the following command:

    ```
    hdfs namenode -format -clusterId hdcluster
    ```

     In this command, the `-clusterId` option should be a unique cluster ID in the environment. A unique cluster ID will be automatically generated if not specified.

7. Similarly, format `namenode2` on `master2` with the following command:

    ```
    hdfs namenode -format -clusterId hdcluster
    ```

     Warning!
    The cluster ID for this NameNode should be the same as the cluster ID specified for `namenode1` in order for both NameNodes to be in the same cluster.

8. Now, we can start or stop the HDFS cluster with the following commands on either of the NameNode hosts:

    ```
    start-dfs.sh
    ```

    ```
    stop-dfs.sh
    ```

How it works...

On a non-federated HDFS cluster, all the DataNodes register with and send heartbeats to the single NameNode. On a federated HDFS cluster, all the DataNodes will register with all the NameNodes in the cluster, and heartbeats and block reports will be sent to these NameNodes.

A Federated HDFS cluster is composed of one or multiple namespace volumes, which consist of a namespace and a block pool that belongs to the namespace. A namespace volume is the unit of management in the cluster. For example, cluster management operations such as `delete` and `upgrade` will be operated on a namespace volume. In addition, federated NameNodes can isolate namespaces for different applications or situations.

The following table shows the properties for configuring NameNode federation:

Daemon	Property	Description
NameNode	`dfs.namenode.rpc-address`	For NameNode RPC communication with clients
	`dfs.namenode.servicerpc-address`	For NameNode RPC communication with HDFS services
	`dfs.namenode.http-address`	NameNode HTTP web UI address
	`dfs.namenode.https-addressw`	NameNode Secured HTTP web UI address
	`dfs.namenode.name.dir`	NameNode local directory
	`dfs.namenode.edits.dir`	Local directory for NameNode edits logs
	`dfs.namenode.checkpoint.dir`	SecondaryNameNode local directory
	`dfs.namenode.checkpoint.edits.dir`	Directory for SecondaryNameNode edits logs
SecondaryNameNode	`dfs.secondary.namenode.keytab.file`	The SecondaryNameNode `keytab` file
	`dfs.namenode.backup.address`	The address for the backup node
BackupNode	`dfs.secondary.namenode.keytab.file`	Backup node `keytab` file

There's more...

A NameNode federated Hadoop cluster has different administrative tasks than the old version (MRv1), which does not support federation.

Decommissioning a NameNode from the cluster

Add the NameNode ID into the `$HADOOP_CONF_DIR/namenode_exclude.txt` file. For example, if we want to decommission `namenode1` from the cluster, the content of the file should be:

```
namenode1
```

Distribute the `exclude` file to all the NameNodes with the following command:

```
distributed-exclude.sh $HADOOP_CONF_DIR/namenode_exlude.txt
```

Refresh the NameNode list with the following command:

```
refresh-namenodes.sh
```

We can use the following URL to access the web UI for the HDFS cluster:

```
http://namenode2:50070/dfsclusterhealth.jsp
```

Running balancer

Similar to the old Hadoop version, balancer is used to balance the data blocks over the cluster. On a HDFS federated Hadoop cluster, we can run a balancer with the following command:

```
hadoop-daemon.sh --config $HADOOP_HOME/conf --script hdfs start balancer
-policy node
```

This command will balance the data blocks on the node level. Another balancing policy is `blockpool`, which balances the storage at the block pool level as well as the data node level.

Adding a new NameNode

Suppose we have configured a NameNode-federated Hadoop cluster with two running NameNodes. We want to add the third NameNode `namenode3` on host `master3`. We can use the following steps to do this:

1. Log in to the new NameNode machine `master3`.

2. Configure MRv2 on the `master3` node.

3. Add the following lines into the `$HADOOP_CONF_DIR/hdfs-site.xml` file:

```
<property>
  <name>dfs.nameservices</name>
  <value>namenode1,namenode2,namenode3</value>
</property>

<property>
  <name>dfs.namenode.rpc-address.namenode1</name>
  <value>master1:54310</value>
</property>

<property>
  <name>dfs.namenode.http-address.namenode1</name>
  <value> master1:50070</value>
</property>
```

```
<property>
  <name>dfs.namenode.secondaryhttp-address.namenode1</name>
  <value>master1:50071</value>
</property>

<property>
  <name>dfs.namenode.rpc-address.namenode2</name>
  <value>master2:54310</value>
</property>

<property>
  <name>dfs.namenode.http-address.namenode2</name>
  <value> master2:50070</value>
</property>
<property>
  <name>dfs.namenode.secondaryhttp-address.namenode2</name>
  <value>master2:50071</value>
</property>

<property>
  <name>dfs.namenode.rpc-address.namenode3</name>
  <value>master3:54310</value>
</property>

<property>
  <name>dfs.namenode.http-address.namenode3</name>
  <value> master3:50070</value>
</property>
<property>
  <name>dfs.namenode.secondaryhttp-address.namenode3</name>
  <value>master3:50071</value>
</property>
```

4. Format `namenode3` with the following command:

    ```
    hdfs namenode -format -cluserId hdcluster
    ```

5. Sync the configuration into all the other NameNodes with the following commands:

    ```
    scp $HADOOP_CONF_DIR/hdfs-site.xml master1:$HADOOP_CONF_DIR/
    scp $HADOOP_CONF_DIR/hdfs-site.xml master2:$HADOOP_CONF_DIR/
    ```

6. Sync the configuration into all the slave nodes in the cluster with the following commands:

    ```
    for host in `cat $HADOOP_CONF_DIR/slaves`; do
      echo 'Sync configuration files to ' $host
      scp $HADOOP_CONF_DIR/hdfs-site.xml $host:$HADOOP_CONF_DIR/
    done
    ```

7. Start the HDFS cluster with the following command:

    ```
    start-dfs.sh
    ```

8. Tell the DataNodes the change of the NameNodes with the following command:

    ```
    for slavehost in `$HADOOP_CONF_DIR/slaves`;  do
      echo "Processing on host " $slavehost
      ssh $slavehost -C "hdfs dfsadmin -refreshNameNode master3:54310"
    done
    ```

See also

- ▸ The *Configuring NameNode high availability* recipe in *Chapter 5, Hardening a Hadoop Cluster*
- ▸ http://hadoop.apache.org/docs/r2.0.2-alpha/hadoop-yarn/hadoop-yarn-site/Federation.html
- ▸ http://hadoop.apache.org/docs/current/hadoop-project-dist/hadoop-hdfs/hdfs-default.xml
- ▸ http://hadoop.apache.org/docs/current/hadoop-yarn/hadoop-yarn-site/HDFSHighAvailabilityWithQJM.html

6
Monitoring a Hadoop Cluster

In this chapter, we will cover:

- ▸ Monitoring a Hadoop cluster with JMX
- ▸ Monitoring a Hadoop cluster with Ganglia
- ▸ Monitoring a Hadoop cluster with Nagios
- ▸ Monitoring a Hadoop cluster with Ambari
- ▸ Monitoring a Hadoop cluster with Chukwa

Introduction

System monitoring is critical for maintaining the health and availability for large distributed systems such as Hadoop. General monitoring tasks include monitoring the health of cluster nodes and networks, for example, the usage of memory, heap, CPU, network, and so on. For a Hadoop cluster, we may also want to monitor some specific metrics, such as the status of jobs and tasks in the cluster, the status of the JobTracker, TaskTracker, NameNode, and DataNode.

Hadoop is lucky to be born in an open source world! A number of very stable open source tools for system monitoring are there waiting to join the Hadoop family, and many of these systems have been adopted by Hadoop for monitoring purposes.

In this chapter, we will first introduce the management framework, **Java Management Extension** (**JMX**) for system monitoring. Next, we will introduce two famous open source cluster monitoring systems: **Ganglia** and **Nagios**. Ganglia is an open source scalable monitoring system. Monitoring daemons running on monitoring hosts send data to monitoring server hosts for storage, statistical analysis, and visualization. Nagios is another famous monitoring system. It monitors hosts in the cluster using plugins.

Next, we will introduce Hadoop-specific monitoring systems **Ambari** and **Chukwa**. Ambari was designed to be a full-fledged system for the deployment, management, and monitoring of Hadoop clusters. It was developed based on the monitoring framework of Ganglia and Nagios. But different from Ganglia and Nagios, Apache Chukwa monitors a Hadoop cluster by analyzing system logs collected from the Hadoop cluster. Apache **Flume** is another general purpose data analytics framework for streaming data such as system logs. It can be configured to do system monitoring, which is similar to Chukwa.

Monitoring a Hadoop cluster with JMX

JMX is the technology used by Java to build, monitor, and manage distributed systems and network applications. It has been incorporated into Java from **J2SE** platform 5.0. For more information about JMX, please visit the official website at `http://www.oracle.com/technetwork/java/javase/tech/javamanagement-140525.html`. In this recipe, we will outline steps to configure Hadoop cluster monitoring with JMX.

In this chapter, we assume to monitor Hadoop Version 1.1.y or the corresponding 0.20.x Hadoop release. Configurations for monitoring Hadoop Versions 2.0.x or 0.23.x should follow the recipe with some changes.

Getting ready

We assume that Oracle JDK has been installed, and our Hadoop cluster has been configured properly, and all the daemons are running without any problems.

How to do it...

Use the following steps to configure JMX for monitoring a Hadoop cluster:

1. Create a JMX password file for remote monitoring with the following command:

    ```
    cp $JAVA_HOME/jre/lib/management/jmxremote.password.template
    $HADOOP_HOME/conf/jmxremote.password
    ```

2. Open the template password $HADOOP_HOME/conf/jmxremote.password file with a text editor and the last few lines of this file will be similar to the following:

    ```
    # Following are two commented-out entries.  The "measureRole" role
    has
    # password "QED".  The "controlRole" role has password "R&D".
    #
    # monitorRole   QED
    # controlRole   R&D
    ```

Remove the comment symbol # for the two highlighted lines.

These two lines specify the passwords for `monitorRole` and `controlRole`. JMX will use them for authentication purposes in a remote monitoring.

Change the permission of the password file to `600` with the following command:

```
chmod 600 $HADOOP_HOME/conf/jmxremote.password
```

Warning!

If this file is too open, you will get an error similar to the following when starting the Hadoop cluster daemons:

```
master: Error: Password file read access must be
restricted: /usr/local/hadoop/conf/jmxremote.password
```

3. Open the `$HADOOP_HOME/conf/hadoop-env.sh` file with a text editor.

4. In this file, we will be able to find JMX monitoring configurations for the Hadoop daemons including NameNode, SecondaryNameNode, DataNode, balancer, JobTracker, and TaskTracker. The default configuration will be similar to the following:

```
export HADOOP_NAMENODE_OPTS="-Dcom.sun.management.jmxremote
$HADOOP_NAMENODE_OPTS"
export HADOOP_SECONDARYNAMENODE_OPTS="-Dcom.sun.management.
jmxremote $HADOOP_SECONDARYNAMENODE_OPTS"
export HADOOP_DATANODE_OPTS="-Dcom.sun.management.jmxremote
$HADOOP_DATANODE_OPTS"
export HADOOP_BALANCER_OPTS="-Dcom.sun.management.jmxremote
$HADOOP_BALANCER_OPTS"
export HADOOP_JOBTRACKER_OPTS="-Dcom.sun.management.jmxremote
$HADOOP_JOBTRACKER_OPTS"
```

Now, we need to configure the remote monitoring port for Hadoop daemons by changing the original configuration to the following:

```
# Extra Java runtime options. Empty by default.
export HADOOP_OPTS="-Dcom.sun.management.jmxremote.
authenticate=true -Dcom.sun.management.jmxremote.ssl=false -Dcom.
sun.management.jmxremote.password.file=$HADOOP_CONF_DIR/jmxremote.
password"

export HADOOP_NAMENODE_OPTS="-Dcom.sun.management.jmxremote
$HADOOP_NAMENODE_OPTS -Dcom.sun.management.jmxremote.port=8004"
export HADOOP_SECONDARYNAMENODE_OPTS="-Dcom.sun.management.
jmxremote $HADOOP_SECONDARYNAMENODE_OPTS -Dcom.sun.management.
jmxremote.port=8005"
```

```
export HADOOP_DATANODE_OPTS="-Dcom.sun.management.jmxremote
$HADOOP_DATANODE_OPTS -Dcom.sun.management.jmxremote.port=8006"
export HADOOP_BALANCER_OPTS="-Dcom.sun.management.jmxremote
$HADOOP_BALANCER_OPTS -Dcom.sun.management.jmxremote.port=8007"
export HADOOP_JOBTRACKER_OPTS="-Dcom.sun.management.jmxremote
$HADOOP_JOBTRACKER_OPTS -Dcom.sun.management.jmxremote.port=8008"
export HADOOP_TASKTRACKER_OPTS="-Dcom.sun.management.jmxremote.
port=8009"
```

5. Use the following command to start the monitor user interface:

   jconsole

   We can see a window that is similar to the following screenshot:

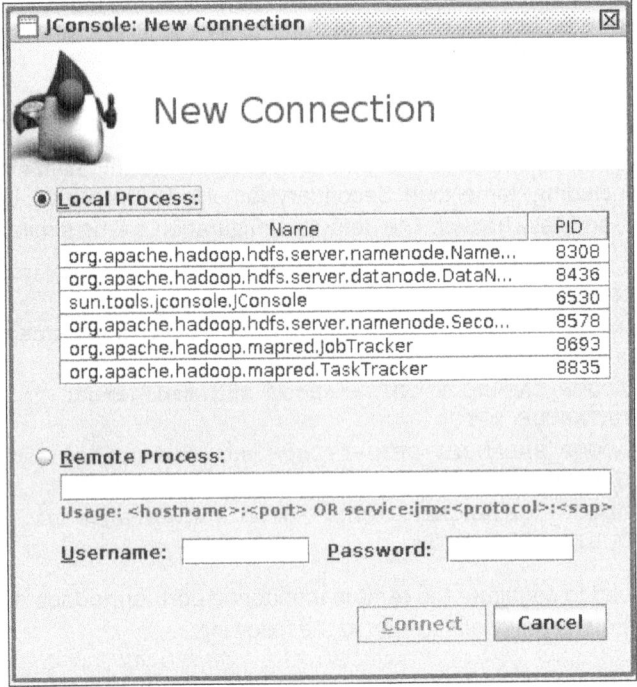

From this window, we can check the status of both local and remote processes. Checking the status of local processes is relatively simple. First, select the desired process to check from the process list. Then, we only need to click on the **Connect** button. Checking the status of remote processes is relatively complicated. We need to specify the location of the service by either specifying the hostname and port or protocol and sap as shown in the screenshot. We also need to enter the **Username** and **Password** values for authentication purposes. In the following steps, we assume to check the status of local JobTracker processes.

6. Select the **Local Process** radio button and then click on the **Connect** button. We can get a monitoring window after waiting for a few moments, as shown in the following screenshot:

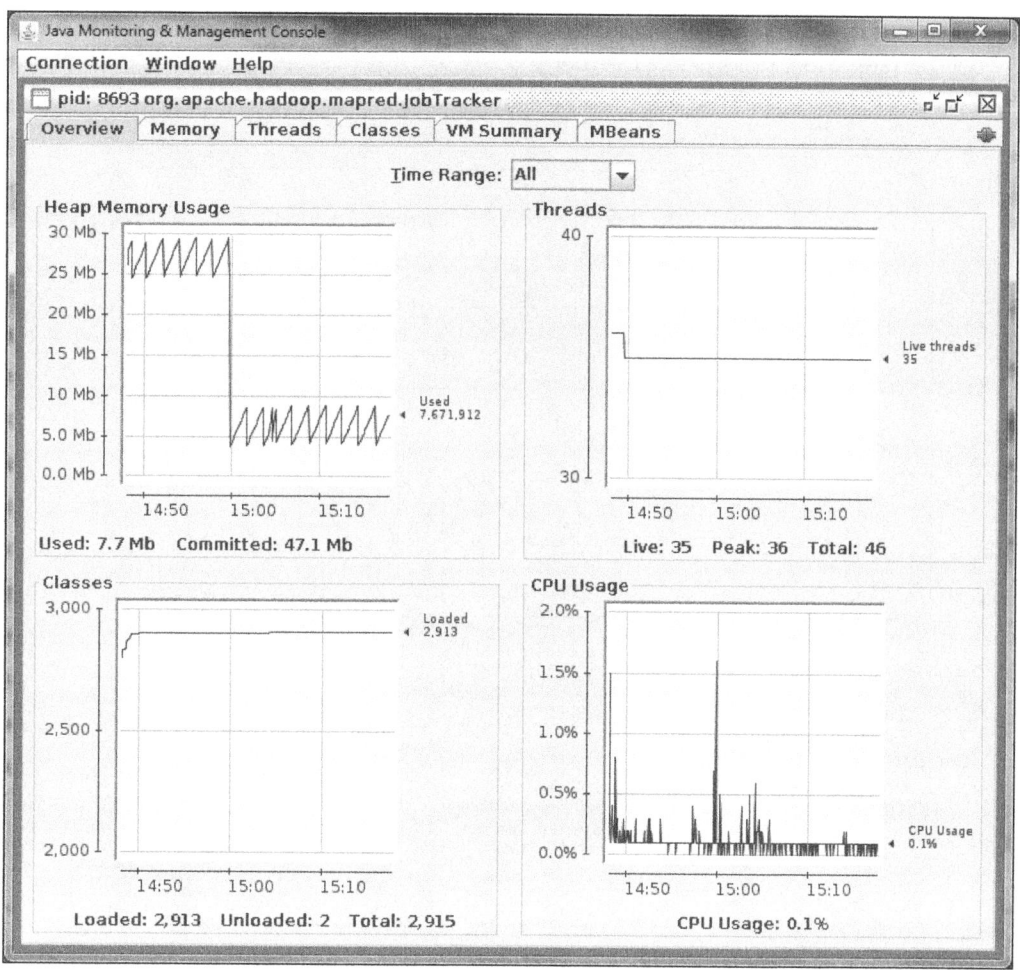

The window shows the daemon status for the JobTracker. From the window, we can check the memory usage, threads, classes, summary of JVM, and details of MBeans.

7. Check the memory of the daemon by clicking on the **Memory** tab of the `jconsole` window, and we will get a window similar to the following:

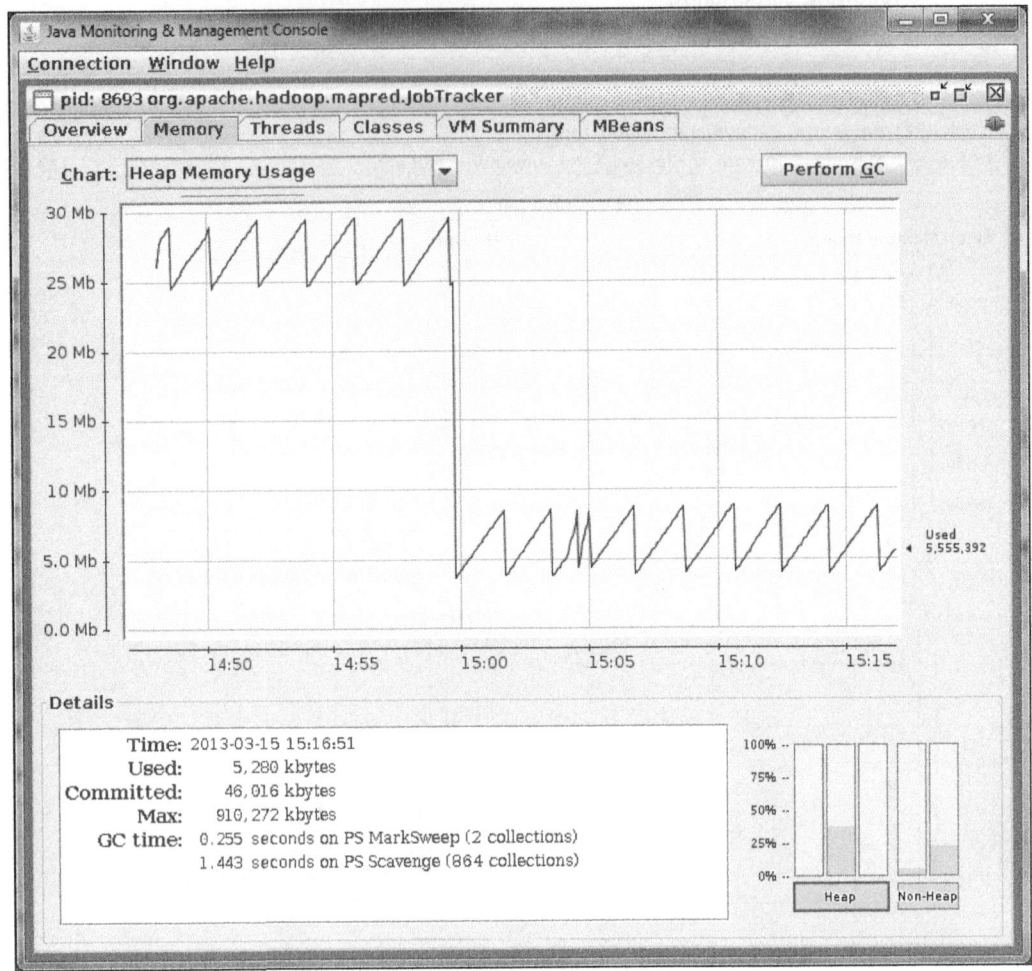

The memory window shows the **Heap Memory Usage** page as a time serial chart. From this window, we can select from different charts and time ranges to display. The bottom part of the window is a summary of the current memory usage.

8. By clicking on the **Threads** tab of the window, we can check the running threads of the JobTracker and we can get a window similar to the following screenshot:

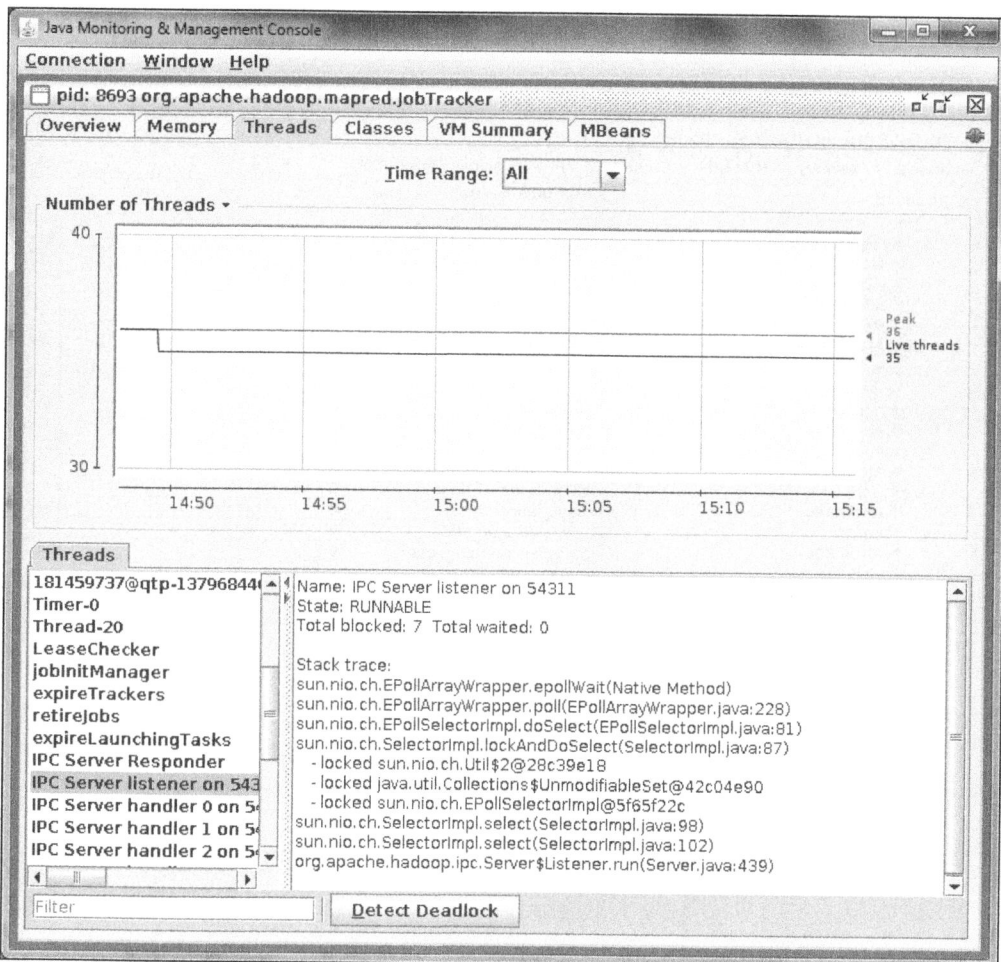

The upper part of the window shows the number of **peak live threads** and the number of **current live threads**. On the lower part of the window, we can see a list of threads, the information of which can be viewed by clicking on the desired thread names.

Similarly, we can check the current classes by clicking on the **Classes** tab of the window and check the summary of the JVM virtual machine by clicking on the **VM Summary** tab of the window.

9. The **MBeans** tab is the most informative one if you want to check the status details of the daemon. For example, the following screenshot shows more metrics details for JobTracker:

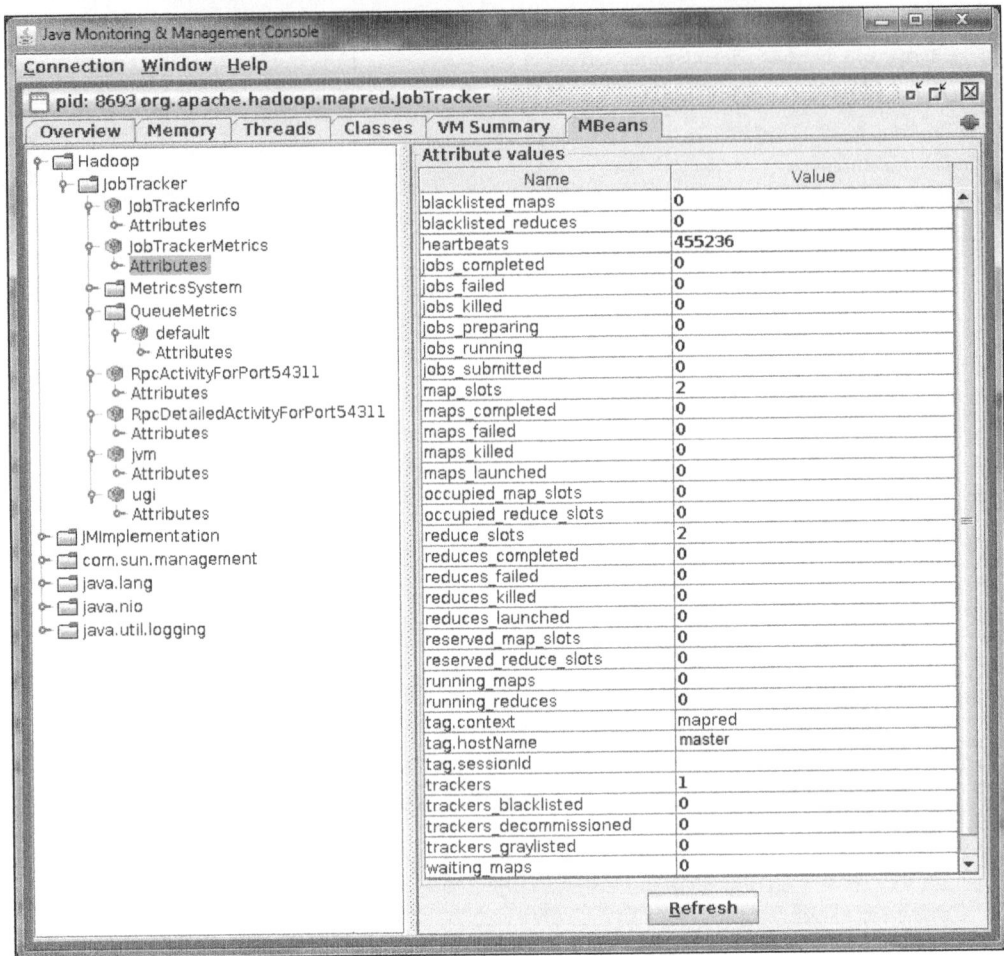

From this window, we can get a number of JobTracker metrics such as number of running jobs, number of map and reduce slots, and number of running map and reduce tasks.

See also

- ▸ The *Monitoring a Hadoop cluster with Ganglia* recipe
- ▸ The *Monitoring a Hadoop cluster with Nagios* recipe
- ▸ The *Monitoring a Hadoop cluster with Ambari* recipe
- ▸ The *Monitoring a Hadoop cluster with Chukwa* recipe
- ▸ Refer to http://docs.oracle.com/javase/tutorial/jmx/
- ▸ Refer to docs.oracle.com/javase/tutorial/jmx/

Monitoring a Hadoop cluster with Ganglia

Ganglia is an open source, scalable, and distributed monitoring system for clusters and computing grids. It has three major components: the **monitoring daemon**, the **metadata daemon**, and the **web UI**. In this recipe, we will outline steps to configure Ganglia for Hadoop cluster monitoring.

Getting ready

Log in to the master node from the administrator machine with the following command:

```
ssh hdadmin@master
```

Use the following yum command to install Ganglia on the master machine:

```
sudo yum install -y ganglia-gmond ganglia-gmetad ganglia-web
```

Install Ganglia monitoring daemon on all the slave nodes with the following commands:

```
for host in `cat $HADOOP_HOME/conf/slaves`
do
  echo 'Installing Ganglia on host ' $host
  sudo ssh $host -C "yum install -y ganglia-gmond"
done
```

In this recipe, we assume that the Ganglia server will run on the master node and the monitoring daemons run on both master and slave nodes.

How to do it...

Use the following steps to configure Ganglia for Hadoop cluster monitoring:

1. Open the gmond configuration file /etc/ganglia/gmond.conf with a text editor.

2. Change the cluster attribute to the following:

```
cluster {
  name = "hadoop"
  owner = "hduser"
  latlong = "unspecified"
  url = "unspecified"
}
```

3. Change the udp_send_channel attribute to the following:

```
udp_send_channel {
  bind_hostname = yes
  # mcast_join = 239.2.11.71
  host = master
  port = 8649
  ttl = 1
}
```

4. Change the udp_recv_channel attribute to the following:

```
udp_recv_channel {
  # mcast_join = 239.2.11.71
  port = 8649
  # bind = 239.2.11.71
}
```

Hadoop supports network communication through both **unicast** (with normal IP addresses, which is the one we use here) and **multicast**, which uses multicast addresses, such as 239.2.11.71. To use multicast, all the monitored hosts should be in the same IP segment. In this book, we assume to use unicast.

5. Add all the hostnames in the cluster to the `gmetad` configuration `/etc/ganglia/gmetad.conf` file, for example, this file should contain the following:

```
data_source "hdcluster" master:8649
```

> Here `hdcluster` is the name of cluster that Ganglia monitors and `master:8649` is the network address of `gmetad`.

6. Open the `$HADOOP_HOME/conf/hadoop-metrics.properties` file with your favorite text editor and add the following contents into the file:

```
jvm.class=org.apache.hadoop.metrics.ganglia.GangliaContext
jvm.period=10
jvm.servers=master:8649
```

The previous three lines configure JVM monitoring.

```
rpc.class=org.apache.hadoop.metrics.ganglia.GangliaContext
rpc.period=10
rpc.servers=master:8649
```

The previous three lines configure RPC monitoring.

```
dfs.class=org.apache.hadoop.metrics.ganglia.GangliaContext
dfs.period=10
dfs.servers=master:8649
```

The previous three lines configure HDFS monitoring.

```
mapred.class=org.apache.hadoop.metrics.ganglia.GangliaContext
mapred.period=10
mapred.servers=master:8649
```

The previous three lines configure to monitor MapReduce metrics.

```
hbase.class=org.apache.hadoop.metrics.ganglia.GangliaContext
hbase.period=10
hbase.servers=master:8649
```

The previous three lines configure monitoring the HBase metrics.

> In the previous configuration, we have specified three common parameters: `class`, `period`, and `servers`. the parameter `class` specifies the message format that Ganglia will use (can be either `GangliaContext` or `GangliaContext31`); `period` specifies the time interval between two consecutive metric updates, and `servers` specifies a list of server that monitoring messages should be sent to.

7. Copy configuration files to all the slave nodes with the following commands:

```
for host in cat $HADOOP_HOME/conf/slaves

do

  echo 'Copying ganglia monitoring configuration file to host'
$host;

    sudo scp /etc/ganglia/gmond.conf $host:/etc/ganglia/gmond.conf

    sudo scp /etc/ganglia/gmetad.conf $host:/etc/ganglia/gmetad.conf

    sudo scp $HADOOP_HOME/conf/hadoop-metrics.properties
$host:$HADOOP_HOME/conf/hadoop-metrics.properties;

  done
```

8. Restart the Hadoop cluster with the following commands:

```
stop-all.sh

start-all.sh
```

9. Start the gmond daemon with the following command on the master node:

```
sudo service gmond start
```

 Run the `sudo chkconfig gmond on` command if you want the process to survive a system reboot.

10. Check the status of gmond with the following command:

```
curl master:8649
```

This command will output the configuration of Ganglia in XML similar to the following:

```
<GANGLIA_XML VERSION="3.1.7" SOURCE="gmond">

<CLUSTER NAME="hdcluster" LOCALTIME="1363403519" OWNER="hduser"
LATLONG="unspecified" URL="hdcluster.com">

<HOST NAME="master" IP="10.147.166.55" REPORTED="1363403500"
TN="19" TMAX="20" DMAX="0" LOCATION="unspecified" GMOND_
STARTED="1363403380">

<METRIC NAME="proc_run" VAL="3" TYPE="uint32" UNITS=" " TN="42"
TMAX="950" DMAX="0" SLOPE="both">

<EXTRA_DATA>

<EXTRA_ELEMENT NAME="GROUP" VAL="process"/>

<EXTRA_ELEMENT NAME="DESC" VAL="Total number of running
processes"/>

<EXTRA_ELEMENT NAME="TITLE" VAL="Total Running Processes"/>

</EXTRA_DATA>
```

```
</METRIC>

<METRIC NAME="dfs.datanode.heartBeats_avg_time" VAL="1.0"
TYPE="double" UNITS="" TN="2" TMAX="60" DMAX="0" SLOPE="both">

<EXTRA_DATA>

<EXTRA_ELEMENT NAME="GROUP" VAL="dfs.datanode"/>

</EXTRA_DATA>

</METRIC>

<METRIC NAME="mapred.shuffleOutput.shuffle_output_bytes"
VAL="0" TYPE="float" UNITS="" TN="1225" TMAX="60" DMAX="0"
SLOPE="positive">

<EXTRA_DATA>

<EXTRA_ELEMENT NAME="GROUP" VAL="mapred.shuffleOutput"/>

</EXTRA_DATA>

</METRIC>

...

<EXTRA_ELEMENT NAME="GROUP" VAL="system"/>

<EXTRA_ELEMENT NAME="DESC" VAL="Operating system release date"/>

<EXTRA_ELEMENT NAME="TITLE" VAL="Operating System Release"/>

</EXTRA_DATA>

</METRIC>

</HOST>

</CLUSTER>

</GANGLIA_XML>
```

 The highlighted lines show that some HDFS and MapReduce metrics are being monitored by Ganglia.

11. Start the `gmetad` daemon with the following command on the master node:

```
sudo service gmetad start
```

12. Start the `gmond` on all slave nodes with the following commands:

```
for host in cat $HADOOP_HOME/conf/slaves
do
  echo 'Starting gmond service on host: ' $host;
  sudo ssh $host -C "service gmond start";
done
```

13. Open the `/etc/httpd/conf.d/ganglia.conf` file with your favorite text editor and add the following content:

```
<Location /ganglia>
    Order deny,allow
    Allow from all
</Location>
```

 The `access control` setting in this file allows everyone to visit the Ganglia web UI. For security reasons, we can restrict the IP addresses, hosts, or domains with the `Allow from` and `Deny from` statements in the configuration.

14. Start the `httpd` daemon with the following command:

    sudo service httpd start

15. Check the status of Ganglia by opening URL `http://master:80/ganglia`, and we can get a web page similar to the following screenshot:

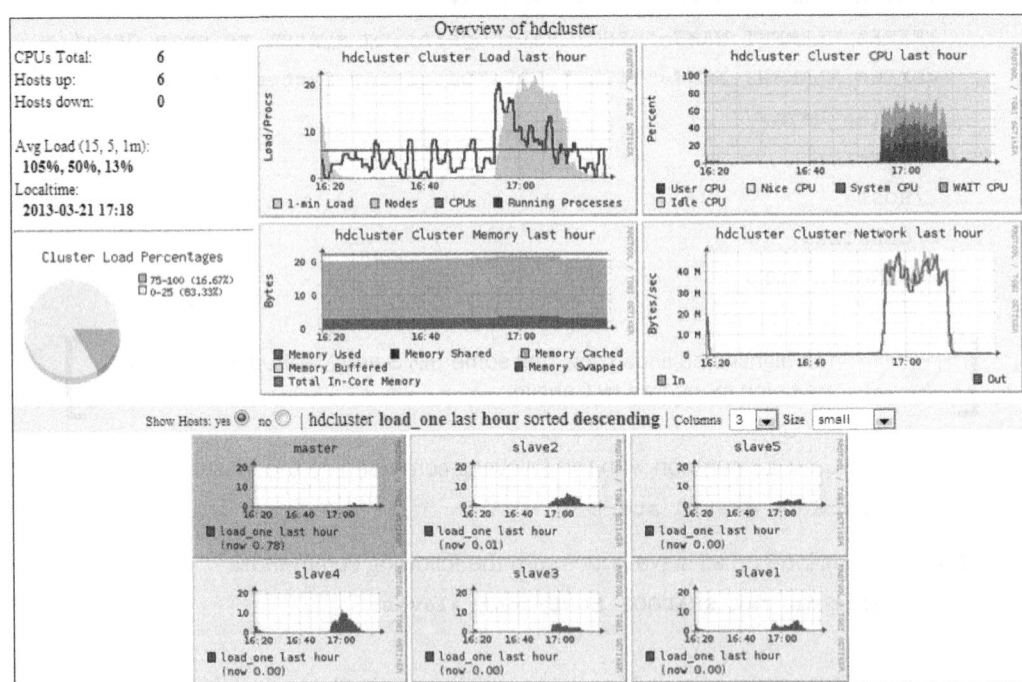

The upper-left portion of the UI is a summary of the cluster, including number of hosts, host status, average load, and so on.

The upper-right part of the screenshot shows an overview of the whole cluster, including cluster total load, CPU usage, memory, and network traffic. The screenshot contains a clear jump for about 20 minutes when one `teragen` job is running, which consumes cluster resources.

The lower part of the screenshot shows the status for each node in the cluster, including the master node and all the slave nodes. We can change the metric to display by selecting from the combo box, as shown in the following screenshot:

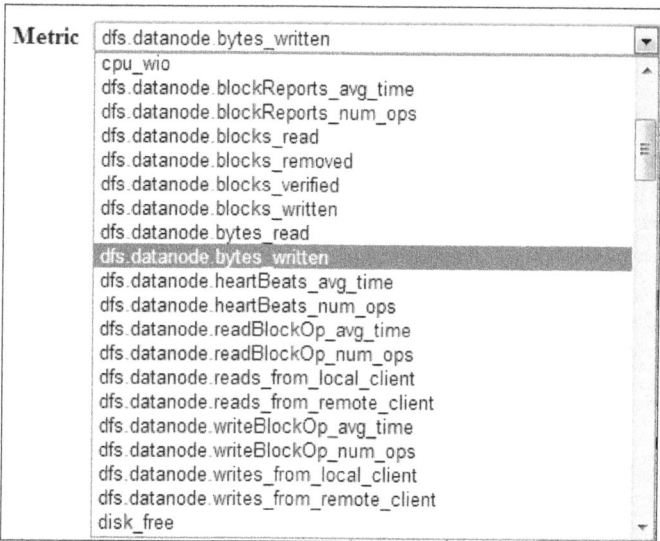

For example, by selecting the metric **dfs_datenode.bytes_written**, we can get the following screenshot for each node:

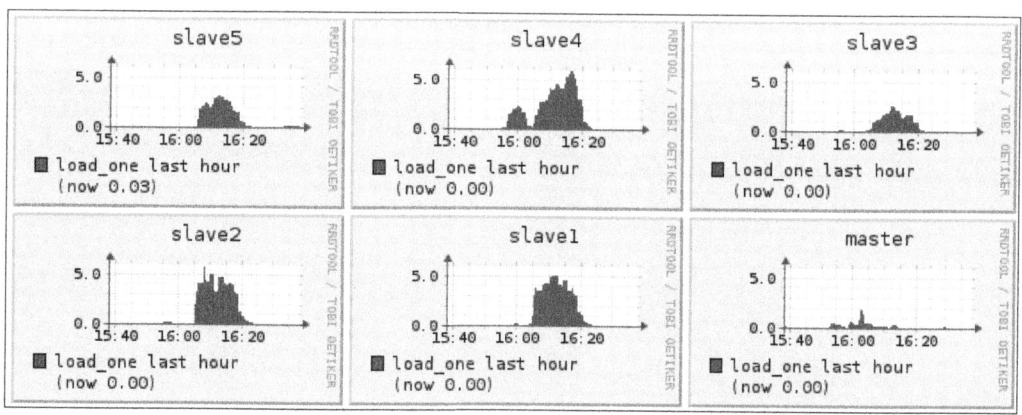

The previous screenshot confirms that a DataNode is the actual place where data blocks are stored, and NameNode only keeps track of the metadata for the data blocks. So the written data size is much smaller for NameNode.

16. Check the details of each cluster node by selecting the option from the combo box, which has the initial value of **--Choose a Node**. For example, if we want to check all the metric values for the master node, we will be able to get a web page similar to the following screenshot:

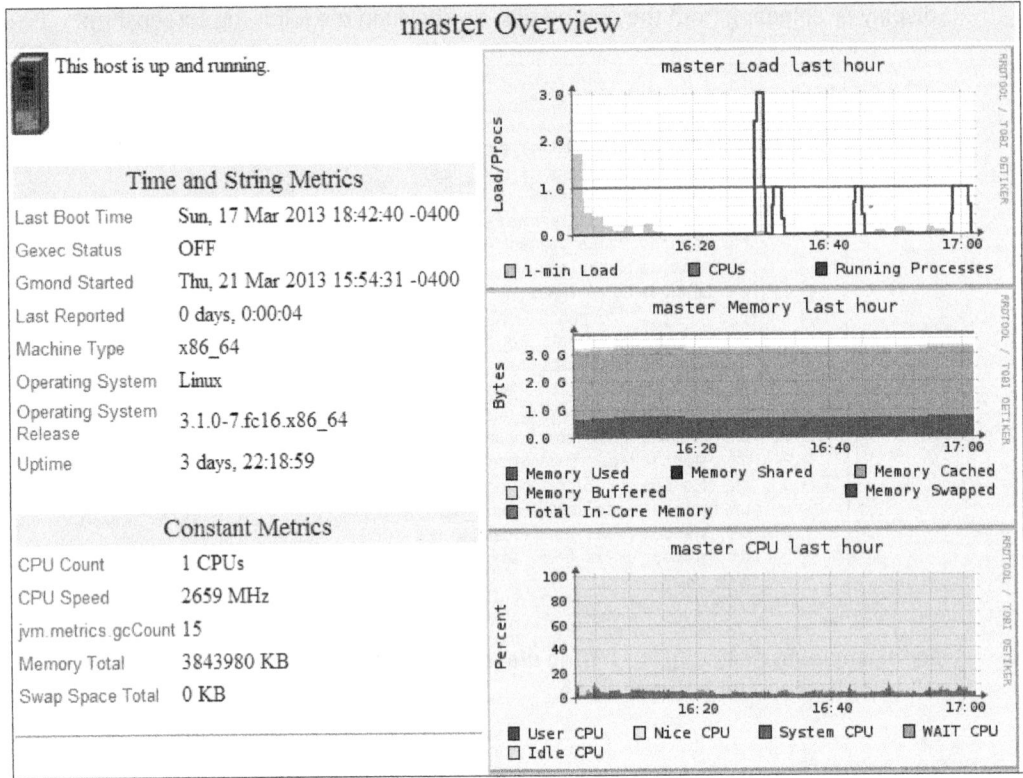

17. By scrolling down the window, we can check the Hadoop JobTracker metrics as shown in the following screenshot:

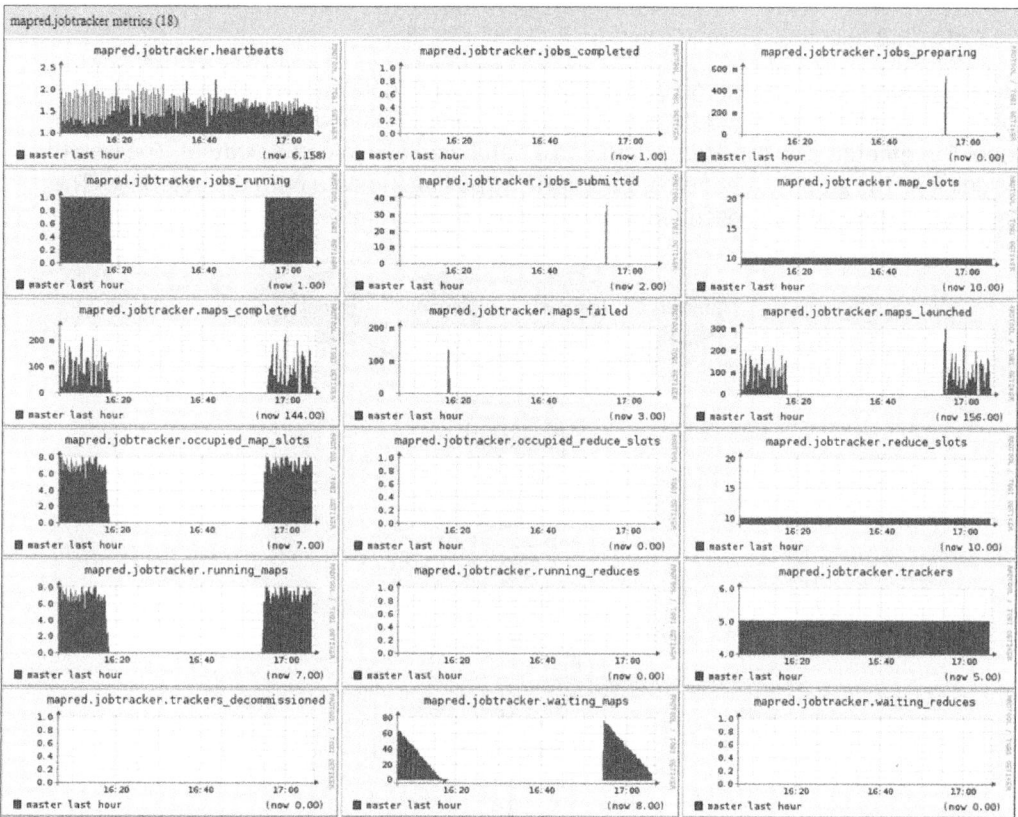

The previous screenshot contains the status information of the JobTracker including the number of running jobs, the number of map reduce slots, and so on.

How it works...

A Ganglia monitoring system is composed of three parts: the monitoring daemons `gmond`, the meta-data handling daemon `gmetad`, and the web UI.

Ganglia **gmond** daemons run on each node that is being monitored in the cluster. They continuously collect metrics data and send to the **gmetad** daemon running on the master node. The **gmetad** daemon stores data into a database maintained by **rrdtool**. The web UI, including all the graphs, is generated with PHP by pulling the data from the database. The Ganglia data flow can be described with the following diagram:

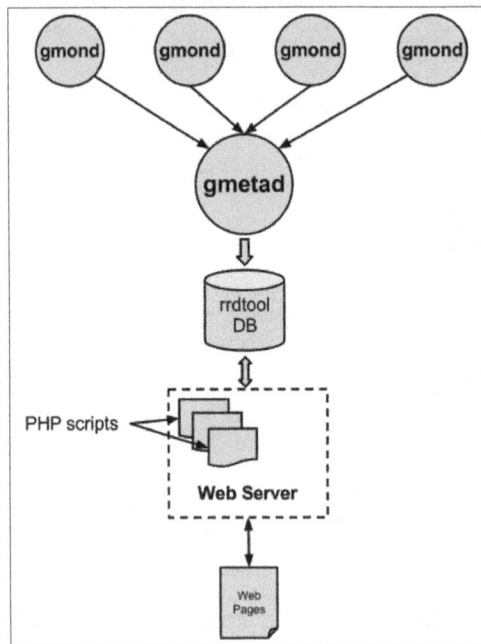

See also

► The *Monitoring a Hadoop cluster with JMX* recipe
► The *Monitoring a Hadoop cluster with Chukwa* recipe
► The *Monitoring a Hadoop cluster with Nagios* recipe
► The *Monitoring a Hadoop cluster with Ambari* recipe

- ▶ Refer to http://ganglia.sourceforge.net/
- ▶ Refer to http://www.ibm.com/developerworks/wikis/display/ WikiPtype/ganglia

Monitoring a Hadoop cluster with Nagios

Nagios is a powerful open source cluster monitoring system. It can monitor not only hosts and servers but also interconnecting devices such as routers and switches. The alerting services provide notification mechanisms for fast response on system problems.

Designed to be a generic monitoring system, Nagios can be configured to monitor Hadoop clusters. In this recipe, we will outline steps to configure Nagios for Hadoop cluster monitoring.

Getting ready

Perform the following steps before monitoring a Hadoop cluster with Nagios:

1. To get started with Nagios monitoring, we need to install it first. On CentOS and other Red Hat-compatible Linux systems, we can use the following `yum` command to install Nagios:

   ```
   sudo yum install nagios nagios-plugins
   ```

   This command will automatically install the dependency software packages such as `libgd` and `libgd-devel`. After installation, the Nagios configuration files will be under the `/etc/nagios` directory and the Nagios daemon will be under the `/etc/init.d/` directory.

2. Install the **Nagios Remote Plugin Executor** (**NRPE**) package with the following command:

   ```
   sudo yum install nrpe
   ```

   NRPE is a Nagios add-on that allows us to execute Nagios plugins on a remote machine. For more information, please check: http://nagios.sourceforge. net/docs/3_0/addons.html and http://nagios.sourceforge.net/docs/ nrpe/NRPE.pdf.

3. Download the `check_jmx` Nagios plugin from http://exchange.nagios.org/ directory/Plugins/Java-Applications-and-Servers/ check_jmx/details.

   We want to use Java JMX as a Nagios plugin to monitor Hadoop metrics.

   Use the following commands to build the `check_jmx` package:

   ```
   tar xvf check_jmx.tgz
   cd check_jmx
   ant
   ```

4. After this, we want to get the following directory structure:

```
check_jmx
├── ...
├── nagios
|   ├── plugin
|   |   ├── check_jmx
|   |   └── jmxquery.jar
|   └── readme.txt
└── ...
```

5. Copy the two highlighted files in the `/usr/local/nagios/libexec` directory:

```
cp check_jmx/nagios/plugin/check_jmx /usr/local/nagios/libexec
cp check_jmx/nagios/plugin/jmxquery.jar /usr/local/nagios/libexec
```

By doing this, we will be able to use the `check_jmx` command in the Nagios monitoring configuration.

How to do it...

Use the following steps to configure Nagios for Hadoop cluster monitoring:

1. Open the `/etc/nagios/nagios.cfg` file with a text editor.

 This file is the main configuration file of Nagios. It references a number of files with the extension `.cfg`, which contains specific monitoring configurations.

2. Change the contacts information for alerting services by changing the e-mail address in the `/usr/local/nagios/etc/objects/contacts.cfg` file:

```
define contact{
  contact_name    nagiosadmin
  use    generic-contact
  alias    Nagios
  email    nagios@localhost
}
```

 Other alerting methods such as SMS messages and paging, are also available. Please refer to the following web page for more information:

`http://nagios.sourceforge.net/docs/3_0/objectdefinitions.html`

3. Change the Apache web server configuration file `/etc/httpd/conf/httpd.conf` by adding the following line:

```
Include /etc/httpd/conf/nagios.conf
```

The `/etc/httpd/conf/nagios.conf` file is the configuration file for the Nagios web interface; the content of this file should be similar to the following:

```
# Specifies the location of the cgi scripts.
ScriptAlias /nagios/cgi-bin /usr/local/nagios/sbin
<Directory "/usr/local/nagios/sbin">
  AllowOverride AuthConfig
  Options ExecCGI
  Allow from all
  Order allow,deny
</Directory>

# Specifies the Nagios root directory.
# This will enable us to visit Nagios through http://<host>/nagios
Alias /nagios /usr/local/nagios/share
<Directory "/usr/local/nagios/share">
  Options None
  AllowOverride AuthConfig
  Order allow,deny
  Allow from all
</Directory>
```

The previous configuration specifies the root as well as the CGI directories for the Nagios web UI; to enable access for users, we need to create the `/usr/local/nagios/sbin/.htaccess` and `/usr/local/nagios/share/.htaccess` files, with the following content:

```
AuthName "Nagios Access"
AuthType Basic
AuthUserFile /etc/nagios/htpasswd.users
require valid-user
```

4. Create an administrator user for the Nagios web UI with the following command:

sudo htpasswd -c /etc/nagios/htpasswd.users nagiosadmin

 We are supposed to type in a password for the `nagiosadmin` user twice. The username and password will be used to log in to the web UI.

Now, we are ready to specify the Hadoop cluster monitoring configurations with the following steps:

1. Open the `/etc/nagios/nagios.cfg` file and add the following content:

```
cfg_file=/etc/nagios/hosts.cfg
cfg_file=/etc/nagios/services.cfg
```

   The previous two lines tell the main configuration file `nagios.cfg` to include two user specific configuration files: `hosts.cfg` and `services.cfg`.

2. Configuration file `hosts.cfg` specifies the hosts we want to monitor, and it should have content similar to the following:

```
####################################
## Declare host groups.
####################################
define hostgroup {
 hostgroup_name hdgroup
 alias Hadoop cluster groups.
}


####################################
# Define a host template.
# All the hosts configuration in our
# cluster should be derived from this
# template.
####################################
define host {
    name        hdhost
    use         linux-server
    hostgroups hdgroup
    register    0
}


##########################################
# This are the real hosts in the cluster.
##########################################
define host{
    host_name    master
    alias        The master node.
    address      10.194.19.16
    use          hdhost
}

    define host{
```

```
        host_name    slave1
        alias        The slave 1.
        address      10.40.193.19
        use          hdhost
    }

    define host{
        host_name    slave2
        alias        The slave 2.
        address      10.36.117.108
        use          hdhost
    }

    define host{
        host_name    slave3
        alias        The slave 3.
        address      10.40.66.245
        use          hdhost
    }

    define host{
        host_name    slave4
        alias        The slave 4.
        address      10.245.133.242
        use          hdhost
    }

    define host{
        host_name    slave5
        alias        The slave 5.
        address      10.12.73.254
        use          hdhost
    }
```

The file configures six hosts to monitor in the cluster, including one master node and the five slave nodes.

3. The configuration file `services.cfg` specifies the services we want to monitor. The contents of this file should be similar to the following:

```
#################################################
## Service definitions.
## For example, we want to monitor the status of
## the system, including the load, cpu usage,
## memory usage etc.
```

```
## For the monitoring of Hadoop clsuters,
#################################################
# Monitor system metrics.
define service{
    use                 generic-service
    hostgroup_name      hdgroup
    service_description SSH
    check_command       check_ssh
}

define service{
    use                 local-service
    hostgroup_name      hdgroup
    service_description Swap Usage
    check_command       check_local_swap!20!10
}

define service{
    use                 local-service
    hostgroup_name      hdgroup
    service_description Total processes
    check_command       check_local_procs!250!400!RSZDT
}
```

The service configured in this file will be applied to each host claiming to be in the `hdgroup` group, which is configured in the `hosts.cfg` file.

4. Verify the configurations with the following command:

```
sudo nagios --verify-config /etc/nagios/nagios.cfg
```

We will get output similar to the following screenshot:

```
Nagios Core 3.5.0
Copyright (c) 2009-2011 Nagios Core Development Team and Community Contributors
Copyright (c) 1999-2009 Ethan Galstad
Last Modified: 03-15-2013
License: GPL
...
Checking for circular paths between hosts...
Checking obsessive compulsive processor commands...
Checking misc settings...

Total Warnings: 0
Total Errors:   0

Things look okay - No serious problems were detected during the pre-flight check
```

5. Start the Nagios service with the following command:

```
sudo service nagios start
```

6. Check the status of the service with the following command:

```
sudo service nagios status
```

If Nagios is running, the output should be similar to:

```
nagios (pid 21542) is running...
```

If SELinux is on, we need to change the context of the web directory with:

```
chcon -R -t httpd_sys_content_t /usr/local/nagios/sbin/
chcon -R -t httpd_sys_content_t /usr/local/nagios/share/
```

7. Restart the web server with the following command:

```
sudo service httpd restart
```

Now, we should be able to check the web UI by opening URL:
`http://master/nagios`.

>  If you are opening the web UI for the first time, you need to type in the username and password. The username should be `nagiosadmin` and the password should be the one you entered for the `htpasswd` command.

How it works...

Nagios is an open source centralized network monitoring system. A typical Nagios deployment consists of a monitoring server and a number of hosts that are being monitored. An administrator defines monitoring specifications (what services on which hosts) using one or more configuration files. For more information about Nagios, please refer to: `http://www.nagios.org`.

See also

- ▸ The *Monitoring a Hadoop cluster with JMX* recipe
- ▸ The *Monitoring a Hadoop cluster with Chukwa* recipe

> ▶ The *Monitoring a Hadoop cluster with Ganglia* recipe
>
> ▶ The *Monitoring a Hadoop cluster with Ambari* recipe
>
> ▶ Refer to http://library.nagios.com/library/products/ nagioscore/manuals

Monitoring a Hadoop cluster with Ambari

The Apache **Ambari** project (http://incubator.apache.org/ambari/) is an open source project aiming to ease the management and monitoring of Hadoop clusters. Currently, Ambari supports the management of the software: HDFS, MapReduce, HBase, and Hive. In this recipe, we will outline steps to configure Hadoop Ambari for cluster installation, monitoring, and management.

Getting ready

We assume that the Hadoop cluster has been configured properly. Perform the following steps:

1. Enable the NTP server with the following command:

    ```
    sudo service ntpd start
    sudo chkconfig ntpd on
    ```

2. SELinux should have been disabled on the servers where Ambari is installed. We can use the following command to temporarily disable SELinux:

    ```
    sudo setenforce 0
    ```

3. To permanently disable SELinux, we need to edit the SELinux configuration file /etc/ selinux/config by changing the state of the SELINUX attribute to the following:

    ```
    SELINUX=disabled0
    ```

    > After changing the /etc/selinux/config file, we need to restart the system to make it effective.

4. Disable the iptables service with the following command:

    ```
    sudo service iptables stop
    sudo chkconfig iptables off
    ```

5. Check the status of iptables with the following command:

    ```
    sudo iptables -L
    ```

The output should be similar to the following:

```
Chain INPUT (policy ACCEPT)
target      prot opt source              destination


Chain FORWARD (policy ACCEPT)
target      prot opt source              destination


Chain OUTPUT (policy ACCEPT)
target      prot opt source              destination
```

How to do it...

Use the following steps to configure Ambari for Hadoop monitoring and management:

1. Download the repository file from the Horntonworks website with the following commands:

   ```
   sudo wget http://public-repo-1.hortonworks.com/ambari/centos6/1.x/
   GA/ambari.repo -P /etc/yum.repos.d
   ```

2. Install the `epel` repository with the following command:

   ```
   sudo yum install epel-release
   ```

3. Verify the repository list with the following command:

   ```
   yum repolist
   ```

   The output should be similar to the following:

   ```
   Loaded plugins: langpacks, presto, refresh-packagekit
   ...
   repo id                repo name                            status
   HDP-UTILS-1.1.0.15     HDP-UTILS-1.1.0.15                   52
   Updates-ambari-1.x     ambari-1.x - Updates                 10
   ambari-1.x             Ambari 1.x                           5
   epel                   Extra Packages for Enterprise Linux 5 -
   x86_64
   ```

4. Install Ambari with the following command:

   ```
   sudo yum install ambari-server
   ```

   The command will automatically install the **PostgreSQL** database, which is required by Ambari.

5. Set up the Ambari server with the following command:

```
sudo ambari-server setup
```

 We will get a warning if SELinux is not disabled and the `iptables` service will be disabled if it hasn't been. During the configuration process, we will be asked to configure the username and password for the PostgreSQL database. If you choose not to do so, which is the default option, the default username and password will be `ambari-server` and `bigdata`. The setup process will then prompt for downloading the Oracle JDK, and we should accept the license. The downloaded JDK will be installed to hosts when deploying packages on the cluster.

The output of the setup process is shown in the following screenshot:

```
Run postgresql initdb
Initializing database:                                          [ OK ]
Run postgresql start
Starting postgresql service:                                    [ OK ]
Setup ambari-server
Checking SELinux...
SELinux status is 'disabled'
Checking iptables...
iptables is disabled now
Checking PostgreSQL...
Configuring database...
Enter advanced database configuration [y/n] (n)?
Configuring PostgreSQL...
Restarting PostgreSQL
Checking JDK...
Downloading JDK from http://public-repo-1.hortonworks.com/ARTIFACTS/j
dk-6u31-linux-x64.bin to /var/lib/ambari-server/resources/jdk-6u31-li
nux-x64.bin
JDK distribution size is 85581913 bytes
jdk-6u31-linux-x64.bin... 100% (81.6 MB of 81.6 MB)
Successfully downloaded JDK distribution to /var/lib/ambari-server/re
sources/jdk-6u31-linux-x64.bin
To install the Oracle JDK you must accept the license terms found at
http://www.oracle.com/technetwork/java/javase/downloads/jdk-6u21-lice
nse-159167.txt. Not accepting will cancel the Ambari Server setup.
Do you accept the Oracle Binary Code License Agreement [y/n] (y)?
Installing JDK to /usr/jdk64
Successfully installed JDK to /usr/jdk64/jdk1.6.0_31
Completing setup...
Ambari Server 'setup' finished successfully
```

6. Now, we can start the Ambari server with the following command:

```
sudo service ambari-server start
```

7. Visit the web UI by opening URL: `http://master:8080`.

 Now, we need to log in to the Ambari server with the username and password both as `admin`.

8. After logging in, we will be able to install and manage our Hadoop cluster from the Ambari web UI, which is similar to the following screenshot:

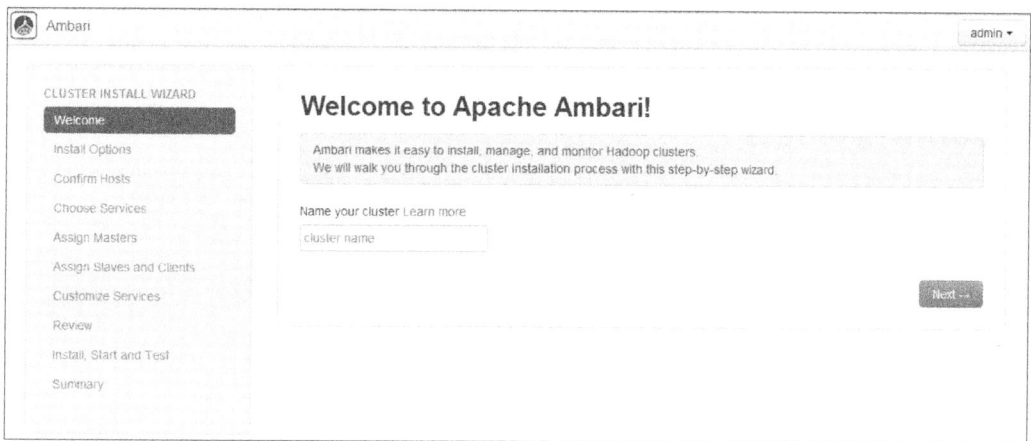

9. Next, we need to configure **Install Options** as shown in the following screenshot:

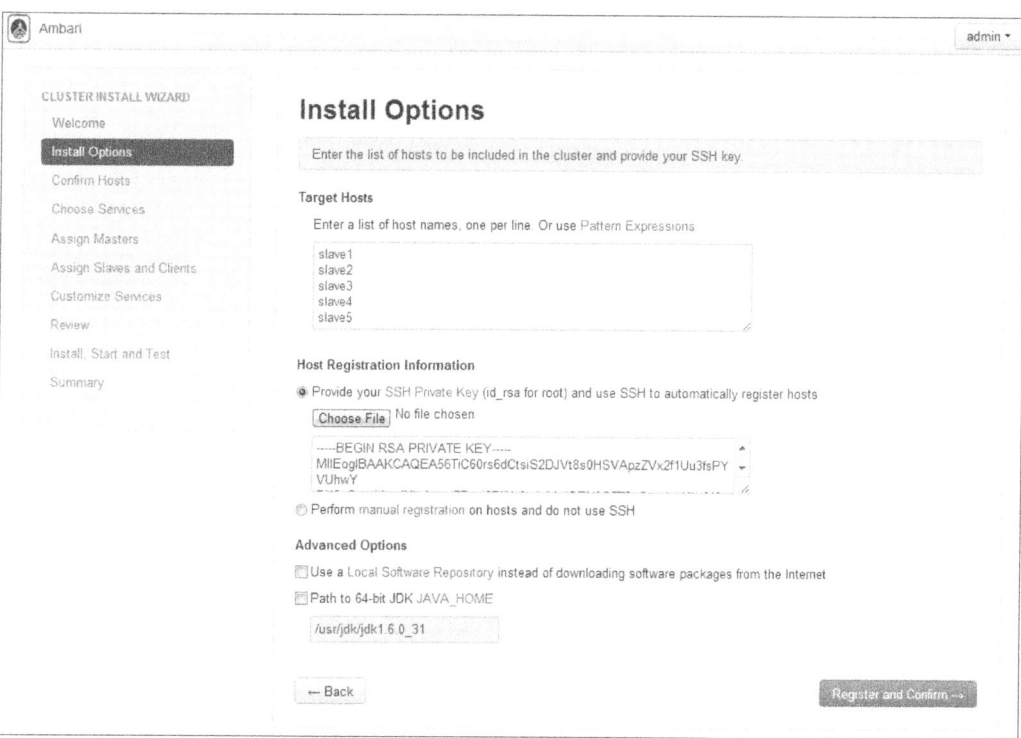

10. After specifying the installation options as shown in the previous screenshot, we can click on the **Register and Confirm** button to start the installation process. This will lead to the host registration progress page as shown in the following screenshot. In this step, we need to confirm the hosts to install Hadoop:

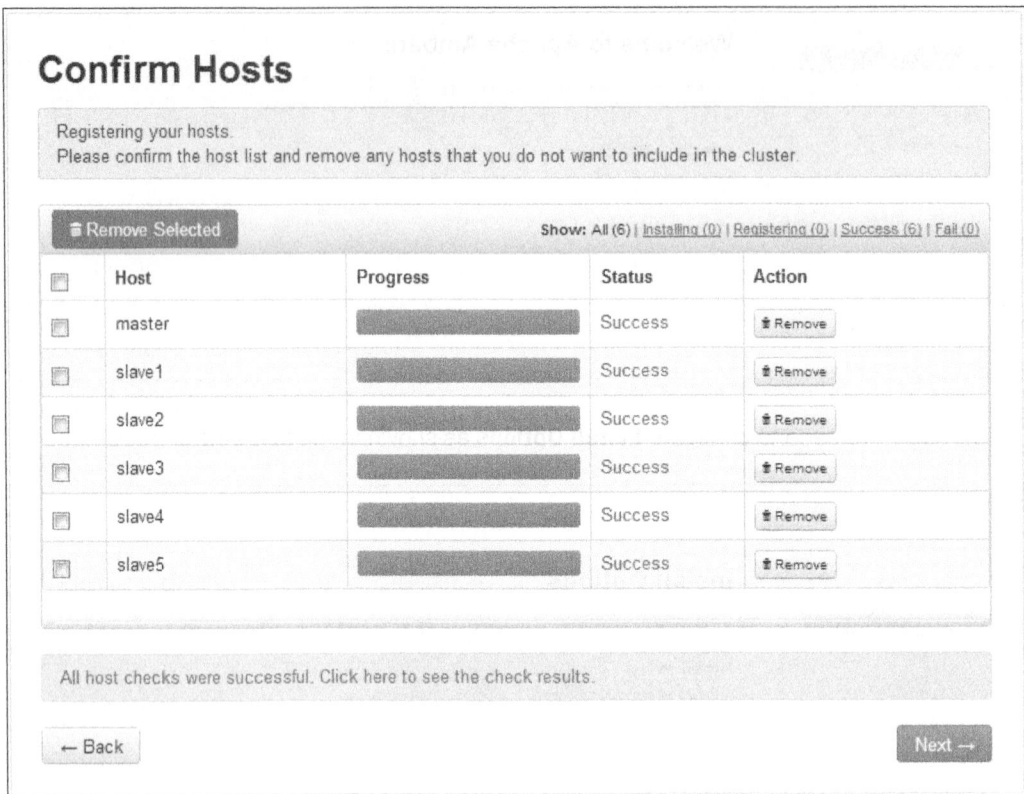

11. By clicking on the **Next** button, we will allow the web page to choose the services to install, as shown in the following screenshot:

Choose Services

Choose which services you want to install on your cluster.

Service all | minimum	Version	Description
☑ HDFS	1.1.2	Apache Hadoop Distributed File System
☑ MapReduce	1.1.2	Apache Hadoop Distributed Processing Framework
☑ Nagios	3.2.3	Nagios Monitoring and Alerting system
☑ Ganglia	3.2.0	Ganglia Metrics Collection system
☑ Hive + HCat + ZooKeeper	0.10.0	Data warehouse system for ad-hoc queries & analysis of large datasets and table & storage management service
☑ HBase + ZooKeeper	0.94.2	Non-relational distributed database and centralized service for configuration management & synchronization
☑ Pig	0.10.1	Scripting platform for analyzing large datasets
☑ Sqoop	1.4.2	Tool for transferring bulk data between Apache Hadoop and structured data stores such as relational databases
☑ Oozie	3.2.0	System for workflow coordination and execution of Apache Hadoop jobs

← Back

Next →

12. By default, all the services are selected to be installed; we can make changes based on the requirements and then click on the **Next** button. We will go to a web page to assign hosts as masters, slaves, and clients, as shown in the following screenshot:

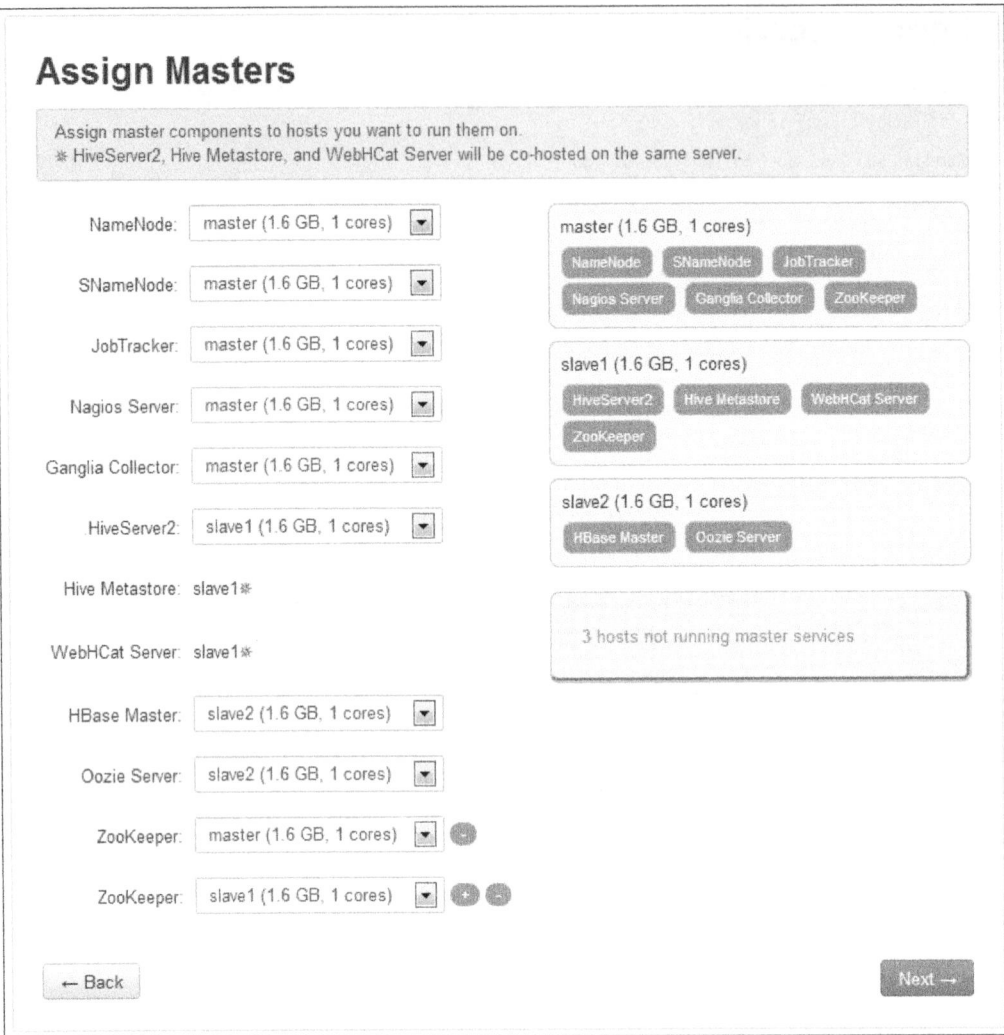

13. Next, we will go to a web page for customizing services, for example, configuring the location for the `NameNode` directory. In this step, some services such as Hive and Nagios may ask you to enter administrative usernames and passwords, which are required for service installation.

Assign Slaves and Clients

Assign slave and client components to hosts you want to run them on.
Hosts that are assigned master components are shown with ✱.
"Client" will install HDFS Client, MapReduce Client, Hive Client, HCat Client, HBase Client, Pig, Sqoop, Oozie Client and ZooKeeper Client.

Host	all | none	all | none	all | none	all | none
master ✱	☐ DataNode	☐ TaskTracker	☐ RegionServer	☑ Client
slave1 ✱	☑ DataNode	☑ TaskTracker	☑ RegionServer	☐ Client
slave2 ✱	☑ DataNode	☑ TaskTracker	☑ RegionServer	☐ Client
slave3	☑ DataNode	☑ TaskTracker	☑ RegionServer	☐ Client
slave4	☑ DataNode	☑ TaskTracker	☑ RegionServer	☐ Client
slave5	☑ DataNode	☑ TaskTracker	☑ RegionServer	☐ Client

← Back

Next →

14. After everything is configured, we will get a summary page about our configurations, as shown in the following screenshot:

Review

Please review the configuration before installation

Print

Admin Name : admin

Cluster Name : hdcluster

Total Hosts : 6 (6 new)

Local Repository : No

Services

  HDFS
    NameNode : master
    SecondaryNameNode : master
    DataNodes : 5 hosts

  MapReduce
    JobTracker : master
    TaskTrackers : 5 hosts

  Nagios
    Server : master
    Administrator : nagiosadmin / (guo.18@wright.edu)

  Ganglia
    Server : master

← Back

Deploy →

15. By clicking on the **Deploy** button, the cluster deployment will start and a progress bar will appear for each service that is being installed, as shown in the following screenshot:

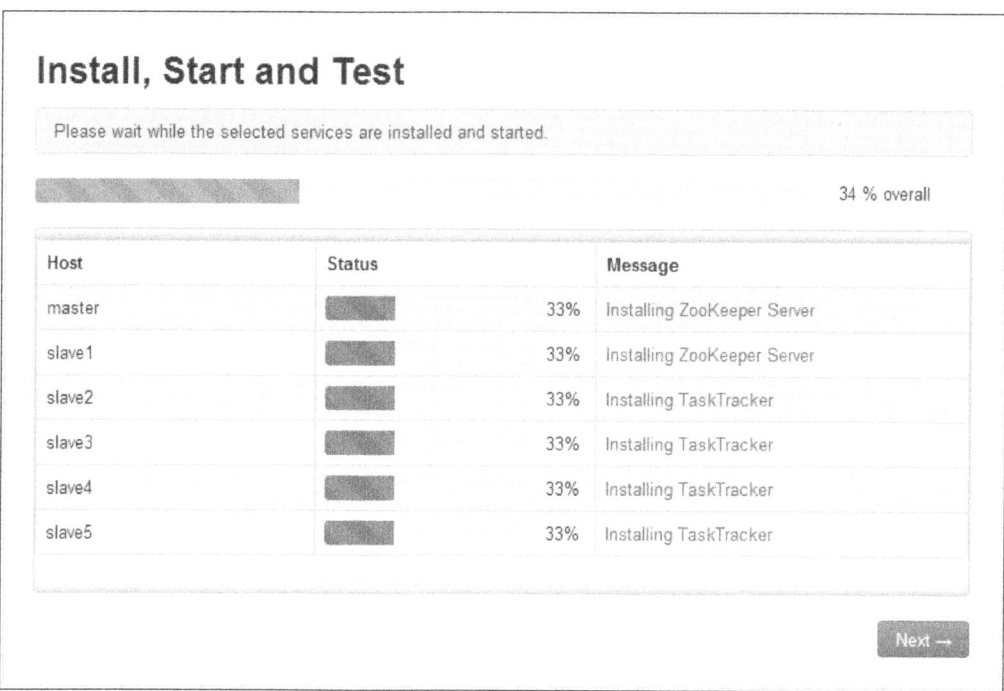

Install, Start and Test

Please wait while the selected services are installed and started.

34 % overall

Host	Status		Message
master		33%	Installing ZooKeeper Server
slave1		33%	Installing ZooKeeper Server
slave2		33%	Installing TaskTracker
slave3		33%	Installing TaskTracker
slave4		33%	Installing TaskTracker
slave5		33%	Installing TaskTracker

Next →

16. After the deployment completes, we will get a **Summary** page as shown in the following screenshot:

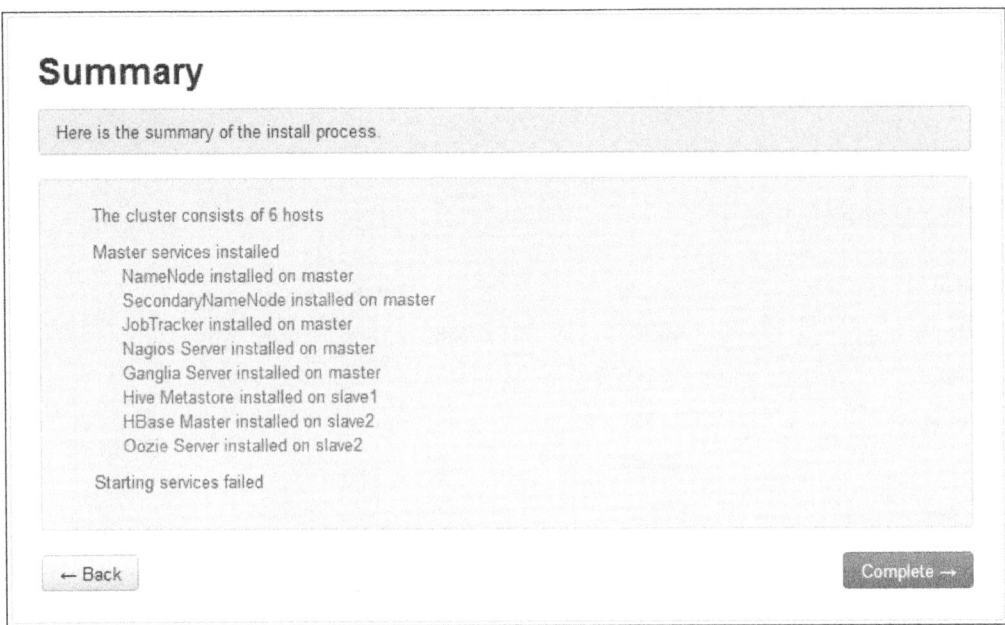

17. By clicking on the **Complete** button, the cluster installation process will finish, and we will be able to see the status of the cluster as shown in the following screenshot:

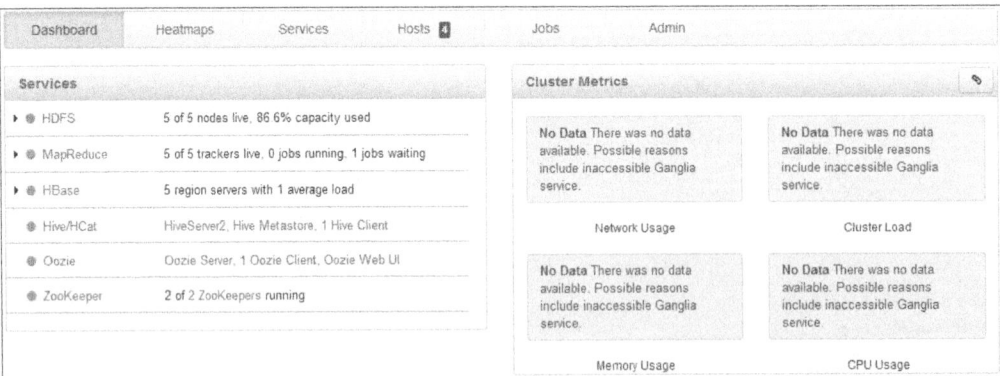

See also

- The *Monitoring a Hadoop cluster with JMX* recipe
- The *Monitoring a Hadoop cluster with Chukwa* recipe
- The *Monitoring a Hadoop cluster with Ganglia* recipe
- The *Monitoring a Hadoop cluster with Nagios* recipe
- Refer to http://incubator.apache.org/ambari/
- Refer to http://incubator.apache.org/ambari/1.2.1/installing-hadoop-using-ambari/content/index.html

Monitoring a Hadoop cluster with Chukwa

Chukwa is a project developed for collecting and analyzing Hadoop logs. It uses HDFS as its storage architecture and contains a number of toolkits for log analysis and cluster monitoring. In this recipe, we will guide you through steps to configure Chukwa to monitor a Hadoop cluster.

Getting ready

The latest release of Chukwa uses HBase for key-value storage. So, before getting started, we assume that Hadoop and HBase have been installed and properly configured.

Next, we can use the following steps to install Chukwa:

1. Download the latest release from the official website http://incubator.apache.org/chukwa, for example, use the following command:

   ```
   sudo wget http://mirror.symnds.com/software/Apache/incubator/
   chukwa/chukwa-0.5.0/chukwa-incubating-src-0.5.0.tar.gz -P /usr/
   local
   ```

2. Decompress the archive with the following command:

   ```
   sudo tar xvf chukwa-incubating-src-0.5.0.tar.gz
   ```

3. Create a symbolic link for the directory with the following command:

   ```
   sudo ln -s chukwa-incubating-src-0.5.0 chukwa
   ```

4. Change the ownership for the directories with the following commands:

```
sudo chown hduser.hduser chukwa-incubating-src-0.5.0 -R
sudo chown hduser.hduser chukwa -R
```

5. Change the environment variables by adding the following content into the `~/.bashrc` file:

```
export CHUKWA_HOME=/usr/local/chukwa
PATH=$CHUKWA_HOME/bin:$PATH
```

6. Build Chukwa from the source with the following commands:

```
source ~/.bashrc
cd $CHUKWA_HOME
mvn clean package
```

7. When the compilation finishes, the directory structure of Chukwa will be similar to the following:

```
chukwa
├── bin
│   ├── chukwa
│   ├── chukwa-config.sh
│   ├── slaves.sh
│   ├── start-agents.sh
│   ├── start-chukwa.sh
│   ├── start-collectors.sh
│   └── VERSION
├── conf
│   ├── auth.conf
│   ├── chukwa-agent-conf.xml
│   ├── chukwa-collector-conf.xml
│   ├── chukwa-demux-conf.xml
│   ├── chukwa-env.sh
│   ├── chukwa-log4j.properties
│   ├── collectors
│   ├── agents
│   ├── hadoop-log4j.properties
│   ├── hadoop-metrics.properties
```

```
|  ├── hbase.schema
|  ├── initial_adaptors
|  └── system-data-loader.properties
└── ...

29 directories, 93 files
```

 If you are downloading the binary version of Chukwa, the directory structure might be different from this.

8. Install `telnet` with the following command:

   `sudo yum install telnet`

9. Log in to the master node from the administrator machine with the following command:

   `ssh hduser@master`

How to do it...

Use the following steps to configure Chukwa for Hadoop monitoring:

1. Change the `log4j.appender.DRFA` variable in the `$HADOOP_HOME/conf/log4j.properties` file to the following:

   `log4j.appender.DRFA=org.apache.log4j.net.SocketAppender`

2. Copy the Hadoop `metrics` file from the `Chukwa` directory to the Hadoop configuration directory with the following command:

   `cp $CHUKWA_HOME/etc/chukwa/hadoop-metrics.properties $HADOOP_HOME/conf`

3. Copy the `client.jar` file from the Chukwa installation directory to the Hadoop shared directory using the following command:

   `cp $CHUKWA_HOME/share/chukwa/chukwa-0.5.0-client.jar $HADOOP_HOME/lib`

4. Copy the `json` library from the Chukwa library to the Hadoop library using the following command:

   `cp $CHUKWA_HOME/share/chukwa/lib/json-simple-1.1.jar $HADOOP_HOME/lib`

5. Sync the files and configurations to the slave nodes with the following commands:

```
for host in cat $HADOOP_HOME/conf/slaves

do

  echo 'Copying file to ' $host

  scp $HADOOP_HOME/lib/chukwa-0.5.0-client.jar $host:$HADOOP_HOME/
lib;

  scp $HADOOP_HOME/lib/json-simple-1.1.jar $host: $HADOOP_HOME/
lib;

  scp $HADOOP_HOME/conf/hadoop-metrics.properties $host:$HADOOP_
HOME/conf

done
```

6. Restart the Hadoop cluster with the following commands:

```
stop-all.sh
start-all.sh
```

7. Start the HBase daemon with the following command:

```
start-hbase.sh
```

8. Import the Chukwa `schema` file to HBase with the following command:

```
hbase shell < $CHUKWA_HOME/etc/chukwa/hbase.schema
```

The command will give output similar to the following:

```
HBase Shell; enter 'help<RETURN>' for list of supported commands.
Type "exit<RETURN>" to leave the HBase Shell
Version 0.94.5, r1443843, Fri Feb  8 05:51:25 UTC 2013


create "Hadoop",
{NAME => "ClientTrace", VERSIONS => 65535},
{NAME => "dfs_namenode", VERSIONS => 65535},
{NAME => "dfs_FSNamesystem", VERSIONS => 65535},
{NAME => "dfs_datanode", VERSIONS => 65535},
{NAME => "mapred_jobtracker", VERSIONS => 65535},
{NAME => "mapred_shuffleOutput", VERSIONS => 65535},
{NAME => "mapred_tasktracker", VERSIONS => 65535},
{NAME => "jvm_metrics", VERSIONS => 65535},
{NAME => "mapred_Queue", VERSIONS => 65535},
{NAME => "metricssystem_MetricsSystem", VERSIONS => 65535},
{NAME => "rpc_rpc", VERSIONS => 65535},
```

```
{NAME => "rpcdetailed_rpcdetailed", VERSIONS => 65535},
{NAME => "ugi_ugi", VERSIONS => 65535}
0 row(s) in 2.7920 seconds


create "HadoopLog",
{NAME => "NameNode", VERSIONS => 65535},
{NAME => "Audit", VERSIONS => 65535}
0 row(s) in 1.0740 seconds


create "Jobs",
{NAME => "summary" }
0 row(s) in 1.0610 seconds


create "SystemMetrics",
{NAME => "cpu", VERSIONS => 65535},
{NAME => "system", VERSION => 65535},
{NAME => "disk", VERSION => 65535},
{NAME => "memory", VERSION => 65535},
{NAME => "network", VERSION => 65535},
{NAME => "tags", VERSION => 65535}
0 row(s) in 1.1030 seconds


create "ClusterSummary",
{NAME=> "cpu", VERSIONS => 65535},
{NAME => "system", VERSION => 65535},
{NAME => "disk", VERSION => 65535},
{NAME => "memory", VERSION => 65535},
{NAME => "network", VERSION => 65535},
{NAME => "hdfs", VERSION => 65535},
{NAME => "mapreduce", VERSION => 65535}
0 row(s) in 1.0830 seconds


create "chukwa",
{NAME=>"chukwaAgent_chunkQueue", VERSIONS => 65535},
{NAME => "chukwaAgent_metrics", VERSION => 65535},
{NAME => "chukwaAgent_httpSender", VERSION => 65535}
0 row(s) in 1.0860 seconds
```

The output shows that six HBase tables have been created.

9. Use a text editor to open the `$CHUKWA_HOME/etc/chukwa/chukwa-collector-conf.xml` file and comment the `chukwaCollector.pipeline` property by adding the following string before the property:

   `<!--`

   Add the following string at the end of the property:

   `-->`

   By doing this, we have configured Chukwa to use HBase for log collection storage.

10. Configure the environment variables in the `$CHUKWA_HOME/etc/chukwa/chukwa-env.sh` file to the following:

    ```
    export JAVA_HOME=/usr/java/latest
    export HADOOP_HOME=/usr/local/hadoop
    export HBASE_HOME=/usr/local/hbase
    export HADOOP_CONF_DIR=$HADOOP_HOME/conf
    export HBASE_CONF_DIR=$HBASE_HOME/conf
    ```

11. Configure Chukwa to collect data from slave nodes by adding the following hostnames to the `$CHUKWA_HOME/etc/chukwa/agents` file:

    ```
    slave1
    slave2
    slave3
    . . .
    ```

12. We can run multiple collectors (for example, we want to run collectors on the `master` and `slave1` nodes) by adding the following content into the `$CHUKWA_HOME/etc/chukwa/collectors` file:

    ```
    http://master:8081
    http://slave1:8081
    ```

 Multiple collectors can increase the throughput of the data collection process.

13. Start the Chukwa agents with the following command:

    `start-agents.sh`

We will get output similar to the following screenshot:

```
slave4: starting agent, logging to /tmp/chukwa/logs/chukwa-hduser-agent-slave4.out
slave5: starting agent, logging to /tmp/chukwa/logs/chukwa-hduser-agent-slave5.out
slave1: starting agent, logging to /tmp/chukwa/logs/chukwa-hduser-agent-slave1.out
slave3: starting agent, logging to /tmp/chukwa/logs/chukwa-hduser-agent-slave3.out
slave2: starting agent, logging to /tmp/chukwa/logs/chukwa-hduser-agent-slave2.out
```

14. Start the Chukwa collector with the following command:

```
start-collectors.sh
```

The output of this command is similar to the following:

```
master: starting collector, logging to /tmp/chukwa/logs/chukwa-hduser-collector-master.out
slave1: starting collector, logging to /tmp/chukwa/logs/chukwa-hduser-collector-slave1.out
```

15. Add the configuration directory of Hadoop and HBase to the Pig CLASSPATH entry with:

```
export PIG_CLASSPATH=$HADOOP_HOME/conf:$HBASE_HOME/conf
```

16. Use pig to analyze the data with the following command:

```
pig -Dpig.additional.jars=$HBASE_HOME/hbase-0.94.5.jar:$PIG_
HOME/pig-0.11.0.jar $CHUKWA_HOME/share/chukwa/script/pig/
ClusterSummary.pig
```

17. Start the web UI for **Hadoop Infrastructure Care Center** (**HICC**) with the following command:

```
chukwa hicc
```

18. Open the URL http://master:4080 and use admin as both the username and password for login.

> We can modify the $CHUKWA_HOME/etc/chukwa/auth.conf file to change the login credential.
>
> By default the file will have the following content:
>
>   admin: admin, user
>
> The meaning of this is username: password[, role].

How it works...

Chukwa was designed to collect data that are dynamically generated across distributed machines in a cluster. It has four major components: *adaptor*, *collector*, *MapReduce* or *other data processing jobs*, and the web UI called *HICC*.

Chukwa adaptors are deployed on each data source machine. Adaptors run on these machines in the umbrella of agents, which send the collected data to collectors on local or remote machines.

Chukwa collectors pipeline data from agents to data storage systems such as HDFS. For performance reasons, data are typically written as sequence files, which will be processed by MapReduce jobs.

The MapReduce jobs will generate key-value pairs for visualization by the last component—HICC. Chukwa uses the embedded web server **Jetty** for the deployment of the web archive file $CHUKWA_HOME/ share/chukwa/webapps/hicc.war.

Sometimes, you might have problem running the HICC and visiting the web UI; the most probable reason is that you have incompatible .jar files for Hadoop, HBase, and Chukwa. In such cases, my suggestion is to clone the source code from GitHub (https://github.com/apache/chukwa) and compile the hicc.war web archive file from the source. For more information, please check the README.txt file in the source code root directory.

In summary, the data flow of Chukwa can be described with the following diagram:

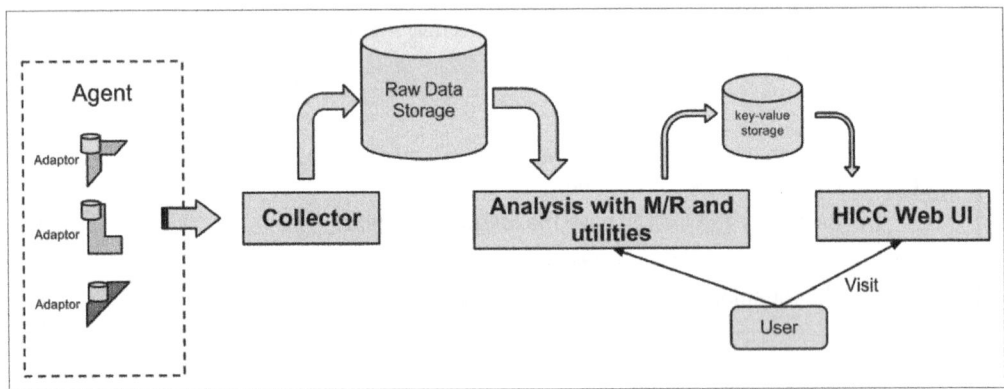

For more information about the design of Chukwa, please check the URL:
http://incubator.apache.org/chukwa/docs/r0.5.0/design.html.

There's more...

Due to the instability of this software package, you might need to do some debugging when deploying it onto the cluster. But to get started with Chukwa, it is always advisable to run it in local or pseudo-distributed mode, which will start one agent and one collector on the local machine. To do this, the following commands can be used:

```
chukwa agent local
```

The previous command will give the following output:

```
OK chukwaAgent.checkpoint.dir [File] = /tmp/chukwa/log/
OK chukwaAgent.checkpoint.interval [Time] = 5000
OK chukwaAgent.control.port [Portno] = 9093
OK chukwaAgent.sender.fastRetries [Integral] = 4
```

We can also use the following command:

```
chukwa collector local
```

This command will give the following output:

```
OK chukwaCollector.http.port [Integral] = 8081
OK chukwaCollector.pipeline [ClassName list] = org.apache.hadoop.
chukwa.datacollection.writer.SocketTeeWriter,org.apache.hadoop.chukwa.
datacollection.writer.hbase.HBaseWriter
OK chukwaCollector.rotateInterval [Time] = 300000
OK chukwaCollector.writerClass [ClassName] = org.apache.hadoop.chukwa.
datacollection.writer.PipelineStageWriter
OK writer.hdfs.filesystem [URI] = hdfs://master:54310
started Chukwa http collector on port 8081
```

We can check the status of the daemons by tailing on the logfiles with the following commands:

```
tail -f /tmp/chukwa/logs/agent.log
tail -f /tmp/chukwa/logs/collector.log
```

Currently, Chukwa is an incubator project under the **Apache Free Software** (**AFS**) foundation. We can check the development plan and progress on its wiki page at wiki.apache.org/hadoop/chukwa or on the official website at: http://incubator.apache.org/chukwa/. Similar to many open source projects, new bugs are reported and new features added; a nice way to keep up to date with the most recent changes is to work with the source code repository, which can be found at https://github.com/apache/chukwa.

See also

- ▶ The *Monitoring a Hadoop cluster with JMX* recipe
- ▶ The *Monitoring a Hadoop cluster with Ganglia* recipe
- ▶ The *Monitoring a Hadoop cluster with Nagios* recipe
- ▶ The *Monitoring a Hadoop cluster with Ambari* recipe
- ▶ Refer to `http://incubator.apache.org/chukwa/docs/r0.5.0/admin.html`

7
Tuning a Hadoop Cluster for Best Performance

In this chapter, we will cover:

- ▸ Benchmarking and profiling a Hadoop cluster
- ▸ Analyzing job history with Rumen
- ▸ Benchmarking a Hadoop cluster with GridMix
- ▸ Using Hadoop Vaidya to identify performance problems
- ▸ Balancing data blocks for a Hadoop cluster
- ▸ Choosing a proper block size
- ▸ Using compression for input and output
- ▸ Configuring speculative execution
- ▸ Setting proper number of map and reduce slots for TaskTracker
- ▸ Tuning the JobTracker configuration
- ▸ Tuning the TaskTracker configuration
- ▸ Tuning shuffle, merge, and sort parameters
- ▸ Configuring memory for a Hadoop cluster
- ▸ Setting proper number of parallel copies
- ▸ Tuning JVM parameters
- ▸ Configuring JVM Reuse
- ▸ Configuring the reducer initialization time

Introduction

Hadoop performance tuning is a challenging task, mainly due to the distributed feature of the system. The sheer number of configuration properties can tell, from another perspective, how complicated it is to configure a Hadoop cluster. Many of the configuration parameters have an effect on the performance of the cluster. Sometimes, different settings of the properties can lead to dramatic performance differences. And some properties are more relevant and sensitive than others with regard to the performance of a Hadoop cluster.

A Hadoop cluster is composed of many components. A systematic way of performance tuning is to tune the components based on their contribution on the cluster performance. Most of the Big Data applications are I/O bound, so is Hadoop. So, configurations that are closely related to I/O requests should be the first priority for performance tuning. For example, suboptimal configuration on data replication properties can cause a large number of data block copies over the network, which will pose a negative effect on the performance of a cluster. Similarly, improper JVM configurations can cause large data swaps for intermediate data. And, unbalanced data block distribution on the DataNodes can cause the suboptimal execution of map and reduce tasks.

The first step of Hadoop performance tuning is to understand how Hadoop MapReduce works with different configuration property settings. Based on this, optimized configurations or best practices can be derived. But this is not a trivial task. It requires techniques, such as data collection by running controlled experiments under different parameter settings, data analysis using optimization techniques, and analytical and reasoning skills. As a matter of fact, due to the challenges and novelty, of Hadoop cluster performance tuning, the research community has recent projects and publications about learning and tuning the performance of a Hadoop cluster (for example, the starfish project at `http://www.cs.duke.edu/starfish/`).

While the method of finding the optimal parameter configurations is straightforward for tuning the performance of a Hadoop cluster, the implementation is demanding, both theoretically and in practice. Various tools and strategies for optimizing Hadoop performance have been developed and adopted by the Hadoop community. For example, **balancer** is a tool used for balancing skewed data blocks and **speculative execution** is a strategy for launching a speculative task for a slowly progressing task.

In this chapter, we will introduce the following topics in general:

- Identifying the performance problems by benchmarking a Hadoop cluster
- Tuning Hadoop configuration parameters for best performance
- Using strategies and tools for Hadoop best performance tuning

 Optimal settings for different Hadoop clusters can be different. In other words, the optimal configuration for one cluster might not be optimal for another cluster under different hardware configurations. So, to find the optimal settings for a specific cluster, real field work is needed

Benchmarking and profiling a Hadoop cluster

Benchmarking of a Hadoop cluster is the first step to tune the performance of a Hadoop cluster. We can also use Hadoop benchmarks to identify configuration problems and use it as reference for performance tuning. For example, by comparing the local benchmark with clusters with similar configurations, we can have a general understanding of the cluster performance.

Typically, we benchmark a Hadoop cluster after the cluster is newly configured and before putting it to service to accept jobs. This is because, when clients can submit jobs, the benchmarks can be perplexed by the client's jobs to show the real performance of a Hadoop cluster, and also the benchmark jobs can cause inconveniences for the clients.

In this section, we will introduce how to benchmark and stress test a Hadoop cluster using the `tests` and `examples` package included in the Hadoop distribution. More specifically, we will test the read/write performance of the HDFS cluster. In addition, we will test the failure resilience of the MapReduce framework and the performance of the MapReduce cluster under stress.

Getting ready

To get started with Hadoop cluster benchmarks, we assume that a working Hadoop cluster has been configured and all the daemons are running without any issues. We also assume that the required environment variables have been properly set in proper locations. For example, we should have `HADOOP_HOME` point to the home directory of Hadoop installation and have `JAVA_HOME` set in the `$HADOOP_HOME/conf/hadoop-env.sh` file.

Log in from the Hadoop cluster administrative machine to the cluster master node with the following command:

```
ssh hduser@master
```

How to do it...

Use the following recipe to perform HDFS benchmarks:

1. Test the filesystem with the following command:

    ```
    hadoop jar $HADOOP_HOME/hadoop-test-1.1.2.jar testfilesystem
    -files 10 -megaBytes 10
    ```

    This command will generate 10 files with 10 MB each for testing, and the message for this benchmark will be similar to the following:

    ```
    13/04/18 21:25:36 INFO fs.FileSystem: seed = -7801967327500182430
    13/04/18 21:25:36 INFO fs.FileSystem: files = 10
    ```

```
13/04/18 21:25:36 INFO fs.FileSystem: megaBytes = 10
13/04/18 21:25:37 INFO fs.FileSystem: creating control file:
10485760 bytes, 10 files
13/04/18 21:25:38 INFO fs.FileSystem: created control file for:
11691305 bytes
13/04/18 21:25:38 WARN mapred.JobClient: Use GenericOptionsParser
for parsing the arguments. Applications should implement Tool for
the same.
. . .
```

> If there are no errors, the test is considered successful.

2. Benchmark the distributed write consistency on the distributed filesystem with the following command:

    ```
    hadoop jar $HADOOP_HOME/adoop-test-*.jar DistributedFSCheck -write
    -nrFiles 10 -fileSize 50
    ```

    This command will write 10 (controlled by the -nrFiles option) files of 50 MB (controlled by the -fileSize option) with random content to the HDFS. It will generate a result file named TestDFSIO_results.log with the following content:

    ```
    ----- TestDFSIO ----- : write
               Date & time: Mon Apr 01 18:25:12 EDT 2013
           Number of files: 10
    Total Mbytes processed: 500
         Throughput mb/sec: 8.585459665510491
    Average IO rate mb/sec: 9.46606731414795
     IO rate std deviation: 2.906442884562995

    Test exec time sec: 42.338
    ```

3. Similarly, we can benchmark the distributed read consistency on the distributed filesystem with the following command:

    ```
    hadoop jar $HADOOP_HOME/hadoop-test-*.jar DistributedFSCheck -read
    -nrFiles 10 -fileSize 50
    ```

    The command will read 10 files with the size of 50 MB from the cluster and will generate a result file with the following content:

    ```
    ----- TestDFSIO ----- : read
               Date & time: Mon Apr 01 18:26:13 EDT 2013
           Number of files: 10
    Total MBytes processed: 500
    ```

```
Throughput mb/sec: 15.531809145129225
Average IO rate mb/sec: 17.578426361083984
IO rate std deviation: 6.313778174121274
Test exec time sec: 42.205
```

 From the output of the two (read/write consistency check) commands, we know that writing is more expensive than reading for the HDFS cluster. This is because the write operations, in turn, involve more operations, such as computing and recording the checksums of the data blocks and many more.

The following recipe can be used to benchmark a MapReduce cluster:

1. Benchmark MapReduce jobs with the following command:

   ```
   hadoop jar $HADOOP_HOME/hadoop-test-*.jar mapredtest 5 1000
   ```

   The `mapredtest` benchmark does a load test on the MapReduce computing framework. This benchmark is done with random integers, which are generated, written to files, read read back from files, and tested with the original files.

2. Test the reliability of the MapReduce distributed computing framework with the following command:

   ```
   hadoop jar $HADOOP_HOME/hadoop-test-*.jar MRReliabilityTest
   -libjars $HADOOP_HOME/hadoop-examples-*.jar
   ```

   The command will intentionally cause task and TaskTracker failures on a running job. So, during the test, we will be able to see messages such as: **Killing a few tasks**. A sample message will be similar to the following:

   ```
   13/04/17 17:49:22 INFO mapred.ReliabilityTest: Wed Apr 17 17:49:22
   EDT 2013 Killing a few tasks
   13/04/17 17:49:22 INFO mapred.ReliabilityTest: Wed Apr 17 17:49:22
   EDT 2013 Killed task : attempt_201304051222_0116_m_000000_0
   13/04/17 17:49:22 INFO mapred.ReliabilityTest: Wed Apr 17 17:49:22
   EDT 2013 Killed task : attempt_201304051222_0116_m_000000_2
   13/04/17 17:49:22 INFO mapred.ReliabilityTest: Wed Apr 17 17:49:22
   EDT 2013 Killed task : attempt_201304051222_0116_m_000001_0
   ...
   java.lang.Throwable: Child Error
           at org.apache.hadoop.mapred.TaskRunner.run(TaskRunner.
   java:271)
   Caused by: java.io.IOException: Task process exit with nonzero
   status of 126.
           at org.apache.hadoop.mapred.TaskRunner.run(TaskRunner.
   java:258)
   ```

```
13/04/17 17:49:38 WARN mapred.JobClient: Error reading task
outputhttp://slave1:50060/tasklog?plaintext=true&attemptid=attempt
_201304051222_0119_m_000037_0&filter=stdout
13/04/17 17:49:38 WARN mapred.JobClient: Error reading task
outputhttp://slave1:50060/tasklog?plaintext=true&attemptid=attempt
_201304051222_0119_m_000037_0&filter=stderr
```

 The failed tasks will be re-executed on a different TaskTracker. So, killing one or a few tasks should not fail a job if the cluster is resilient to failures. If a job fails after a few killed tasks, it is possibly because MapReduce is not reliable enough or not resilient to failures, and hence reliability tuning (such as by adding more computing TaskTrackers) is needed.

3. Benchmark MapReduce to deal with a large number of small jobs with the following command:

   ```
   hadoop jar $HADOOP_HOME/hadoop-test-*.jar mrbench -numRuns 20
   ```

   `mrbench` executes a small job a number of times (20 in this command) and checks if these small jobs are *responsive* and can run *efficiently* on the cluster. This command will generate an output similar to the following:

   ```
   DataLines    Maps    Reduces AvgTime (milliseconds)
   1            2       1          45231
   ```

 This output tells us that the average runtime is about 45 seconds.

4. Benchmark the MapReduce load generator with the following command:

   ```
   hadoop jar $HADOOP_HOME/hadoop-test-1.1.2.jar loadgen -m 100 -r 10
   -keepmap 50 -keepred 50 -indir input -outdir output
   ```

   The result of this command will be similar to the following:

   ```
   Original sum: 1000
   ```

   ```
   Recomputed sum: 1000
   ```

   ```
   Success=true
   ```

5. Do a stress test with the NameNode:

   ```
   hadoop jar $HADOOP_HOME/hadoop-test-*.jar nnbench -create_write
   ```

   We will get output similar to the following:

   ```
   -------------- NNBench -------------- :
                             Version: NameNode Benchmark 0.4
   ```

```
                 Date & time: 2013-04-01 18:24:10,491

             Test Operation: create_write
                 Start time: 2013-04-01 18:22:53,382
                Maps to run: 2
             Reduces to run: 1
          Block Size (bytes): 1
             Bytes to write: 0
        Bytes per checksum: 1
            Number of files: 1
         Replication factor: 1
    Successful file operations: 2

   # maps that missed the barrier: 0
                 # exceptions: 0

        TPS: Create/Write/Close: 0
   Avg exec time (ms): Create/Write/Close: 30037.5
         Avg Lat (ms): Create/Write: 30030.5
              Avg Lat (ms): Close: 6.5

         RAW DATA: AL Total #1: 60061
         RAW DATA: AL Total #2: 13
      RAW DATA: TPS Total (ms): 60075
   RAW DATA: Longest Map Time (ms): 60045.0
         RAW DATA: Late maps: 0
      RAW DATA: # of exceptions: 0
```

6. Test the Hadoop performance with large non-splittable files:

    hadoop jar $HADOOP_HOME/hadoop-test-*.jar testbigmapoutput -input input -output output -create 2048

    This benchmark will generate an output similar to the following:

```
13/04/18 22:16:12 INFO mapred.BigMapOutput: Writing 2147483648
bytes to in/part-0 with minKeySize: 10 keySizeRange: 990
minValueSize: 0 valueSizeRange: 20000
13/04/18 22:17:32 INFO mapred.BigMapOutput: Created in/part-0 of
size: 2048MB in 79secs
Job started: Thu Apr 18 22:17:32 EDT 2013
13/04/18 22:17:33 INFO mapred.FileInputFormat: Total input paths
to process : 1
13/04/18 22:17:33 INFO net.NetworkTopology: Adding a new node: /
default-rack/slave1:50010
13/04/18 22:17:33 INFO net.NetworkTopology: Adding a new node: /
default-rack/slave2:50010
```

```
13/04/18 22:17:33 INFO net.NetworkTopology: Adding a new node: /
default-rack/slave3:50010
...
```

7. Test thread map spills with the following command:

   ```
   hadoop jar $HADOOP_HOME/hadoop-test-*.jar threadedmapbench
   ```

   `threadedmapbench` is a MapReduce benchmark that compares the performance of maps with multiple spills to maps with one spill. The output message will be similar to the following:

   ```
   13/04/18 23:16:01 INFO mapred.ThreadedMapBenchmark: Starting the
   benchmark for threaded spills
   ThreadedMapBenchmark.0.0.1
   13/04/18 23:16:02 INFO mapred.ThreadedMapBenchmark: Generating
   random input for the benchmark
   13/04/18 23:16:02 INFO mapred.ThreadedMapBenchmark: Total data :
   128 mb
   13/04/18 23:16:02 INFO mapred.ThreadedMapBenchmark: Data per map:
   128 mb
   13/04/18 23:16:02 INFO mapred.ThreadedMapBenchmark: Number of
   spills : 2
   13/04/18 23:16:02 INFO mapred.ThreadedMapBenchmark: Number of maps
   per host : 1
   13/04/18 23:16:02 INFO mapred.ThreadedMapBenchmark: Number of
   hosts : 1
   ```

Sort is a typical operation of MapReduce jobs. By sorting random data, we can peek the health of our Hadoop cluster. The following steps can be used to benchmark Hadoop sort:

1. Generate some random text data with the following command:

   ```
   hadoop jar $HADOOP_HOME/hadoop-examples-*.jar randomwriter random.
   writer.out
   ```

2. Sort the generated random data with the following command:

   ```
   hadoop jar $HADOOP_HOME/hadoop-examples-*.jar sort random.writer.
   out random.writer.out.sorted
   ```

3. Validate the MapReduce sort algorithm with the following command:

   ```
   hadoop jar $HADOOP_HOME/hadoop-test-*.jar testmapredsort -m 50
   -r 5 -sortInput random.writer.out -sortOutput random.writer.out.
   sorted
   ```

   This command will validate the accuracy of the sort algorithm. If there is no problem on the sort algorithm, we will get the following message:

   SUCCESS! Validated the MapReduce framework's 'sort' successfully.

How it works...

We can get the usage of the Hadoop benchmark of the test package with the following command:

```
hadoop jar $HADOOP_HOME/hadoop-test-*.jar
```

This command will give us the following output:

```
An example program must be given as the first argument.
Valid program names are:
  DFSCIOTest: Distributed i/o benchmark of libhdfs.
  DistributedFSCheck: Distributed checkup of the file system
consistency.
  MRReliabilityTest: A program that tests the reliability of the MR
framework by injecting faults/failures
  TestDFSIO: Distributed i/o benchmark.
  dfsthroughput: measure hdfs throughput
  filebench: Benchmark SequenceFile(Input|Output)Format (block,record
compressed and uncompressed), Text(Input|Output)Format (compressed and
uncompressed)
  loadgen: Generic map/reduce load generator
  mapredtest: A map/reduce test check.
  mrbench: A map/reduce benchmark that can create many small jobs
  nnbench: A benchmark that stresses the namenode.
  testarrayfile: A test for flat files of binary key/value pairs.
  testbigmapoutput: A map/reduce program that works on a very big non-
splittable file and does identity map/reduce
  testfilesystem: A test for FileSystem read/write.
  testipc: A test for ipc.
  testmapredsort: A map/reduce program that validates the map-reduce
framework's sort.
  testrpc: A test for rpc.
  testsequencefile: A test for flat files of binary key value pairs.
  testsequencefileinputformat: A test for sequence file input format.
  testsetfile: A test for flat files of binary key/value pairs.
  testtextinputformat: A test for text input format.
  threadedmapbench: A map/reduce benchmark that compares the
performance of maps with multiple spills over maps with 1 spill
```

We can get the usage for the `testfilesystem` benchmark with the following command:

```
hadoop jar $HADOOP_HOME/hadoop-test-1.1.2.jar testfilesystem
```

The command will give the following output:

```
Usage: TestFileSystem -files N -megaBytes M [-noread] [-nowrite]
[-noseek] [-fastcheck]
```

The following table shows the meaning of each option of this benchmark command:

Option	Description
-files	Number of files to generate for the benchmark.
-megaBytes	Size in megabytes of the generated files.
-noread	Disable the data reading test.
-nowrite	Disable the data writing test.
-noseek	Disable the seek test.
-fastcheck	Whether to use fast check or not. If the value is true, the test buffer will be filled with the same value, otherwise random numbers are generated for each location in the test buffer.

We can get the help for the mrbench benchmark with the following command:

```
hadoop jar $HADOOP_HOME/hadoop-test-*.jar mrbench --help
```

The output will be as follows:

```
MRBenchmark.0.0.2
Usage: mrbench [-baseDir <base DFS path for output/input, default is /
benchmarks/MRBench>]
          [-jar <local path to job jar file containing Mapper and
Reducer implementations, default is current jar file>]
          [-numRuns <number of times to run the job, default is 1>]
          [-maps <number of maps for each run, default is 2>]
          [-reduces <number of reduces for each run, default is 1>]
          [-inputLines <number of input lines to generate, default is
1>]
          [-inputType <type of input to generate, one of ascending
(default), descending, random>]
          [-verbose]
```

We can get the usage of the loadgen benchmark with the following command:

```
hadoop jar $HADOOP_HOME/hadoop-test-*.jar loadgen
```

The output of this command will be the following:

```
Usage: [-m <maps>] [-r <reduces>]
          [-keepmap <percent>] [-keepred <percent>]
          [-indir <path>] [-outdir <path]
```

```
[-inFormat[Indirect] <InputFormat>] [-outFormat <OutputFormat>]
[-outKey <WritableComparable>] [-outValue <Writable>]
```

We can use nnbench with the command:

hadoop jar softwares/hadoop/hadoop-test-*.jar nnbench

The usage will be displayed as the following:

```
NameNode Benchmark 0.4
Usage: nnbench <options>
Options:
        -operation <Available operations are create_write open_read
        rename delete. This option is mandatory>
        * NOTE: The open_read, rename and delete operations assume
        that
        the files they operate on, are already available. The
        create_write operation must be run before running the other
        operations.
        -maps <number of maps. default is 1. This is not mandatory>
        -reduces <number of reduces. default is 1. This is not
        mandatory>
        -startTime <time to start, given in seconds from the epoch.
        Make sure this is far enough into the future, so all maps
        (operations) will start at the same time>. default is launch
        time + 2 mins. This is not mandatory
        -blockSize <Block size in bytes. default is 1. This is not
        mandatory>
        -bytesToWrite <Bytes to write. default is 0. This is not
        mandatory>
        -bytesPerChecksum <Bytes per checksum for the files. default
        is 1.
        This is not mandatory>
        -numberOfFiles <number of files to create. default is 1. This
        is
        not mandatory>
        -replicationFactorPerFile <Replication factor for the files.
        default is 1. This is not mandatory>
        -baseDir <base DFS path. default is /benchmarks/NNBench.
        This is
        not mandatory>
        -readFileAfterOpen <true or false. if true, it reads the file
        and
        reports the average time to read. This is valid with the
        open_read operation. default is false. This is not mandatory>
        -help: Display the help statement
```

The output tells us that only the -operation option is mandatory, all the others are optional.

We can use the `testbigmapoutput` benchmark with the following command:

```
hadoop jar $HADOOP_HOME/hadoop-test-*.jar testbigmapoutput
```

The output will be as follows:

```
BigMapOutput -input <input-dir> -output <output-dir> [-create
<filesize in MB>]
```

The `-input` and `-output` options are mandatory for this benchmark and the `-create` option, which specifies the file size that is to read created, is optional.

We can get the usage of the `mapredtest` benchmark with the following command:

```
hadoop jar $HADOOP_HOME/hadoop-test-*.jar mapredtest
```

We will get the following output:

```
Usage: TestMapRed <range> <counts>
```

 A good test will have a `<counts>` value that is substantially larger than that of `<range>`.

The `<range>` option specifies the range of the integer to be generated, random integers will be generated between 0 and range -1. The `<counts>` option specifies how many random integers is to be generated for the benchmark; it should have a substantially larger value than the `<range>` option.

We can use the `testmapredsort` benchmark with the following command:

```
hadoop jar $HADOOP_HOME/hadoop-test-*.jar testmapredsort
```

The output will be similar to the following:

```
sortvalidate [-m <maps>] [-r <reduces>] [-deep] -sortInput <sort-
input-dir> -sortOutput <sort-output-dir>
```

The following table shows the meaning of the options:

Option	Description
`-m`	Number of mappers.
`-r`	Number of reducers.
`-deep`	Performs deep validation.

Option	Description
-sortInput	Directory for the input data used for sort. The specified directory must exist, otherwise the benchmark will fail.
-sortOutput	Output directory after the data specified by the -sortInput directory is sorted. The specified directory must exist, otherwise the benchmark will fail.

There's more...

Besides the Hadoop `tests` package, Hadoop is shipped with an `example` package, which can also be used to benchmark a Hadoop cluster. We can get all the examples benchmarks with the following command:

```
hadoop jar $HADOOP_HOME/hadoop-example-*.jar
```

This command will give us the following output:

```
Valid program names are:
  aggregatewordcount: An Aggregate based map/reduce program that
counts the words in the input files.
  aggregatewordhist: An Aggregate based map/reduce program that
computes the histogram of the words in the input files.
  dbcount: An example job that count the pageview counts from a
database.
  grep: A map/reduce program that counts the matches of a regex in the
input.
  join: A job that affects a join over sorted, equally partitioned
datasets
  multifilewc: A job that counts words from several files.
  pentomino: A map/reduce tile laying program to find solutions to
pentomino problems.
  pi: A map/reduce program that estimates Pi using monte-carlo method.
  randomtextwriter: A map/reduce program that writes 10GB of random
textual data per node.
  randomwriter: A map/reduce program that writes 10GB of random data
per node.
  secondarysort: An example defining a secondary sort to the reduce.
  sleep: A job that sleeps at each map and reduce task.
  sort: A map/reduce program that sorts the data written by the random
writer.
  sudoku: A sudoku solver.
  teragen: Generate data for the terasort
  terasort: Run the terasort
  teravalidate: Checking results of terasort
  wordcount: A map/reduce program that counts the words in the input
files.
```

Some commands are very handy for testing the configuration of a Hadoop cluster. For example, we can use the following command to test the cluster by computing π (pi):

```
hadoop jar $HADOOP_HOME/hadoop-example-*.jar pi 10 1000000
```

This command will start a MapReduce job to compute π with 10 mappers with each mapper generating 1,000,000 samples.

The usage for `randomwriter` is as follows:

```
hadoop jar $HADOOP_HOME/hadoop-example-*.jar randomwriter <out-dir>
```

`<out-dir>` specifies the output directory of `randomwriter`.

The usage for `sort` is as follows:

```
sort [-m <maps>] [-r <reduces>] [-inFormat <input format class>]
[-outFormat <output format class>] [-outKey <output key class>]
[-outValue <output value class>] [-totalOrder <pcnt> <num samples>
<max splits>] <input> <output>
```

The meaning of each option is shown in the following table:

Option	Description
-m	Number of map tasks.
-r	Number of reduce tasks.
-inFormat	The input format class.
-outFormat	The output format class.
-outKey	The output key class.
-outValue	The output value class.
-totalOrder	Specifies the use of `TotalOrderPartitioner` to partition the input data. Three parameters are needed: `<pcnt>` specifies the number of partitions, `<num samples>` specifies the number of samples, and `<max splits>` specifies the maximum number of splits for the data.
input	The sort input directory.
output	The sort output directory.

The usage for `wordcount` is as follows:

```
hadoop jar $HADOOP_HOME/hadoop-example-*.jar wordcount <in> <out>
```

`in` specifies the directory for input and `out` specifies the directory for output.

▸   The _Benchmarking a Hadoop cluster with GridMix_ recipe

Analyzing job history with Rumen

Rumen is a tool for extracting well-formatted information from job logfiles. It parses logs and generates statistics for the Hadoop jobs. The job traces can be used for performance tuning and simulation.

Current Rumen implementation includes two components: **TraceBuilder** and **folder**. The TraceBuilder takes job history as input and generates easily parsed `json` files. The folder is a utility to manipulate on input traces, and, most of the time, it is used to scale the summarized job traces from the TraceBuilder. For example, we can use the folder tool to scale up (make time longer) or down (make time shorter) the job runtime. In this recipe, we will outline steps to analyze the job history with Rumen.

Getting ready

Before getting started, we assume that the Hadoop cluster has been properly configured and all the daemons are running without any issues.

Log in from the Hadoop cluster administrator machine to the cluster master node using the following command:

```
ssh hduser@master
```

How to do it...

Use the following steps to analyze job history with Rumen:

1. Use the TraceBuilder to extract the **Gold Trace** from the Hadoop job history files. The syntax of the command is as follows:

    ```
    hadoop org.apache.hadoop.tools.rumen.TraceBuilder [options]
    <jobtrace-output> <topology-output> <inputs>
    ```

    For example, we can use the following command to extract a job trace and topology from the job history directory:

    ```
    hadoop org.apache.hadoop.tools.rumen.TraceBuilder -recursive
    file:///tmp/jobtraces.json file:///tmp/topology.out file:///usr/
    local/hadoop/logs/history/done
    ```

This command will *recursively* extract job history traces as well as the topology of the cluster from the Hadoop job history directory `$HADOOP_HOME/logs/history/done`. The `-recursive` option tells the TraceBuilder to scan the job history directory recursively.

The `jobtraces.json` output file will contain all the metrics of MapReduce jobs, similar to the following:

```
{
  "priority" : "NORMAL",
  "jobID" : "job_201304012206_0001",
  "user" : "hduser",
  "jobName" : "PiEstimator",
  "mapTasks" : [ {
    "startTime" : 1364868424530,
    "attempts" : [ {
      "location" : {
        "layers" : [ "default-rack", "master" ]
      },
      "hostName" : "/default-rack/master",
      "result" : "SUCCESS",
      "startTime" : 1364868424536,
      "finishTime" : 1364868426761,
      "attemptID" : "attempt_201304012206_0001_m_000000_0",
      "shuffleFinished" : -1,
      "sortFinished" : -1,
      "hdfsBytesRead" : 242,
      "hdfsBytesWritten" : -1,
      "fileBytesRead" : -1,
      "fileBytesWritten" : 51959,
      "mapInputRecords" : 1,
      "mapOutputBytes" : 18,
      "mapOutputRecords" : 2,
      "combineInputRecords" : 0,
      "reduceInputGroups" : -1,
      "reduceInputRecords" : -1,
      "reduceShuffleBytes" : -1,
      "reduceOutputRecords" : -1,
      "spilledRecords" : 2,
      "mapInputBytes" : 24,
      "resourceUsageMetrics" : {
        "cumulativeCpuUsage" : 600,
        "virtualMemoryUsage" : 764727296,
```

```
            "physicalMemoryUsage" : 185315328,
            "heapUsage" : 173867008
          }
        } ],
        "finishTime" : 1364868426971,
        "preferredLocations" : [ {
          "layers" : [ "default-rack", "master" ]
        } ],
        "taskType" : "MAP",
        "taskStatus" : "SUCCESS",
        "taskID" : "task_201304012206_0001_m_000000",
        "inputBytes" : 242,
        "inputRecords" : 1,
  ...
  "outputBytes" : 51959,
    "reduceTasks" : [ {
      "startTime" : 1364868426978,
      "attempts" : [ {
        "location" : {
          "layers" : [ "default-rack", "master" ]
        },
        "hostName" : "/default-rack/master",
        "result" : "SUCCESS",
        "startTime" : 1364868426995,
        "finishTime" : 1364868441901,
        "attemptID" : "attempt_201304012206_0001_r_000000_0",
        "shuffleFinished" : 1364868440476,
  ...
    "failedReduceAttemptCDF" : {
      "maximum" : 9223372036854775807,
      "minimum" : -9223372036854775808,
      "rankings" : [ ],
      "numberValues" : 0
    },
    "mapperTriesToSucceed" : [ 1.0 ],
    "failedMapperFraction" : 0.0,
    "relativeTime" : 0,
    "clusterMapMB" : -1,
    "clusterReduceMB" : -1,
    "jobMapMB" : 200,
    "jobReduceMB" : 200
}
```

2. The second step of using Rumen is to scale the data generated from the previous step. We can use the following syntax to do this:

```
hadoop org.apache.hadoop.tools.rumen.Folder [options] [input]
[output]
```

For example, to scale the runtime of the job trace generated in the previous step to 50 minutes, we can use the following command:

```
hadoop org.apache.hadoop.tools.rumen.Folder -output-duration 50m
-input-cycle 20m file:///home/hduser/jobtraces.json file:///home/
hduser/job-scaled-50min.json
```

In this command, the `-output-duration` option defines the final runtime of the job trace, and the default value for this option is one hour. The `-input-cycle` option is mandatory, and it defines the basic unit of time for the folding operation.

See also

▶ The *Benchmarking a Hadoop cluster with GridMix* recipe

▶ Refer to `http://hadoop.apache.org/docs/r1.1.2/rumen.html`

▶ Refer to `https://issues.apache.org/jira/browse/MAPREDUCE-751`

Benchmarking a Hadoop cluster with GridMix

GridMix is a tool for benchmarking Hadoop clusters. It generates a number of synthetic MapReduce jobs and builds a model based on the performance of these jobs. Resource profiles of the cluster are modeled based on the job execution metrics. The profiles can help us find performance bottlenecks of the cluster. In this section, we will outline steps for benchmarking Hadoop with GridMix.

Getting ready

We assume that our Hadoop cluster has been properly configured and all the daemons are running without any issues.

 Currently, GridMix has three versions. For the purpose of differentiation and notation, we will use `GridMix` to represent GridMix version 1, use `GridMix2` to represent GridMix version 2, and use `GridMix3` to represent GridMix version 3.

Log in to the Hadoop cluster node from the administrator machine using the following command:

```
ssh hduser@master
```

How to do it...

Use the following steps to get GridMix2 benchmarks:

1. Change the current working directory with the following command:

   ```
   cd $HADOOP_HOME/src/benchmarks/gridmix2
   ```

2. Build the GridMix2 package with the following command:

   ```
   ant
   ```

3. Copy the `gridmix.jar` file to the current working directory with the following command:

   ```
   cp build/gridmix.jar .
   ```

4. Open the `gridmix-env-2` file with a text editor and change the environment variables to the following values:

   ```
   export HADOOP_VERSION=hadoop-1.1.2
   export HADOOP_HOME=/usr/local/hadoop
   export HADOOP_CONF_DIR=$HADOOP_HOME/conf
   export USE_REAL_DATASET=FALSE

   export APP_JAR=${HADOOP_HOME}/hadoop-test-*.jar
   export EXAMPLE_JAR=${HADOOP_HOME}/hadoop-examples-*.jar
   export STREAMING_JAR=${HADOOP_HOME}/contrib/streaming/hadoop-streaming-*.jar
   ```

5. Open the `gridmix_config.xml` GridMix2 configuration file with a text editor and change the benchmark configuration by changing the properties for the benchmark. For example, the following lines configure the number of jobs for the `streamSort` benchmark with small jobs:

   ```
   <property>
     <name>streamSort.smallJobs.numOfJobs</name>
     <value>10,5</value>
   </property>

   <property>
     <name>streamSort.smallJobs.numOfReduces</name>
     <value>6,3</value>
   </property>
   ```

These two properties specify that we will use 10 small stream sort jobs with 6 reducers, and 5 small stream sort jobs with 3 reducers. All other configurations should follow rules similar to this one.

6. Make the `generateGridmix2Data.sh` script executable with the following command:

```
chmod +x generateGridmix2Data.sh
```

7. Generate data with the following command:

```
./generateGridmix2Data.sh
```

This command will generate data on HDFS. By default the generated data will be compressed with a block compression ratio of 4. Three jobs will be started as shown in the output message:

```
Job started: Fri Apr 19 16:02:48 EDT 2013

Running 492 maps.

Job started: Fri Apr 19 16:02:48 EDT 2013

Running 492 maps.

Job started: Fri Apr 19 16:02:48 EDT 2013

13/04/19 16:02:49 INFO mapred.JobClient: Running job:
job_201304051222_0233

13/04/19 16:02:49 INFO mapred.JobClient: Running job:
job_201304051222_0234

13/04/19 16:02:49 INFO mapred.JobClient: Running job:
job_201304051222_0235

...
```

8. Make the `rungridmix_2` script be executable with the following command:

```
chmod +x rungridmix_2
```

9. Run the `GridMix2` benchmark with the command:

```
./rungridmix_2
```

This command will take a while to finish. We can see an output message similar to the following:

```
Jobs in waiting state: 30
Jobs in ready state: 0
Jobs in running state: 140
Jobs in success state: 32
Jobs in failed state: 0
```

How it works...

GridMix is a benchmark for Hadoop clusters. It is generally used to model the performance profile of a Hadoop cluster by running a number of jobs.

The data required by GridMix is generated by running the `generateGridmix2data.sh` script. We can configure this file to change, for example, the size of the generated data file. Then, when executing the `rungridmix_2` script, a number of jobs will be generated and submitted in batch mode. In the end, the running time of these jobs will be computed.

GridMix2 is shipped with the following representative jobs: `streamSort`, `javaSort`, `webdataSort`, `combiner`, and `monsterSort`. These jobs can be classified into the following categories:

- ▸ A three-stage MapReduce job, which is motivated by the multistage or pipelined MapReduce jobs
- ▸ Large sort of variable key/value sizes, which is motivated by the processing of large datasets
- ▸ Reference select jobs, which is motivated by jobs that sample from a large, reference data set
- ▸ API text sort jobs, which is motivated by the application of MapReduce APIs for sorting

A GridMix benchmark is a mix of a number of small, medium, and large jobs from different categories. We can specify the mix in the `gridmix_config.xml` file. Based on the specification, a number of jobs will be created and submitted to the Hadoop cluster until it finishes.

There's more...

Besides benchmarking with GridMix2, we can also benchmark a Hadoop cluster with GridMix1 and GridMix3.

Benchmarking Hadoop cluster with GridMix1

The usage of GridMix1 is similar to GridMix2. The following steps can be used:

1. Change to the GridMix1 directory:

   ```
   cd $HADOOP_HOME/src/benchmarks/gridmix
   ```

2. Open the `gridmix-env` file with a text editor and change the configuration to the following:

   ```
   export HADOOP_HOME=/usr/local/Hadoop
   export GRID_MIX_HOME=$HADOOP_HOME/src/benchmarks/gridmix
   export APP_JAR=${HADOOP_HOME}/hadoop-test-*.jar
   ```

```
export EXAMPLE_JAR=${HADOOP_HOME}/hadoop-examples-*.jar
export STREAMING_JAR=${HADOOP_HOME}/contrib/streaming/hadoop-
streaming-*.jar
export GRID_MIX_DATA=/gridmix1/data
export GRID_MIX_PROG=/gridmix1/programs
```

>  The last two environment variables GRID_MIX_DATA and GRID_MIX_PROG specify two directories on HDFS. So, the generated data and programs will be on HDFS.

3. Make the `generateData.sh` script executable with the following command:

   ```
   chmod +x generateData.sh
   ```

4. Generate data with the following command:

   ```
   sh ./generateData.sh
   ```

   GridMix1 is composed of a number of high-level scripts to control how benchmark jobs work. The tree structure of the GridMix1 directory is similar to the following:

```
gridmix
├── generateData.sh
├── gridmix-env
├── gridmix.jar
├── javasort
│   ├── text-sort.large
│   ├── text-sort.medium
│   └── text-sort.small
├── maxent
│   └── maxent.large
├── monsterQuery
│   ├── monster_query.large
│   ├── monster_query.medium
│   └── monster_query.small
├── pipesort
│   ├── text-sort.large
│   ├── text-sort.medium
│   └── text-sort.small
├── README
├── streamsort
│   ├── text-sort.large
│   ├── text-sort.medium
│   └── text-sort.small
├── submissionScripts
│   ├── allThroughHod
```

```
    |   ├── allToSameCluster
    |   ├── maxentHod
    |   ├── maxentToSameCluster
    |   ├── monsterQueriesHod
    |   ├── monsterQueriesToSameCluster
    |   ├── sleep_if_too_busy
    |   ├── textSortHod
    |   ├── textSortToSameCluster
    |   ├── webdataScanHod
    |   ├── webdataScanToSameCluster
    |   ├── webdataSortHod
    |   └── webdataSortToSameCluster
    ├── webdatascan
    |   ├── webdata_scan.large
    |   ├── webdata_scan.medium
    |   └── webdata_scan.small
    └── webdatasort
        ├── webdata_sort.large
        ├── webdata_sort.medium
        └── webdata_sort.small

8 directories, 36 files
```

 The GridMix1 directory contains a few template jobs with different sizes. For example, the three scripts (text-sort.small, text-sort. medium, and text-sort.large) in the javasort directory are templates for small, medium, and large javasort jobs.

5. To run a small javasort job, we can use the following command:

   sh javasort/text-sort.small

 We can use similar commands to run medium and large jobs.

Benchmarking Hadoop cluster with GridMix3

Use the following steps to build a GridMix3 benchmark for a Hadoop cluster:

1. Copy the required JAR files to the Hadoop lib directory using the following commands:

   cp $HADOOP_HOME/hadoop-tools-*.jar $HADOOP_HOME/lib

   cp $HADOOP_HOME/contrib/gridmix/hadoop-gridmix-*.jar $HADOOP_HOME/ lib

The `hadoop-tools-*.jar` file contains tools such as Rumen, which is needed by GridMix3. And the `hadoop-gridmix-*.jar` file contains the GridMix3 benchmark tool. In addition, the GridMix3 job mix for a Hadoop cluster is typically described with a job trace file, which is generated from job configuration files using Rumen.

2. Use Rumen to generate a job trace file with the following command:

```
hadoop org.apache.hadoop.tools.rumen.TraceBuilder -recursive
file:///tmp/jobtrace.json file:///tmp/topology.out file:///usr/
local/hadoop/logs/history/done
```

The command will generate a job trace file `/tmp/jobtrace.json`, and in the next step, we are going to use this file as input for the GridMix3 Hadoop benchmarks.

Sometimes, we might get a CRC exception when running this command. A quick fix for this problem is to delete the `.crc` file for the corresponding job configuration file, for example, the checksum file for the job configuration file `job_201304051222_0192_conf.xml` is `job_201304051222_0192_conf.xml.crc`. We can delete the latter file to ignore the `.crc` check.

3. Run the GridMix3 benchmark with the following command:

```
hadoop org.apache.hadoop.mapred.gridmix.Gridmix -generate 100m
gridmixdata  /tmp/jobtraces.json
```

This command will generate an output similar to the following:

```
13/04/01 22:57:11 INFO gridmix.SubmitterUserResolver:  Current
user resolver is SubmitterUserResolver
13/04/01 22:57:11 INFO gridmix.Gridmix:  Submission policy is
STRESS
13/04/01 22:57:11 INFO util.NativeCodeLoader: Loaded the native-
hadoop library
13/04/01 22:57:11 WARN snappy.LoadSnappy: Snappy native library
not loaded
13/04/01 22:57:11 INFO gridmix.CompressionEmulationUtil:
GridMix is configured to generate compressed input data with  a
compression ratio of 0.5
13/04/01 22:57:11 INFO gridmix.Gridmix: Generating 100.0m of test
data...
13/04/01 22:57:11 INFO gridmix.Statistics: Not tracking job
GRIDMIX_GENERATE_INPUT_DATA as seq id is less than zero: -1
```

4. To acquire the usage and available parameters for GridMix3, we can use the following command:

```
hadoop org.apache.hadoop.mapred.gridmix.Gridmix
```

The output of this command will be as follows:

```
The general command line syntax is
bin/hadoop command [genericOptions] [commandOptions]

Usage: gridmix [-generate <MiB>] [-users URI] [-Dname=value ...]
<iopath> <trace>
  e.g. gridmix -generate 100m foo - Configuration parameters:
    General parameters:
        gridmix.output.directory                  : Output directory
        gridmix.client.submit.threads             : Submitting threads
...
```

See also

▸ The *Benchmarking and profiling a Hadoop cluster* recipe

▸ Refer to `http://hadoop.apache.org/docs/r1.1.2/rumen.html`

▸ Refer to `$HADOOP_HOME/src/benchmarks/README.gridmix2`

Using Hadoop Vaidya to identify performance problems

Hadoop **Vaidya** is an open source, rule-based performance diagnostic framework for Apache Hadoop. Each rule can identify a specific performance problem. For example, Hadoop cluster administrators can use Vaidya to identify slow progressing jobs that are wasting cluster resources. Hadoop clients can use Vaidya to identify configuration mistakes for their submitted jobs.

Hadoop Vaidya is extensible; users can analyze Hadoop job with their own rules. In this recipe, we will outline steps to configure Hadoop Vaidya for Hadoop cluster performance diagnosis.

Getting ready

Before getting started, we assume that the Hadoop cluster has been properly configured and all the daemons are running without any issues.

Log in from the Hadoop cluster administrator machine to the master node machine using the following command:

```
ssh hduser@master
```

How to do it...

Perform the following steps to use Hadoop Vaidya:

1. Locate the directory for the job configuration file you want to analyze. The default location of this folder is $HADOOP_HOME/logs.

2. Locate the job history files under the job history directory with the following command:

    ```
    find $HADOOP_HOME/logs -name 'job_201304012330_0001*'
    ```

 This command assumes that at least one job has been run so that at least one job configuration file can be found. For purpose of illustration, we assume that a teragen job has finished before running this command.

For example, in this command, we want to get the configuration file for the job with JobID job_201304012330_0001. We can get the following two lines as output:

```
logs/history/job_201304012330_0001_conf.xml
logs/history/job_201304012330_0001_1364874504561_hduser_TeraGen
```

 The first XML file in the output is the job configuration file and the second one is the job logfile.

3. Use Vaidya to analyze the job trace files with the following command:

    ```
    sh $HADOOP_HOME/contrib/vaidya/bin/vaidya.sh -jobconf file:///usr/
    local/hadoop/logs/history/job_201304012330_0002_conf.xml -joblog
    file:///usr/local/hadoop/logs/history/job_201304012330_0002_136487
    4504561_hduser_TeraGen -report report.txt
    ```

 Note that the file location should be an absolute path including the schema, which is either hdfs:// or file://.

This command will generate the `report.txt` file with content similar to the following:

```
<?xml version="1.0" encoding="UTF-8" standalone="no"?><PostE
xPerformanceDiagnosticReport><JobInformationElement><JobTra
ckerID/><JobName>PiEstimator</JobName><JobType>MAP_REDUCE</
JobType>hduser<SubmitTime>2013-04-17 19:46:49.213</Su
bmitTime><LaunchTime>2013-04-17 19:46:49.369</LaunchTime><FinishTi
me>2013-04-17 19:54:06.833</FinishTime><Status>SUCCESS</Status></
JobInformationElement><TestReportElement><TestTitle>Balanaced
Reduce Partitioning</TestTitle><TestDescription>This rule tests as
to how well the input to reduce tasks is balanced</TestDescription
><TestImportance>HIGH</TestImportance>
<TestResult>NEGATIVE(PASSED)</TestResult>
<TestSeverity>0.0</TestSeverity><ReferenceDetails>*
TotalReduceTasks: 1
* BusyReduceTasks processing 0.85% of total records: 1
* Impact: 0.0</ReferenceDetails><TestPrescription>* Use the
appropriate partitioning function
* For streaming job consider following partitioner and hadoop
config parameters
   * org.apache.hadoop.mapred.lib.KeyFieldBasedPartitioner
   * -jobconf stream.map.output.field.separator, -jobconf stream.
num.map.output.key.fields</TestPrescription></TestReportElement>
<TestReportElement><TestTitle>Impact of Map tasks Re-Execution</
TestTitle><TestDescription>This test rule checks percentage of map
task re-execution impacting the job performance</TestDescription><
TestImportance>HIGH</TestImportance>
<TestResult>NEGATIVE(PASSED)</TestResult>
<TestSeverity>0.0</TestSeverity><ReferenceDetails>* Total Map
Tasks: 10
* Launched Map Tasks: 10
* Percent Maps ReExecuted: 0
* Impact: 0.0</ReferenceDetails><TestPrescription>* Need careful
evaluation of why maps are re-executed.
   * It could be due to some set of unstable cluster nodes.
   * It could be due to application-specific failures.</
TestPrescription></TestReportElement><TestReportElem
ent><TestTitle>Impact of Reduce tasks Re-Execution</
TestTitle><TestDescription>This test rule checks percentage of
reduce task re-execution impacting the job performance</TestDescri
ption><TestImportance>HIGH</TestImportance>
```

```
<TestResult>NEGATIVE(PASSED)</TestResult>
<TestSeverity>0.0</TestSeverity><ReferenceDetails>* Total Reduce
Tasks: 1
* Launched Reduce Tasks: 1
* Percent Reduce Tasks ReExecuted: 0
* Impact: 0.0</ReferenceDetails><TestPrescription>* Need careful
evaluation of why reduce tasks are re-executed.
   * It could be due to some set of unstable cluster nodes.
   * It could be due to application-specific failures.</
TestPrescription></TestReportElement><TestReportElement><TestTit
le>Map and/or Reduce tasks reading HDFS data as a side effect</
TestTitle><TestDescription>This test rule checks if map/reduce
tasks are reading data from HDFS as a side effect. The more data
read as a side effect can potentially be a bottleneck across
parallel execution of map/reduce tasks.</TestDescription><TestImpo
rtance>HIGH</TestImportance>
<TestResult>POSITIVE(FAILED)</TestResult>
<TestSeverity>0.99</TestSeverity><ReferenceDetails>* Total HDFS
Bytes read: 2440
* Total Map Input Bytes read: 240
* Impact: 1.0</ReferenceDetails><TestPrescription>Map and/or
Reduce tasks are reading application specific files from HDFS.
Make sure the replication factor
of these HDFS files is high enough to avoid the data reading
bottleneck. Typically the replication factor
can be the square root of map/reduce tasks capacity of
the allocated cluster.</TestPrescription></TestReportEle
ment><TestReportElement><TestTitle>Map side disk spill</
TestTitle><TestDescription>This test rule checks if Map tasks are
spilling the data on to the local disk during the map side sorting
due to insufficient sort buffer size. The impact is calculated
as ratio between local bytes written to map output bytes. Impact
is normalized using NormalizationFactor given below and any
value greater than or equal to normalization factor is treated
as the maximum (i.e. 1).</TestDescription><TestImportance>LOW</
TestImportance>
<TestResult>POSITIVE(FAILED)</TestResult>
<TestSeverity>0.33</TestSeverity><ReferenceDetails>*
TotalMapOutputBytes: 180
* Total Local Bytes Written by Maps: 219400
* Impact: 1.0</ReferenceDetails><TestPrescription>* Use the
combiner to lower the map output size.
* Increase map side sort buffer size (io.sort.mb:100).
* Increase index buffer size (io.sort.record.percent:0) if the
number of Map Output Records is large.
* Increase (io.sort.spill.percent:0), default 0.80 i.e. 80% of
sort buffer size and index buffer size.
</TestPrescription></TestReportElement></
PostExPerformanceDiagnosticReport>
```

How it works...

We can get the options for Vaidya with the following command:

```
$HADOOP_HOME/contrib/vaidya/bin/vaidya.sh -help
```

The output is as follows:

```
Invalid arguments: -jobconf or -joblog arguments are missing
Usage:
PostExPerformanceDiagnoser -jobconf <fileurl> -joblog <fileurl>
[-testconf <filepath>] [-report <filepath>]


-jobconf <fileurl>       : File path for job configuration file (e.g.
job_xxxx_conf.xml). It can be on HDFS or
                         : local filesystem. It should be specified in
the URL format.
                         : e.g. local file => file://localhost/Users/
hadoop-user/job_0001_conf.xml
                         : e.g. hdfs file  => hdfs://namenode:port/
Users/hadoop-user/hodlogs/.../job_0001_conf.xml


-joblog <fileurl>        : File path for job history logfile. It can be
on HDFS or local file system.
                         : It should be specified in the URL format.


-testconf <filepath>   : Optional file path for performance advisor
tests configuration file. It should be available
                         : on local file system and be specified as as
an absolute file path.
                         : e.g. => /Users/hadoop-user/postex_diagnosis_
tests.xml. If not specified default file will be used
                         : from the hadoop-{ver}-vaidya.jar in a
classpath.
                         : For user to view or make local copy of
default tests, file is available at $HADOOP_HOME/contrib/vaidya/conf/
postex_diagnosis_tests.xml


-report <filepath>       : Optional file path for for storing diagnostic
report in a XML format. Path should be available
                         : on local file system and be specified as as
an absolute file path.
                         : e.g. => /Users/hadoop-user/postex_diagnosis_
report.xml. If not specified report will be printed on console


-help                    : prints this usage
```

There's more...

HiBench is a benchmarking suite for Hadoop. It has nine typical workloads, including micro, HDFS, web search machine learning, and data analytics benchmarks. For example, it supports benchmarks for **Nutch** (a text indexing software package), **PageRank** (the PageRank algorithm), the Mahout machine learning algorithms, and Hive queries.

The HiBench project and the paper provide good examples of Hadoop benchmarking. For more information, you can refer to `https://github.com/intel-hadoop/Hibench`.

See also

- ▶ The *Benchmarking and profiling a Hadoop cluster* recipe
- ▶ The *Benchmarking a Hadoop cluster with GridMix* recipe
- ▶ Refer to `http://hadoop.apache.org/docs/stable/vaidya.html`

Balancing data blocks for a Hadoop cluster

HDFS stores data blocks on DataNode machines. When Hadoop processes jobs, data is generated and deleted. Over time, some DataNodes can host much more data blocks than others. This unbalanced distribution of data on the cluster is called **data skew**.

Data skew is a big problem for a Hadoop cluster. We know that when the JobTracker assigns tasks to TaskTrackers, it follows the general rule of being **data local**, which means the map tasks will be assigned to those hosts where data blocks reside in. If the data block storage distribution is skewed, or in other words, the data blocks locate only on a small percentage of DataNodes, only those nodes with data blocks can follow the data local rule. Also, if JobTracker assigns tasks to other nodes that do not have data hosted locally, the data needs to be transferred from remote machines to the TaskTracker machine. The data transfer will cost a large amount of network bandwidth, downgrading the overall performance of the cluster.

To deal with the data skew problem on HDFS, Hadoop is shipped with a **balancer** tool. It can be configured either manually or automatically to rebalance the data blocks.

Getting ready

To get started with balancer, we assume that the Hadoop cluster has been properly configured and all the daemons are running without any issues.

Log in from the cluster administrator machine to the master node using the following command:

```
ssh hduser@master
```

How to do it...

Use the following steps to balance HDFS data blocks with balancer:

1. Check the data skew through the web UI, for example, by the opening URL `http://master:50070/`.

   The web page will be similar to the following screenshot:

NameNode 'master:54310'

Started: Sat Feb 16 02:19:03 EST 2013
Version: 1.1.1, r1411108
Compiled: Mon Nov 19 10:48:11 UTC 2012 by hortonfo
Upgrades: There are no upgrades in progress.

Browse the filesystem
Namenode Logs
Go back to DFS home

Live Datanodes : 5

Node	Last Contact	Admin State	Configured Capacity (GB)	Used (GB)	Non DFS Used (GB)	Remaining (GB)	Used (%)	Used (%)	Remaining (%)	Blocks
slave1	1	In Service	78.75	2.73	4.27	71.74	3.47		91.1	69
slave2	2	In Service	78.75	2.76	4.25	71.75	90.7		91.1	74
slave3	2	In Service	78.75	3.3	4.42	71.04	4.19		90.2	71
slave4	1	In Service	78.75	2.88	4.45	71.43	3.65		90.7	60
slave5	2	In Service	78.75	3.38	4.23	71.14	4.29		90.34	66

This is Apache Hadoop release 1.1.1

The screenshot shows that the data blocks are skewed. Hence, rebalancing is necessary.

2. Use the following command to balance the data blocks on the DataNode machines:

```
hadoop balancer -threshold 0.2
```

This command will take some time to finish depending on the status of the distributed filesystem as well as the value for the `-threshold` option. The `-threshold` option specifies the threshold for whether the cluster is balanced. It is a real number within range [0, 1] with a default value of 0.1. A smaller value for this option leads to a more even distribution of the data blocks. On the other hand, it will require more time to finish. Setting this option to be 0 is not recommended because it is not practical to achieve an ideal balance.

3. Alternatively, we can start the Hadoop balancer daemon to automatically balance the data blocks on HDFS. We can use the following command to do this:

```
start-balancer.sh
```

The balancer will move data blocks among the DataNodes according to the space utilization. For example, it will move data blocks from highly utilized nodes to the less utilized nodes. This process is done iteratively. We can get the updated DataNode information from the NameNode after each iteration. If the cluster is already balanced, we will get an output similar to the following:

```
Time Stamp                 Iteration#  Bytes Already Moved   Bytes
Left To Move   Bytes Being Moved
13/04/02 00:56:27 INFO net.NetworkTopology: Adding a new node: /
default-rack/127.0.0.1:50010
13/04/02 00:56:27 INFO balancer.Balancer: 0 over utilized nodes:
13/04/02 00:56:27 INFO balancer.Balancer: 1 under utilized nodes:
127.0.0.1:50010
The cluster is balanced. Exiting...
Balancing took 567.0 milliseconds
```

4. To stop the balancer, we can use the following command:

```
stop-balancer.sh
```

How it works...

The Hadoop balancer balances data blocks on HDFS according to a preconfigured threshold value, which sets the target for whether the cluster is balanced or not. A node is considered balanced if the difference between space utilization of the node and space utilization of the cluster is less than the threshold.

Sometimes, we want to limit the percentage of bandwidth used by the balancer. By default, Hadoop defines a property dfs.balance.bandwidthPerSec, which determines the maximum speed that a data block will be moved from one DataNode to another. Its default value is 1 MB/s. By configuring this property to be a higher value, the balancing speed will be faster, but more resources will be used. For example, to change the value of this property to be 10 MB/s, we can open the $HADOOP_HOME/conf/hdfs-site.xml file and add the following lines:

```
<property>
  <name>dfs.balance.bandwidthPerSec</name>
  <value>10485760</value>
</property>
```

 We need to restart HDFS to make this change take effect.

Choosing a proper block size

HDFS stores data as data blocks distributed on multiple machines. So, when a large file is put onto HDFS, it will first be split into a number of data blocks. These data blocks are then distributed by the NameNode to the DataNodes in the cluster. The granularity of the data blocks can affect the distribution and parallel execution of the tasks.

Based on the property of the jobs being executed, one **block size** might result in better performance than others. We will guide you through steps to configure a proper block size for the Hadoop cluster.

Getting ready

We assume that the Hadoop cluster has been properly configured and all the daemons are running without any issues.

Log in from the Hadoop cluster administrator machine to the master node using the following command:

```
ssh hduser@master
```

How to do it...

Configure the proper HDFS block size using the following steps:

1. Run a typical job on the configured cluster. For example, we can run a sample `terasort` on the cluster with the following command:

    ```
    hadoop jar $HADOOP_HOME/hadoop-example-*.jar terasort input output
    ```

2. Use Rumen to generate job traces from the job history file and the job logfile with the following command:

    ```
    hadoop org.apache.hadoop.tools.rumen.TraceBuilder file:///tmp/
    jobtraces.json file:///tmp/topology.out file:///usr/local/hadoop/
    logs/history/done/ job_201304012206_0002_conf.xml
    ```

3. Use GridMix3 to generate a Hadoop cluster benchmark with different block sizes:

    ```
    hadoop org.apache.hadoop.mapred.gridmix.Gridmix -generate 10m
    input jobtraces.json
    ```

 Now, we can find the block size that achieves the best performance. For example, by setting block size to be 64 MB, we can get the best performance.

4. Stop the cluster using the following command:

```
stop-all.sh
```

5. Open the $HADOOP_HOME/conf/hdfs-site.xml file with your favorite text editor and change the dfs.block.size property to be the following:

```
<property>
  <name>dfs.block.size</name>
  <value>64</value>
</property>
```

6. Start the Hadoop cluster with the following command:

```
start-all.sh
```

Using compression for input and output

A typical MapReduce job uses parallel mapper tasks to load data from external storage devices, such as hard drives to the main memory. When a job finishes, the reduce tasks write the result data back to the hard drive. In this way, during the life cycle of a MapReduce job, many data copies are created when data is relayed between the hard drive and the main memory. Sometimes, the data is copied over the network from a remote node.

Copying data from and to hard drives and transfers over the network are expensive operations. To reduce the cost of these operations, Hadoop introduced **compression** on the data.

Data compression in Hadoop is done by a compression codec, which is a program that encodes and decodes data streams. Although compression and **decompression** can cause additional cost to the system, the advantages far outweigh the disadvantages.

In this section, we will outline steps to configure data compression on a Hadoop cluster.

Getting ready

We assume that the Hadoop cluster has been properly configured and all the daemons are running without any issues.

Log in from the Hadoop cluster administrator machine to the cluster master node using the following command:

ssh hduser@master

 In this recipe, we assume all the property configurations will make changes in the $HADOOP_HOME/conf/mapred-site.xml file.

How to do it...

Use the following steps to configure input and output data compression for a Hadoop cluster:

1. Stop the cluster with the following command:

   stop-all.sh

2. Enable output compression by adding the following property:

   ```
   <property>
     <name>mapred.output.compress</name>
     <value>true</value>
   </property>
   ```

3. Specify the output compression codec by changing the following property:

   ```
   <property>
     <name>mapred.output.compression.codec</name>
     <value>org.apache.hadoop.io.compress.GzipCodec</value>
   </property>
   ```

 The property specifies Hadoop to use the **Gzip** codec for data compression. Other available compression codecs include org.apache. hadoop.io.compress.GzipCodec, org.apache.hadoop. io.compress.BZip2Codec, and so on. The default value for this property is org.apache.hadoop.io.compress.DefaultCodec.

4. Change the output compression type for sequence file output by changing the following property:

   ```
   <property>
     <name>mapred.output.compression.type</name>
     <value>BLOCK</value>
   </property>
   ```

This will change the sequence file output compression type from the default type RECORD to BLOCK. The other types are NONE and RECORD. By setting this property to be NONE, we will disable the compression of the sequence file outputs. Individual records will be compressed with the RECORD compression type and a number of records will be compressed with the BLOCK compression type. Generally, the BLOCK compression type is more efficient than the RECORD type, so it is recommended.

5. Configure the map output compression by changing the following property:

```
<property>
  <name>mapred.compress.map.output</name>
  <value>true</value>
</property>
```

This configuration will enable the map output compression. To disable it, which is the default, we can change the value to be false or remove this configuration property from the configuration file.

6. Similar to the codec configuration for the MapReduce job output, we can perform configuration compression codecs for the map task output, the default of which is org.apache.hadoop.io.compress.DefaultCodec. For example, we can configure the map output compression to be the Gzip codec by changing the property, as shown in the following code:

```
<property>
  <name>mapred.map.output.compression.codec</name>
  <value>org.apache.hadoop.io.compress.GzipCodec</value>
</property>
```

7. Copy the configuration file from the master node to all the slave nodes in the cluster with the following command:

```
for host in 'cat $HADOOP_HOME/conf/slaves'
do
    echo 'Copying mapred-site.xml file to host: ' $host
    scp $HADOOP_HOME/conf/mapred-site.xml $host:$HADOOP_HOME/conf/
done
```

8. Restart the Hadoop cluster with the following command:

```
start-all.sh
```

How it works...

The following table is a summary of properties for configuring Hadoop data compression:

Property	Default
`mapred.output.compress`	`true`
`mapred.output.compression.type`	`RECORD`
`mapred.output.compression.codec`	`org.apache.hadoop.io.compress.DefaultCodec`
`mapred.compress.map.output`	`false`
`mapred.map.output.compression.codec`	`org.apache.hadoop.io.compress.DefaultCodec`

Available compression codecs are described in the following table:

Codec name	Java class
`DefaultCodec`	`org.apache.hadoop.io.compress.DefaultCodec`
`GzipCodec`	`org.apache.hadoop.io.compress.GzipCodec`
`BZip2Codec`	`org.apache.hadoop.io.compress.BZip2Codec`
`SnappyCodec`	`org.apache.hadoop.io.compress.SnappyCodec`
`LzoCodec`	`org.apache.hadoop.io.compress.LzoCodec`

Configuring speculative execution

Speculative execution is a proactive performance boosting strategy used by JobTracker to execute one task on two TaskTracker instances. When either of these tasks finishes, the other task will be killed. By default, speculative execution is on.

Speculative execution can be helpful to improve the performance of MapReduce jobs by reducing the execution time for slowly progressing tasks. For example, on heterogeneous Hadoop clusters with different hardware configurations, low performance computing nodes can greatly prolong the execution time of a MapReduce job. Speculative execution can remedy this problem by prioritizing the high performance nodes for MapReduce tasks execution. Hence, the MapReduce execution time can be shortened.

On the other hand, speculative execution can negatively affect the performance of the cluster when a lot of resources are used for speculative execution. For example, many tasks will have to wait for slots that are used for speculative execution.

In this recipe, we will list steps to configure Hadoop speculative execution.

Getting ready

We assume that the Hadoop cluster has been properly configured and all the daemons are running without any issues.

Log in from the Hadoop cluster administrator machine to the cluster master node using the following command:

```
ssh hduser@master
```

 In this recipe, we assume all the property configurations will make changes to the $HADOOP_HOME/conf/mapred-site.xml file.

How to do it...

We can use the following recipe to configure Hadoop speculative execution:

1. Stop the MapReduce cluster with the following command:

   ```
   stop-mapred.sh
   ```

2. Disable the map task speculative execution by changing the following property:

   ```
   <property>
     <name>mapred.map.tasks.speculative.execution</name>
     <value>false</value>
   </property>
   ```

    By default, Hadoop speculative execution is turned on.

3. Disable the reduce task speculative execution by changing the following property:

   ```
   <property>
     <name>mapred.reduce.tasks.speculative.execution</name>
     <value>false</value>
   </property>
   ```

4. Configure the maximum percentage of concurrently running speculative tasks by changing the following property:

```
<property>
  <name>mapreduce.job.speculative.speculativecap</name>
  <value>0.2</value>
</property>
```

 This configures, at maximum, 20 percent of the tasks of a job to run speculatively.

5. Configure the job speculative execution threshold for slow tasks by changing the following property:

```
<property>
  <name>mapreduce.job.speculative.slowtaskthreshold</name>
  <value>1.0</value>
</property>
```

 This property is used to test if a task needs to be executed speculatively. Its default value is 1.0.

6. Configure the threshold for a TaskTracker to speculatively execute slow tasks by changing the following property:

```
<property>
  <name>mapreduce.job.speculative.slownodethreshold</name>
  <value>1.0</value>
</property>
```

 This property is used to test if a TaskTracker qualifies to run speculative tasks. Its default value is 1.0.

7. Sync the configurations to the slave nodes with the following command:

```
for host in 'cat $HADOOP_HOME/conf/slaves'; do
  echo 'Copying mapred-site.xml file to host: ' $host
  sudo scp $HADOOP_HOME/conf/mapred-site.xml $host:$HADOOP_HOME/
conf/
done
```

8. Start the MapReduce cluster with the following command:

```
start-mapred.sh
```

How it works...

When speculative execution is enabled, some tasks will get killed. This can be verified by opening the URL `http://master:50030/`.

The web page will be similar to the following screenshot:

Hadoop job_201302281451_0014 failures on master

Attempt	Task	Machine	State	Error	Logs
attempt_201302281451_0014_m_000071_0	task_201302281451_0014_m_000071	slave3	KILLED		Last 4KB Last 8KB All
attempt_201302281451_0014_m_000072_0	task_201302281451_0014_m_000072	slave3	KILLED		Last 4KB Last 8KB All
attempt_201302281451_0014_m_000081_1	task_201302281451_0014_m_000081	slave2	KILLED		Last 4KB Last 8KB All

If speculative execution has been enabled for a Hadoop cluster, we can still disable it for specific jobs. For example, when we write MapReduce jobs using Java programming language, we can use the following code snippet to disable speculative execution for this job:

```
Configuration conf = new Configuration();
conf.set("mapred.map.tasks.speculative.execution", "false");
conf.set("mapred.reduce.tasks.speculative.execution", "false");
```

The following table is a summary of the properties we used in this recipe with their default values:

Property	Default value
mapreduce.map.speculative	true
mapreduce.reduce.speculative	true
mapreduce.job.speculative.speculativecap	0.1
mapreduce.job.speculative.slowtaskthreshold	1.0
mapreduce.job.speculative.slownodethreshold	1.0

The three properties `mapreduce.job.speculative.speculativecap`, `mapreduce.job.speculative.slowtaskthreshold`, and `mapreduce.job.speculative.slownodethreshold` control when the JobTracker should start a speculative task. Specifically, a speculative task for a regular task will start when the following conditions are met:

- Speculative execution is enabled
- The completion rate, in percentage, of the regular task is less than `mapreduce.job.speculative.slowtaskthreshold` times the mean completion rate of all other tasks
- The completion rate, in percentage, of the regular task is less than `mapreduce.job.speculative.slownodethreshold` times the mean completion rate of all other tasks on the current TaskTracker
- The number of launched speculative tasks is smaller than the configured speculative cap

Setting proper number of map and reduce slots for the TaskTracker

The number of map and reduce slots determines the number of concurrent map/reduce tasks for a TaskTracker, which forks multiple JVMs to run these tasks. In this recipe, we will give you a general view of setting proper number of these slots for the TaskTracker.

Getting ready

We assume that the Hadoop cluster has been properly configured and all the daemons are running without any issues.

Log in from the Hadoop cluster administrator machine to the cluster master node using the following command:

```
ssh hduser@master
```

How to do it...

Use the following steps to configure map/reduce slots for a TaskTracker:

1. Stop the MapReduce cluster with the following command:
   ```
   stop-mapred.sh
   ```

2. Configure the map slots by adding the following property into the `$HADOOP_HOME/conf/mapred-site.xml` file:

```
<property>
  <name>mapred.takstracker.map.tasks.maximum</name>
  <value>4</value>
</property>
```

 The TaskTracker is configured to have four map slots.

3. Similarly, we can configure the number of reduce slots for a TaskTracker:

```
<property>
  <name>mapred.takstracker.reduce.tasks.maximum</name>
  <value>4</value>
</property>
```

4. Configure the memory usage for each slot by adding the following property:

```
<property>
  <name>mapred.child.java.opts</name>
  <value>-Xmx1024m</value>
</property>
```

5. Sync the configuration to all the slave nodes with the following command:

```
for host in 'cat $HADOOP_HOME/conf/slaves'; do
  echo 'Copying mapred-site.xml file to host: ' $host
  scp $HADOOP_HOME/conf/mapred-site.xml $host:$HADOOP_HOME/conf/
done
```

6. Start the MapReduce cluster with the following command:

```
start-mapred.sh
```

Tuning the JobTracker configuration

In a Hadoop cluster, the JobTracker is responsible for managing jobs and tasks. The performance of the JobTracker is critical for the whole cluster. Hadoop provides a few properties for administrators to tune the JobTracker. In this recipe, we will list the steps to configure the JobTracker.

Getting ready

We assume that the Hadoop cluster has been properly configured and all the daemons are running without any issues.

Log in from the Hadoop cluster administrator machine to the cluster master node using the following command:

```
ssh hduser@master
```

 In this recipe, we assume all the configurations are making changes to the $HADOOP_HOME/conf/mapred-site.xml file.

How to do it...

Use the following steps to configure the JobTracker:

1. Stop the MapReduce cluster with the following command:

    ```
    stop-mapred.sh
    ```

2. Configure the maximum number of tasks for a job by changing the following property:

    ```
    <property>
        <name>mapred.jobtracker.maxtasks.per.job</name>
        <value>3000</value>
    </property>
    ```

     The default value of this property is -1, which ignores the limit.

3. Configure the JobTracker to recover upon restart by changing the following property:

    ```
    <property>
        <name>mapred.jobtracker.restart.recover</name>
        <value>true</value>
    </property>
    ```

     By default, this property is disabled, and the JobTracker will start afresh.

4. Configure the block size for the job history file by changing the following property:

```
<property>
  <name>mapred.jobtracker.job.history.block.size</name>
  <value>3145728</value>
</property>
```

 The job history data, which will be dumped to disk, will be used for job recovery.

5. Configure the task scheduler for the JobTracker by changing the following property:

```
<property>
  <name>mapred.jobtracker.taskScheduler</name>
  <value>org.apache.hadoop.mapred.JobQueueTaskScheduler</value>
</property>
```

 This configuration enables the `org.apache.hadoop.mapred.JobQueueTaskScheduler` Java class to schedule tasks.

6. Configure the maximum running tasks for a job by changing the following property:

```
<property>
  <name>mapred.jobtracker.taskScheduler.maxRunningTasksPerJob</name>
  <value>20</value>
</property>
```

 This property sets a limit on the maximum number of tasks for each job before it gets preempted by the job scheduler. It is related to the scheduling of jobs and tasks.

7. Sync the configuration from the master node to all the slave nodes with the following command:

```
for host in 'cat $HADOOP_HOME/conf/slaves'; do
  echo 'Copying mapred-site.xml file to host: ' $host
  scp $HADOOP_HOME/conf/mapred-site.xml $host:$HADOOP_HOME/conf/
done
```

8. Restart the Hadoop cluster with the following command:

```
start-mapred.sh
```

How it works...

The following table is a list of properties with descriptions:

Property	Default	Description
`mapred.jobtracker.maxtasks.per.job`	-1	Unlimited
`mapred.jobtracker.restart.recover`	`false`	No Recover
`mapred.jobtracker.job.history.block.size`	3145728	
`mapred.jobtracker.taskScheduler.` `maxRunningTasksPerJob`	EMPTY	No Limits

See also

▸ The *Tuning the TaskTracker configuration* recipe

▸ The *Configuring CapacityScheduler* recipe in *Chapter 4, Managing a Hadoop Cluster*

▸ The *Configuring Fair Scheduler* recipe in *Chapter 4, Managing a Hadoop Cluster*

Tuning the TaskTracker configuration

TaskTrackers accept tasks from the JobTracker in a cluster and forks JVMs to run the tasks. A couple of TaskTracker properties can be configured based on the configuration of the cluster.

In this section, we will list steps to configure the TaskTracker property.

Getting ready

We assume that the Hadoop cluster has been properly configured and all the daemons are running without any issues.

Log in from the Hadoop cluster administrator machine to the cluster master node using the following command:

```
ssh hduser@master
```

 In this recipe, we assume all the configurations are making changes to the `$HADOOP_HOME/conf/mapred-site.xml` file.

How to do it...

Use the following steps to configure TaskTracker properties:

1. Stop the MapReduce cluster with the following command:

   `mapred-stop.sh`

2. Configure the MapReduce cluster heartbeat interval by changing the following property:

   ```
   <property>
     <name>mapred.tasktracker.expiry.interval</name>
     <value>600000</value>
   </property>
   ```

    This property specifies the heartbeat time interval, in milliseconds, after which it will be marked lost by the JobTracker.

3. Configure the sleep time before sending the SIGKILL signal by changing the following property:

   ```
   <property>
     <name>mapred.tasktracker.tasks.sleeptime-before-sigkill</name>
     <value>6000</value>
   </property>
   ```

    This property configures the sleep time, in milliseconds that, the TaskTracker waits before sending a SIGKILL signal to a process after it has been sent a SIGTERM signal. Its default value is 5000 ms.

4. Enable the TaskTracker memory management by changing the following property:

   ```
   <property>
     <name>mapred.tasktracker.tasks.maxmemory</name>
     <value>true</value>
   </property>
   ```

5. Configure the TaskTracker index cache size to be 20 MB by changing the following property:

   ```
   <property>
     <name>mapred.tasktracker.indexcache.mb</name>
     <value>20</value>
   </property>
   ```

This property configures the maximum memory that a TaskTracker uses for an index cache when serving map output to reducers.

6. Configure the monitoring interval for the TaskTracker's task memory manager by changing the following property:

```
<property>
  <name>mapred.tasktracker.taskmemorymanager.monitoring-interval</
name>
  <value>5000</value>
</property>
```

 This property configures the interval, in milliseconds, that the TaskTracker monitors the tasks' memory usage. It is only meaningful when a tasks' memory management has been enabled using the `mapred.tasktracker.tasks.maxmemory` property.

7. Configure the TaskTracker to send an out-of-band heartbeat on task completion by changing the following property:

```
<property>
  <name>mapreduce.tasktracker.outofband.heartbeat</name>
  <value>true</value>
</property>
```

 The default value for this property is `false`, which disables the out-of-band heartbeat. Enabling this property can achieve better latency.

8. Configure the maximum number of retries for a map task by changing the following property:

```
<property>
  <name>mapred.map.max.attempts</name>
  <value>4</value>
</property>
```

 By this configuration, a failed task will be retried up to three times before being declared failed.

9. Configure the maximum number of retries for a failed reduce task by changing the following property:

```
<property>
  <name>mapred.reduce.max.attempts</name>
  <value>4</value>
</property>
```

 Similar to the maximum attempts configuration for a map task, this property configures to retry a failed reduce task up to three times before declaring failed.

10. Sync the configuration from the master node to all the slave nodes with the following command:

```
for host in 'cat $HADOOP_HOME/conf/slaves'; do
    echo 'Copying mapred-site.xml file to host: ' $host
    scp $HADOOP_HOME/conf/mapred-site.xml $host:$HADOOP_HOME/conf/
done
```

11. Restart the MapReduce cluster with the following command:

```
start-mapred.sh
```

How it works...

The following table contains a list of properties with descriptions:

Property	Default	Description
mapred.tasktracker.expiry.interval	600000	In milliseconds
mapred.tasktracker.tasks.sleeptime-before-sigkill	5000	In milliseconds
mapred.tasktracker.indexcache.mb	10	In MB
mapred.tasktracker.taskmemorymanager.monitoring-interval	5000	In milliseconds
mapreduce.tasktracker.outofband.heartbeat	false	
mapred.map.max.attempts	4	
mapred.reduce.max.attempts	4	

▸ The *Tuning the JobTracker configuration* recipe

Tuning shuffle, merge, and sort parameters

In a MapReduce job, map task outputs are aggregated into JVM buffers. The size of the in-memory buffer determines how large the data can be merged and sorted at once. Too small a buffer size can cause a large number of swap operations, incurring big overhead. In this section, we will show best practices for configuring the shuffle, merge, and sort parameters.

Getting ready

We assume that the Hadoop cluster has been properly configured and all the daemons are running without any issues.

Log in from the Hadoop cluster administrator machine to the cluster master node using the following command:

ssh hduser@master

In this recipe, we assume all the configurations are making changes to the $HADOOP_HOME/conf/mapred-site.xml file.

How to do it...

Use the following steps to configure the sorting parameters:

1. Stop the MapReduce cluster with command:

   stop-mapred.sh

2. Configure the buffer size, in megabytes, for sorting by changing the property:

   ```
   <property>
     <name>io.sort.mb</name>
     <value>100</value>
   </property>
   ```

To minimize seeks, we typically assign 1 MB for each merge stream.

3. Configure the merge factor by changing the following property:

```
<property>
  <name>io.sort.factor</name>
  <value>100</value>
</property>
```

 This property configures the number of data streams to merge when sorting files. It determines the number of opening file handles. The default value of this property is 10.

4. Change the percentage of buffer dedicated for record collection by changing the following property:

```
<property>
  <name>io.sort.record.percent</name>
  <value>0.05</value>
</property>
```

 This property configures the percentage of memory used for record boundary tracking. The maximum number of records collected before the collection thread must block is equal to `io.sort.record.percent * io.sort.mb / 4`.

5. Change the spill factor for buffers by changing the following property:

```
<property>
  <name>io.sort.spill.percent</name>
  <value>0.8</value>
</property>
```

 This property enforces a soft limit on the in-memory buffer used for sorting or recording the collection. A background thread will start to spill data to disk if the limit is reached. This value should be no smaller than 0.5.

6. Configure the in-memory merge threshold by changing the following property:

```
<property>
  <name>mapred.inmem.merge.threshold</name>
  <value>1000</value>
</property>
```

This property configures a threshold with regard to the number of files for the in-memory merge process. When the threshold number of files has been accumulated, the merge process will start and results will be spilled to the disk. If the value of this property is set to equal or less than zero, there will be no threshold and the merge process will only be triggered by the memory consumption for data processing.

The default value for this property is 1000.

7. Configure the percentage of memory to be allocated from the maximum heap size to storing map outputs during the shuffle by changing the following property:

```
<property>
  <name>mapred.job.shuffle.input.buffer.percent</name>
  <value>0.70</value>
</property>
```

This property configures the percentage, in terms of the maximum heap size, of memory used to store map outputs during the shuffle phase.

8. Configure the threshold to start the in-memory merge by changing the following property:

```
<property>
  <name>mapred.job.shuffle.merge.percent</name>
  <value>0.66</value>
</property>
```

This property configures the in-memory merge threshold. The percentage is set with regard to the memory allocated for map outputs during the shuffle phase defined by the mapred.job.shuffle.input.buffer. percent property.

The default value of this property is 0.66, or approximately two thirds of the memory.

9. Configure the percentage of memory to retain map outputs during the reduce phase by changing the following property:

```
<property>
  <name>mapred.job.reduce.input.buffer.percent</name>
  <value>0.0</value>
</property>
```

This property configures a percentage threshold, in terms of the maximum heap size, of memory used to store map outputs during the reduce phase. To begin the reduce phase, the memory used by the map output should be less than the configured threshold.

The default value for this property is 0.0, which means no map output memory consumption threshold is needed to start the reduce phase.

10. Configure the maximum retries in case of fetch failures by changing the following property:

```
<property>
  <name>mapreduce.reduce.shuffle.maxfetchfailures</name>
  <value>10</value>
</property>
```

This property configures the maximum number of reducer retries to fetch map outputs in case of fetch failure.

11. Sync the configuration from the master node to all the slave nodes in the cluster with the following command:

```
for host in 'cat $HADOOP_HOME/conf/slaves'; do
  echo 'Copying mapred-site.xml file to host: ' $host
  scp $HADOOP_HOME/conf/mapred-site.xml $host:$HADOOP_HOME/conf/
done
```

12. Restart the MapReduce cluster with the following command:

```
start-mapred.sh
```

How it works...

The following table shows the description of the properties and their default values:

Property	Default
io.sort.mb	100
io.sort.factor	10
io.sort.record.percent	0.05
io.sort.spill.percent	0.80
mapred.inmem.merge.threshold	1000

Property	Default
mapred.job.shuffle.merge.percent	0.66
mapred.job.shuffle.input.buffer.percent	0.70
mapred.job.reduce.input.buffer.percent	0.0
mapreduce.reduce.shuffle.maxfetchfailures	10

See also

▸ The *Configuring memory for a Hadoop cluster* recipe

▸ The *Setting proper number of parallel copies* recipe

Configuring memory for a Hadoop cluster

Hadoop has a few memory configuration properties. Their values should be set according to the configurations of the cluster. In this recipe, we will outline steps to configure these memory properties.

Getting ready

We assume that the Hadoop cluster has been properly configured and all the daemons are running without any issues.

Log in from the Hadoop cluster administrator machine to the cluster master node using the following command:

`ssh hduser@master`

 In this recipe, we assume all the configurations are making changes to the $HADOOP_HOME/conf/mapred-site.xml file.

How to do it...

We can use the following steps to configure memory properties for a Hadoop cluster:

1. Stop the MapReduce cluster with the following command:

   `stop-mapred.sh`

2. Configure the virtual memory size, in megabytes, for a map task used by a scheduler by changing the following property:

```
<property>
    <name>mapred.cluster.map.memory.mb</name>
    <value>200</value>
</property>
```

 This property configures the memory size, in terms of the virtual memory, used by the scheduler for a map slot. The default value of this property is -1, which disables this property.

3. Similarly, we can configure the virtual memory size, in megabytes, for a reduce task used by a scheduler by changing the following property:

```
<property>
    <name>mapred.cluster.reduce.memory.mb</name>
    <value>512</value>
</property>
```

4. Configure the maximum virtual memory size for a map task used by a scheduler by changing the following property:

```
<property>
    <name>mapred.cluster.max.map.memory.mb</name>
    <value>512</value>
</property>
```

 This property is similar to the `mapred.cluster.map.memory.mb` property, although it configures the maximum memory size.

5. Configure the maximum virtual memory size for a reduce task used by a scheduler by changing the following property:

```
<property>
    <name>mapred.cluster.max.reduce.memory.mb</name>
    <value>512</value>
</property>
```

6. Configure the maximum virtual memory size for a single map task for the job used by a scheduler by changing the following property:

```
<property>
    <name>mapred.job.map.memory.mb</name>
    <value>0.8</value>
</property>
```

 The default value for this task is `-1`, which ignores this property.

7. Configure the maximum virtual memory size for a single reduce task for the job used by a scheduler by changing the following property:

```
<property>
  <name>mapred.job.reduce.memory.mb</name>
  <value>0.8</value>
</property>
```

8. Sync the configuration from the master node to all the slave nodes in the cluster with the following command:

```
for host in 'cat $HADOOP_HOME/conf/slaves'
do
  echo 'Copying mapred-site.xml file to host: ' $host
  scp $HADOOP_HOME/conf/mapred-site.xml $host:$HADOOP_HOME/conf/
done
```

9. Start the Hadoop cluster with the following command:

```
start-mapred.sh
```

How it works...

The following table lists the properties with their descriptions:

Property	Default	Description
mapred.cluster.map.memory.mb	-1	Feature unused
mapred.cluster.reduce.memory.mb	-1	Feature unused
mapred.cluster.max.map.memory.mb	-1	Feature unused
mapred.cluster.max.reduce.memory.mb	-1	Feature unused
mapred.job.map.memory.mb	-1	Feature unused
mapred.job.reduce.memory.mb	-1	Feature unused

See also

- ▶ The *Setting proper number of map and reduce slots for the TaskTracker* recipe
- ▶ The *Tuning shuffle, merge, and sort parameters* recipe

Setting proper number of parallel copies

When all or part of the map tasks finish, map outputs will be copied from the map task nodes to the reduce task nodes. The parallel copying strategy is used to increase the transfer throughput. By tuning this property, we can boost the performance of our Hadoop cluster. In this recipe, we will outline steps to configure the number of multiple copies for transferring map outputs to reducers.

Getting ready

We assume that the Hadoop cluster has been properly configured and all the daemons are running without any issues.

Log in from the Hadoop cluster administrator machine to the cluster master node using the following command:

```
ssh hduser@master
```

 In this recipe, we assume all the configurations are making changes to the $HADOOP_HOME/conf/mapred-site.xml file.

How to do it...

Use the following recipe to configure the number of parallel copies:

1. Stop the MapReduce cluster with the following command:

   ```
   stop-mapred.sh
   ```

2. Add or change, if it already exists, the following property:

   ```
   <property>
     <name>mapred.reduce.parallel.copies</name>
     <value>20</value>
   </property>
   ```

This configuration changes the number of parallel copies to 20 from the default value 10.

3. Sync the configuration to all the nodes in the cluster with the following command:

```
for host in 'cat $HADOOP_HOME/conf/slaves'; do
    echo 'Copying mapred-site.xml file to host: ' $host
    scp $HADOOP_HOME/conf/mapred-site.xml $host:$HADOOP_HOME/conf/
done
```

4. Restart the Hadoop cluster with the following command:

```
start-mapred.sh
```

See also

▶ The *Tuning the TaskTracker configuration* recipe
▶ The *Tuning shuffle, merge, and sort parameters* recipe

Tuning JVM parameters

Configuring JVM properties plays a very important role in the performance tuning of a Hadoop cluster. In this recipe, we will outline steps to configure the JVM.

Getting ready

We assume that the Hadoop cluster has been properly configured and all the daemons are running without any issues.

Log in from the Hadoop cluster administrator machine to the cluster master node using the following command:

```
ssh hduser@master
```

How to do it...

Use the following steps to configure JVM parameters:

1. Stop the Hadoop cluster with the following command:

```
stop-all.sh
```

2. Open the `$HADOOP_HOME/conf/mapred-site.xml` file and add or change, if it already exists, the following property:

```
<property>
  <name>mapred.child.java.opts</name>
  <value>-Xmx512M</value>
</property>
```

> This property configures the JVM options for TaskTracker child processes, which, by default, will have the same options as the TaskTracker.
>
> Alternatively, we can separately configure the JVM options for the map and reduce processes by changing the `mapred.map.child.java.opts` and `mapred.reduce.child.java.opts` properties.

3. Copy the configuration from the master node to all the slave nodes in the cluster with the following command:

```
for host in 'cat $HADOOP_HOME/conf/slaves'; do
  echo 'Copying mapred-site.xml file to host: ' $host
  scp $HADOOP_HOME/conf/mapred-site.xml $host:$HADOOP_HOME/conf/
done
```

4. Start the MapReduce cluster with the following command:

```
start-all.sh
```

See also

▸ The *Configuring JVM Reuse* recipe

Configuring JVM Reuse

MapReduce tasks are executed by JVM processes/threads, which are forked by the TaskTracker. The creation of a JVM, which includes the initialization of execution environments, is costly, especially when the number of tasks is large. In the default configuration, the number of JVMs needed to finish a job should be equal to the number of the tasks. In other words, the default setting uses one JVM to execute one task. When the execution of a task completes, its JVM will be killed by the TaskTracker.

JVM Reuse is an optimization of reusing JVMs for multiple tasks. If it is enabled, multiple tasks can be executed sequentially with one JVM.

In this recipe we will outline the steps to configure JVM Reuse.

Getting ready

We assume that the Hadoop cluster has been properly configured and all the daemons are running without any issues.

Log in from the Hadoop cluster administrator machine to the cluster master node using the following command:

```
ssh hduser@master
```

How to do it...

Use the following recipe to configure JVM Reuse:

1. Stop the MapReduce cluster with the following command:

   ```
   stop-mapred.sh
   ```

2. Open the `$HADOOP_HOME/conf/mapred-site.xml` file and add or change, if it already exists, the following property:

   ```
   <property>
     <name>mapred.job.reuse.jvm.num.tasks</name>
     <value>2</value>
   </property>
   ```

 This property configures one JVM to run two tasks. The default value of this property is 1, which disables JVM Reuse. If this property is set to -1, the number of tasks a JVM can execute is unlimited.

3. Sync the configuration file to all the slave nodes with the following command:

   ```
   for host in 'cat $HADOOP_HOME/conf/slaves'; do
     echo 'Copying mapred-site.xml file to host: ' $host
     scp $HADOOP_HOME/conf/mapred-site.xml $host:$HADOOP_HOME/conf/
   done
   ```

4. Start the Hadoop cluster with the following command:

   ```
   start-mapred.sh
   ```

See also

▸ The *Tuning JVM parameters* recipe

Configuring the reducer initialization time

Reduce tasks can be started when a certain percentage of map tasks has been finished. By setting this property with a smaller number, the reduce tasks will start earlier, occupying the computing slots. On the other hand, if the number is set too large, for example, very close to 1, the reduce tasks will have to wait for the majority of the map tasks to finish, prolonging the job execution time. In this recipe, we will outline steps to configure reducer initialization.

Getting ready

We assume that the Hadoop cluster has been properly configured and all the daemons are running without any issues.

Log in from the Hadoop cluster administrator machine to the cluster master node using the following command:

```
ssh hduser@master
```

How to do it...

Use the following recipe to configure reducer initialization time:

1. Stop the MapReduce cluster with the following command:

    ```
    stop-mapred.sh
    ```

2. Open the `$HADOOP_HOME/conf/mapred-site.xml` file and add or change, if it already exists, the following property:

    ```
    <property>
      <name>mapred.reduce.slowstart.completed.maps</name>
      <value>0.05</value>
    </property>
    ```

3. Sync the configuration file to all the slave nodes with the following command:

    ```
    for host in 'cat $HADOOP_HOME/conf/slaves'; do
      echo 'Copying mapred-site.xml file to host: ' $host
      scp $HADOOP_HOME/conf/mapred-site.xml $host:$HADOOP_HOME/conf/
    done
    ```

4. Restart the MapReduce cluster with the following command:

    ```
    start-mapred.sh
    ```

See also

- ▶ The *Tuning the TaskTracker configuration* recipe
- ▶ The *Configuring speculative execution* recipe

8
Building a Hadoop Cluster with Amazon EC2 and S3

In this chapter, we will cover:

- ▸ Registering with Amazon Web Services (AWS)
- ▸ Managing AWS security credentials
- ▸ Preparing a local machine for EC2 connection
- ▸ Creating an Amazon Machine Image (AMI)
- ▸ Using S3 to host data
- ▸ Configuring a Hadoop cluster with the new AMI

Introduction

Amazon **Elastic Cloud Computing (EC2)** and **Simple Storage Service (S3)** are cloud computing web services provided by Amazon Web Services(AWS). EC2 offers **platform as a service (PaaS)**, with which we can start up theoretically an unlimited number of servers on the cloud. S3 offers storage services on the cloud. More information about AWS, EC2, and S3 can be obtained from `aws.amazon.com`.

From the previous chapters of this book, we know that the configuration of a Hadoop cluster requires a big amount of hardware investment. For example, to set up a Hadoop cluster, a number of computing nodes and networking devices are required. Comparatively, with the help of AWS cloud computing, especially EC2, we can set up a Hadoop cluster with minimum cost and much less efforts.

In this chapter, we are going to discuss topics of configuring a Hadoop cluster in the Amazon cloud. We will guide you through the recipes of registering with AWS, creating **Amazon Machine Image** (**AMI**), configuring a Hadoop cluster with the new AMI, and so on.

Registering with Amazon Web Services (AWS)

To use AWS, **registration** is required. The steps to register with AWS are straightforward. In this recipe, we will outline steps to do this.

Getting ready

We assume to use a GUI web browser for AWS registration. So, we are assuming you already have a web browser with Internet access. In addition, personal information needs to be prepared to fill the online registration forms.

How to do it...

We will use the following steps to register with AWS:

1. Use a web browser to open the following link: `http://aws.amazon.com/`.

2. Click on the **Sign Up** button on the upper-right corner of the window.

   You will be directed to a web page as shown in the following screenshot:

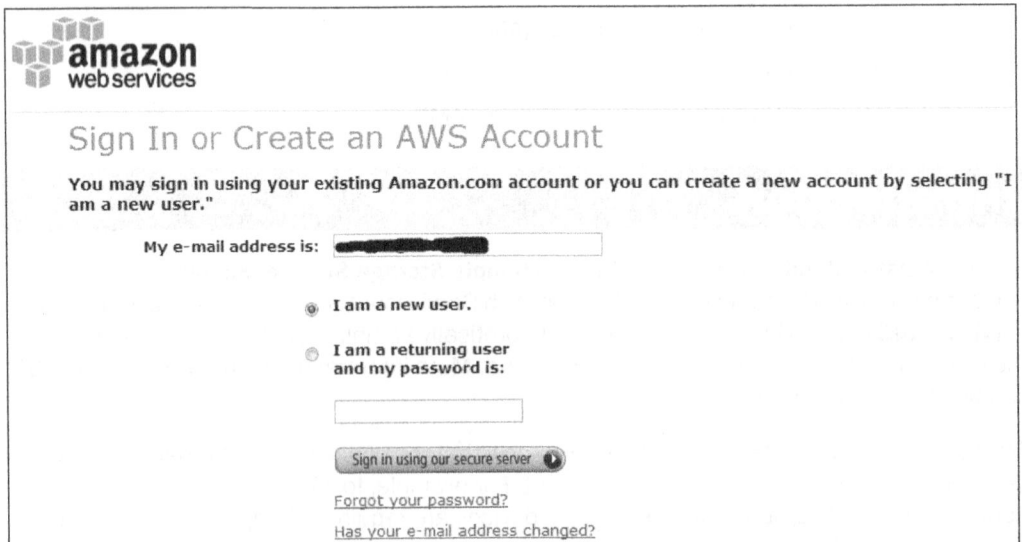

3. Fill in the e-mail address in the text field with the label **My e-mail address is:**, and select the **I am a new user** radio button as shown in the previous screenshot.

4. Click on the **Sign in using our secure server** button at the bottom as shown in the previous screenshot.

5. Fill the **Login Credentials** form, which includes name, e-mail, and password as shown in the following screenshot:

Login Credentials

Use the form below to create login credentials that can be used for AWS as well as Amazon.com.

My name is:

My e-mail address is:

Type it again:

note: this is the e-mail address that we will use to contact you about your account

Enter a new password:

Type it again:

Continue ▶

6. Click on the **Continue** button at the bottom as shown in the previous screenshot.

7. Fill in the **Contact Information**, **Security Check**, and **AWS Customer Agreement** form as shown in the following screenshot:

Contact Information

* required fields

Full Name*:

Company Name:

Country*: United States

Address Line 1*:
Street address, P.O. box, company name, c/o

Address Line 2:
Apartment, suite, unit, building, floor, etc.

City*:

State, Province or Region*:

ZIP or Postal Code*:

Phone number*:

Security Check

Image:

Try a different image

Why do we ask you to type these characters?

Type the characters in the above image*:
Having Trouble? Contact us.

AWS Customer Agreement

☐ **Check here to indicate that you have read and agree to the terms of the Amazon Web Services Customer Agreement.**

Create Account and Continue ▶

8. Click on the **Create Account and Continue** button at the bottom as shown in the previous screenshot.

9. So far, an AWS account has been created. Now we can log in to AWS with the newly created account by using the **I am a returning user and my password is:** option as shown in the following screenshot:

10. By clicking on the **Sign in using our secure server** button at the bottom of the window, we will be able to log in to the AWS management console page with EC2 and S3 service available as shown in the following screenshot:

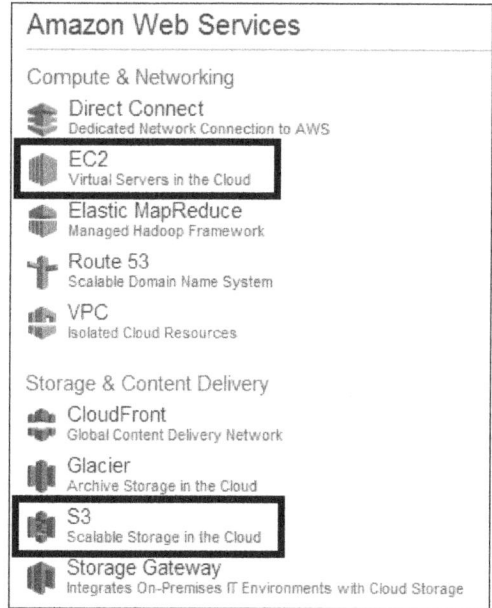

We have finished the registration step successfully.

See also

▶ Refer to `http://docs.aws.amazon.com/AWSEC2/latest/UserGuide/EC2_GetStarted.html?r=1874`

Managing AWS security credentials

Security credentials are critical for web services such as EC2 and S3. They are used for remote access of the cloud servers on AWS. For example, in this chapter, we will use these credentials to log in to the servers remotely from a client machine.

AWS provides a web interface to manage security credentials. This recipe will guide you through the steps to create, download, and manage these security credentials.

Getting ready

Before getting started, we assume that you have successfully registered with AWS; otherwise, you need to follow the steps in the previous recipe to register with AWS.

We also assume that we have a client machine with Linux (such as CentOS) installed. The machine should be able to access the Internet and has at least one GUI web browser installed.

Create a directory for storing AWS credentials using the following command:

```
mkdir -v ~/.ec2
```

How to do it...

Use the following steps to manage AWS security credentials:

1. Open a web browser and go to the URL `aws.amazon.com`.
2. Click on the **My Account / Console** drop-down button on the upper-left of the window as shown in the following screenshot:

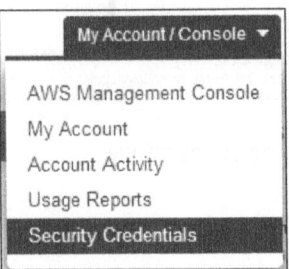

3. Click on the **Security Credentials** option in the drop-down list as shown in the previous screenshot.

   If you have logged in to AWS previously, you will be able to visit the **Security Credentials Management** page. Otherwise, a login window will appear. You need to type in the username and password and log in using the **I am a returning user and my password is:** option.

   Currently, Amazon AWS has a few types of credentials as shown in the following screenshot:

   ↓ **Access Credentials:** Your Access Keys, X.509 Certificates, and Key Pairs
   ↓ **Sign-In Credentials:** Your E-mail Address, Password, and AWS Multi-Factor Authentication Device
   ↓ **Account Identifiers:** Your AWS Account ID and Canonical User ID

4. **Access Credentials** include **Access Keys**, **X.509 Certificates**, and **Key Pairs** as shown in the following screenshot:

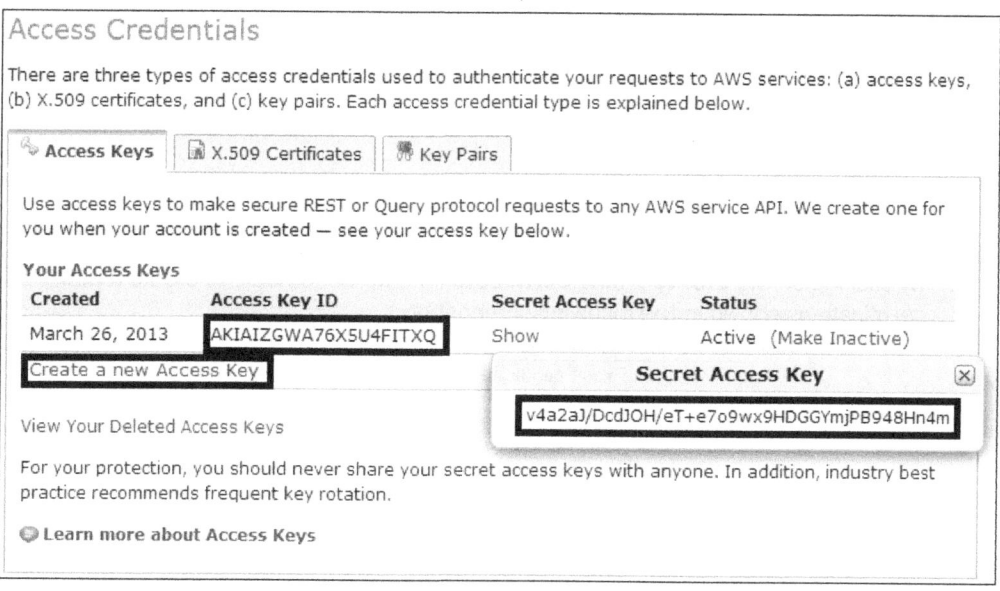

5. By clicking on the **Make Inactive** link on the status column of the access keys table, we can make the access keys inactive. Inactive access keys can be made active again and can be deleted from the list.

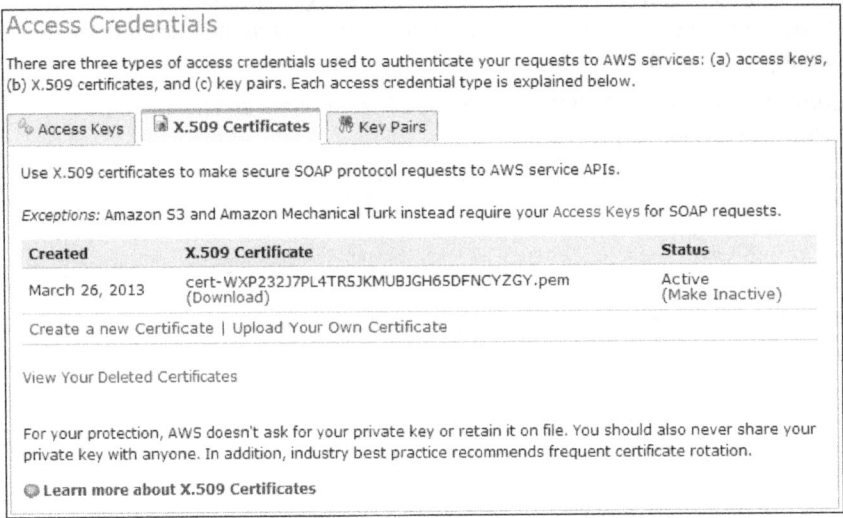

Similarly, we can make an X.509 certificate inactive as seen in the preceding screenshot. Inactive certificates can be made active again or deleted from the list.

6. By clicking on the **Create a new Certificate** link, we will be able to create a new certificate as shown in the following screenshot:

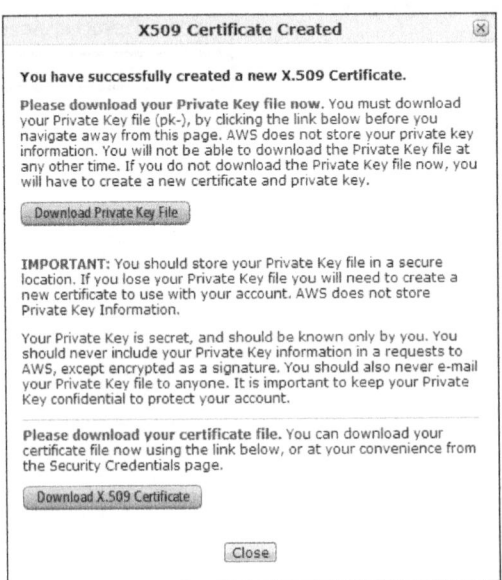

We need to download the private key file as well as the X.509 certificate by clicking on the buttons as shown in the previous screenshot. These files should be kept secured and never shared with any other person.

7. Key pairs used for EC2 can be managed from the management console as shown in the following screenshot:

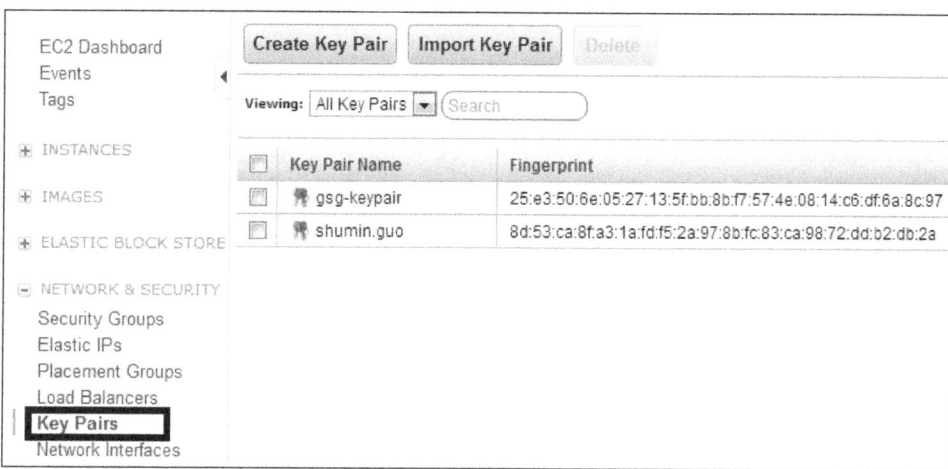

New key pairs can be created by clicking on the **Create Key Pair** button at the top of the window. A pop-up window will be used to type in the name of the key pair. And, the newly created key pair will be downloaded to the local machine.

8. Use the following command to copy the downloaded key pair to the `.ec2` folder:

```
cp *.pem ~/.ec2/
```

How it works...

The following table shows the usage of each security credential:

Security credential		Used for
Access Credentials	Access Keys	Secure REST or query request access to AWS service APIs.
	X.509 Certificates	Make SOAP protocol requests to AWS service APIs.
	Key Pairs	Launch and securely access EC2 instances.
Sign-In Credentials		Log in to AWS from the web portal.
Account Identifiers		Share resources between accounts.

Preparing a local machine for EC2 connection

A local client machine is required for accessing EC2. For example, we can use the local client machine to launch EC2 instances, log in to the instances on EC2, and so on. In this recipe we will list steps to configure a local machine for EC2 connection.

Getting ready

Before getting started, we assume that we have registered with AWS and security credentials have been created. We also assume that a machine with Linux has been installed.

How to do it...

Use the following steps to configure a local machine for EC2 remote access:

1. Get the **Access Key ID** and the **Secret Access Key** from the security credentials web page as shown in the following screenshot:

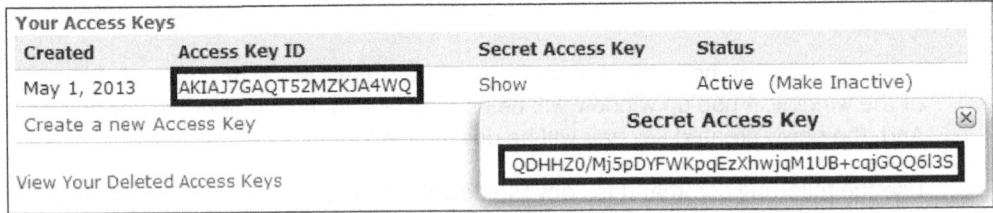

2. Move the key pair to the `.ec2` directory using the following command:

    ```
    mv <key-pair-name>.pem ~/.ec2/
    ```

3. Move the private key file to the `.ec2` directory using the following command:

    ```
    mv pk-*.pem ~/.ec2/
    ```

4. Move the certificate file to the `.ec2` directory using the following command:

    ```
    mv cert-*.pem ~/.ec2/
    ```

    Download EC2 command-line tools from the URL `http://aws.amazon.com/developertools/351`.

5. Decompress the ZIP file using the following command:

    ```
    unzip ec2-ami-tools.zip
    ```

6. Add the following content into the file `~/.profile`:

```
export EC2_HOME=~/ec2/

export AWS_ACCOUNT_ID=example@mail.com

export EC2_PRIVATE_KEY=~/.ec2/pk-WXP232J7PL4TR5JKMUBJGH65DFNCYZGY.pem

export EC2_CERT=~/.ec2/cert-WXP232J7PL4TR5JKMUBJGH65DFNCYZGY.pem

export AWS_ACCESS_KEY_ID=AKIAJ7GAQT52MZKJA4WQ

export AWS_SECRET_ACCESS_KEY=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

export PATH=$PATH:$EC2_HOME/bin
```

7. Add the following content into the file `~/.bashrc`:

```
. ~/.profile
```

8. Test the configuration using the following command:

```
ec2-describe-images
```

   If the configuration has no problem, we will get a list of AMIs; otherwise, we will get an error message similar to the following:

```
Client.AuthFailure: AWS was not able to validate the provided
access credentials
```

Creating an Amazon Machine Image (AMI)

Amazon Machine Image (**AMI**) is the machine image used by EC2. An AMI is a template that contains configuration for operating systems and software packages. We can start EC2 instances from preexisting or personalized AMIs. AWS offers a large number of public AMIs that can be used for free.

Generally, there are two types of AMIs one is EBS-backed AMI (Elastic Block Storage-backed AMI) and the other is instance store-backed AMI. In this recipe, we will first outline steps to create an instance store-backed AMI and briefly introduce how to create an EBS-backed AMI.

Getting ready

Before getting started, we assume that you have successfully registered with AWS.
And, we also assume that a client machine has been configured properly to connect to AWS.

Log in to the local machine and install the

`MAKEDEV` utility using the following command:

```
sudo yum install -y MAKEDEV
```

Install the Amazon AMI tools using the following command:

```
sudo rpm -ivh  http://s3.amazonaws.com/ec2-downloads/ec2-ami-tools.
noarch.rpm
Retrieving http://s3.amazonaws.com/ec2-downloads/ec2-ami-tools.noarch.rpm
Preparing...              ################################### [100%]
   1:ec2-ami-tools         ################################### [100%]
```

How to do it...

Use the following steps to create an instance store-backed AMI:

1. Create an image file using the following command:

    ```
    dd if=/dev/zero of=centos.img bs=1M count=1024
    ```

    This command will emit the following message:

    ```
    1024+0 records in
    1024+0 records out
    1073741824 bytes (1.1 GB) copied, 10.5981 s, 101 MB/s
    ```

    In this command, `if` specifies the input of the data, `/dev/zero` is a special device on Linux systems, `of` specifies the output of the command, where we specify a filename as the image name, `bs` specifies the size of the blocks, and `count` is the number of blocks for input to output. The size of the output file, `centos.img`, is determined by the block size and count. For example, the preceding command creates an image file of size 1M x 1024, which is around 1.0 GB.

2. Check the size of the image file using the following command:

    ```
    ls -lh centos.img
    ```

    And the output will be:

    ```
    -rw-rw-r--. 1 shumin shumin 1.0G May  3 00:14 centos.img
    ```

3. Create a root filesystem inside the image file using the following command:

    ```
    mke2fs -F -j centos.img
    ```

    The output message will be similar to the following:

    ```
    mke2fs 1.42.3 (14-May-2012)
    Discarding device blocks: done
    ```

```
Filesystem label=
OS type: Linux
Block size=4096 (log=2)
Fragment size=4096 (log=2)
Stride=0 blocks, Stripe width=0 blocks
655360 inodes, 2621440 blocks
131072 blocks (5.00%) reserved for the super user
First data block=0
Maximum filesystem blocks=2684354560
80 block groups
32768 blocks per group, 32768 fragments per group
8192 inodes per group
Superblock backups stored on blocks:
        32768, 98304, 163840, 229376, 294912, 819200, 884736,
1605632
Allocating group tables: done
Writing inode tables: done
Creating journal (32768 blocks): done
Writing superblocks and filesystem accounting information: done
```

4. Create a directory under the /mnt directory using the following command:

```
sudo mkdir -v /mnt/centos
```

5. Mount the image file to the folder using the following command:

```
sudo mount -o loop centos.img /mnt/centos
```

6. Create the /dev directory under the root directory of the mounted filesystem using the following command:

```
sudo mkdir -v /mnt/centos/dev
```

7. Create a minimal set of devices using the following commands:

```
sudo /sbin/MAKEDEV -d /mnt/centos/dev -x console
sudo /sbin/MAKEDEV -d /mnt/centos/dev -x null
sudo /sbin/MAKEDEV -d /mnt/centos/dev -x zero
```

These commands will give us the following output:

```
MAKEDEV: mkdir: File exists
MAKEDEV: mkdir: File exists
MAKEDEV: mkdir: File exists
```

The reason for these warning messages is because the parent directories already exist. When the MAKEDEV command tries to create the folder with the mkdir command, it will fail and display this warning message.

8. Create the fstab configuration file using the following command:

   ```
   sudo mkdir -pv /etc/fstab
   ```

9. Put the following content into the file:

   ```
   /dev/sda1   /                   ext3    defaults            1 1
   none        /dev/pts    devpts  gid=5,mode=620      0 0
   none        /dev/shm    tmpfs   defaults            0 0
   none        /proc       proc    defaults            0 0
   none        /sys        sysfs   defaults            0 0
   ```

10. Create the proc folder under the root filesystem of the image file using the following command:

    ```
    sudo mkdir -pv /mnt/centos/proc
    ```

11. Mount a proc filesystem to the /mnt/centos/proc directory using the following command:

    ```
    sudo mount -t proc none /mnt/centos/proc
    ```

12. Create the CentOS yum repository file, /etc/yum.repos.d/centos.repo, using the following content:

    ```
    [centos]

    name=centos

    #mirrorlist=http://mirrorlist.centos.org/?release=$releasever&arch
    =$basearch&repo=os

    #baseurl=http://mirror.centos.org/centos/$releasever/os/$basearch/

    baseurl=http://mirror.centos.org/centos-6/6.4/os/x86_64/

    gpgkey=http://mirror.centos.org/centos-6/6.4/os/x86_64/RPM-GPG-
    KEY-CentOS-6

    gpgcheck=1

    protect=1
    ```

13. Install the latest CentOS 6.3 operating system using the following command:

    ```
    sudo yum --disablerepo=* --enablerepo=centos   --installroot=/mnt/
    centos -y groupinstall Base
    ```

    The --disablerepo option disables all the available repositories, and the--enablerepo option enables only the CentOS repository specified in the previous step.

This command will start the installation of CentOS 6.3 on the mounted directory, which will take a while depending on the network speed and host system hardware configurations.

14. When the installation is complete, we can verify the installation using the following command:

```
ls -lh /mnt/centos/
```

The directory structure of the installed operating system should be the same as the directory structure of a regularly installed Linux. For example, the output will be similar to the following:

```
total 108K
dr-xr-xr-x.  2 root root 4.0K May  3 01:12 bin
dr-xr-xr-x.  3 root root 4.0K May  3 01:13 boot
drwxr-xr-x.  2 root root 4.0K Sep 23  2011 dev
drwxr-xr-x. 73 root root 4.0K May  3 02:00 etc
drwxr-xr-x.  2 root root 4.0K Sep 23  2011 home
dr-xr-xr-x. 10 root root 4.0K May  3 01:12 lib
dr-xr-xr-x.  9 root root  12K May  3 01:11 lib64
drwx------.  2 root root  16K May  3 00:17 lost+found
drwxr-xr-x.  2 root root 4.0K Sep 23  2011 media
drwxr-xr-x.  2 root root 4.0K Sep 23  2011 mnt
drwxr-xr-x.  3 root root 4.0K May  3 01:12 opt
dr-xr-xr-x.  2 root root 4.0K Sep 23  2011 proc
dr-xr-x---.  2 root root 4.0K Sep 23  2011 root
dr-xr-xr-x.  2 root root  12K May  3 01:12 sbin
drwxr-xr-x.  2 root root 4.0K Sep 23  2011 selinux
drwxr-xr-x.  2 root root 4.0K Sep 23  2011 srv
drwxr-xr-x.  2 root root 4.0K Sep 23  2011 sys
drwxrwxrwt.  2 root root 4.0K May  3 01:13 tmp
drwxr-xr-x. 13 root root 4.0K May  3 01:02 usr
drwxr-xr-x. 19 root root 4.0K May  3 01:12 var
```

We will configure the system with the following steps:

1. Create the network adapter configuration file, /mnt/centos/etc/sysconfig/network-scripts/ifcfg-eth0, using the following content:
   ```
   DEVICE=eth0
   BOOTPROTO=dhcp
   ```

```
ONBOOT=yes
TYPE=Ethernet
USERCTL=yes
PEERDNS=yes
IPV6INIT=no
```

In this configuration, BOOTPROTO specifies to use DHCP IP address assignment.

2. Enable networking by adding or changing the NETWORKING option in the network configuration file /mnt/centos/etc/sysconfig/network:

    ```
    NETWORKING=yes
    ```

3. Add the following content into the file /mnt/centos/etc/fstab:

    ```
    /dev/sda2   /mnt      ext3      defaults          0  0
    /dev/sda3   swap      swap      defaults          0  0
    ```

    These two lines configure the mount points for the swap and root partitions.

4. Configure to start necessary services using the following commands:

    ```
    sudo chroot /mnt/centos /bin/sh
    chkconfig --level 345 network on
    exit
    ```

5. Unmount the image file using the following commands:

    ```
    sudo umount /mnt/centos/proc
    sudo umount -d /mnt/centos
    ```

6. Copy the private key and the X.509 certificate file into the instance using the following command:

    ```
    scp -i shumin.guo ~/.ec2/pk-*pem ~/.ec2/cert-*pem root@ec2-58-214-
    29-104.compute-1.amazonaws.com:~/.ec2/
    ```

7. Log in to the instance using the following command:

    ```
    ssh -i ~/.ec2/shumin.guo.pem root@ec2-58-214-29-104.compute-1.
    amazonaws.com
    ```

    In this command, ec2-58-214-29-104.compute-1.amazonaws.com is the public domain name of the instance.

8. Configure password-less login with the following commands:

    ```
    ssh-keygen
    mkdir -v /mnt/centos/root/.ssh
    sudo cp ~/.ssh/id_* /mnt/centos/root/.ssh
    ```

When you are prompted to enter the paraphrase, leave it empty by pressing the *Enter* key.

9. Copy the public key to the `authorized_keys` file using the following command:

```
cat /mnt/centos/root/.ssh/id_rsa.pub >> /mnt/centos/root/.ssh/
authorized_keys
```

10. Copy the local Java installation file to the image folder using the following command:

```
sudo cp -r /usr/java/mnt/centos/usr
```

11. Download the latest Hadoop distribution from the official mirror website `http://www.apache.org/dyn/closer.cgi/hadoop/common/`.

12. Use the following command to decompress the Hadoop package and create the symbolic link:

```
sudo tar xvf hadoop-*.tar.gz -C /mnt/centos/usr/local/
sudo ln -s /mnt/centos/usr/local/hadoop-* /mnt/centos/usr/
local/hadoop
```

13. Add the following environment variables to the file `.bashrc`:

```
export JAVA_HOME=/usr/java/latest
export HADOOP_HOME=/usr/local/hadoop
export PATH=$PATH:$HADOOP_HOME/bin
```

14. Add the following content into the file `$HADOOP_HOME/conf/core-site.xml`:

```
<configuration>
<property>
<name>fs.default.name</name>
<value>hdfs://localhost:54310</value>
</property>
<configuration>
```

15. Add the following content into the file `$HADOOP_HOME/conf/mapred-site.xml`:

```
<configuration>
<property>
<name>dfs.replication</name>
<value>2</value>
</property>

<property>
<name>dfs.data.dir</name>
<value>/hadoop/data/</value>
</property>
<property>
<name>hadoop.tmp.dir</name>
<value>/hadoop/tmp/hadoop-${user.name}/</value>
</property>
</configuration>
```

16. Add the following content into the file `$HAOOP_HOME/conf/hdfs-site.xml`:

```
<configuration>

<property>
<name>mapred.job.tracker</name>
<value>localhost:54311</value>
</property>

<property>
<name>mapred.system.dir</name>
<value>/hadoop/mapred</value>
</property>

</configuration>
```

17. Download and install the other ecosystem components using the steps outlined in the recipes in *Chapter 3, Configuring a Hadoop Cluster*.

We will use the following steps to bundle, upload, and register an AMI:

1. Bundle the loopback image file using the following command:

    ```
    ec2-bundle-image -i centos.img -k .ec2/pk-*.pem -c .ec2/cert-*.pem
    -u 123412341234
    ```

    Option `-i` specifies the image filename, `-k` specifies the private key file, `-c` specifies the certificate file, and `-u` specifies the user account number, which is a 12-digit numeric string.

    We can get the account number from the web user interface through the following URL: `https://portal.aws.amazon.com/gp/aws/manageYourAccount?`. The account number is on the upper-left of the window as shown in the following screenshot:

    The command will ask for the architecture of the image, and then it will bundle the image with the user's security credentials and split the bundled image file into smaller files.

The output message will be similar to the following:

```
Please specify a value for arch [x86_64]:
Bundling image file...
Splitting /tmp/centos.img.tar.gz.enc...
Created centos.img.part.00
Created centos.img.part.01
Created centos.img.part.02
Created centos.img.part.03
Created centos.img.part.04
Created centos.img.part.05
Created centos.img.part.06
Created centos.img.part.07
Created centos.img.part.08
Created centos.img.part.09
Created centos.img.part.10
...
Generating digests for each part...
Digests generated.
Creating bundle manifest...
ec2-bundle-image complete.
```

2. Create a bucket from the S3 web interface as shown in the following screenshot:

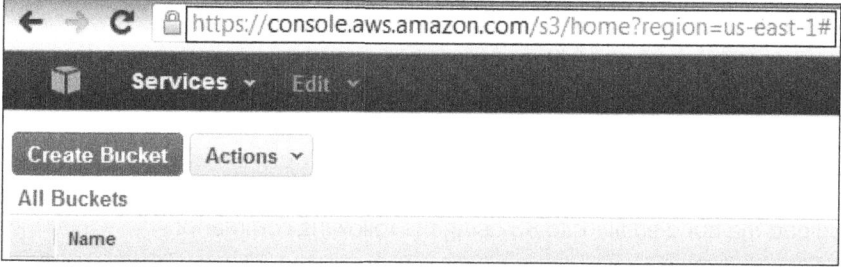

3. Type in the bucket name and select the region based on your location as shown in the following screenshot:

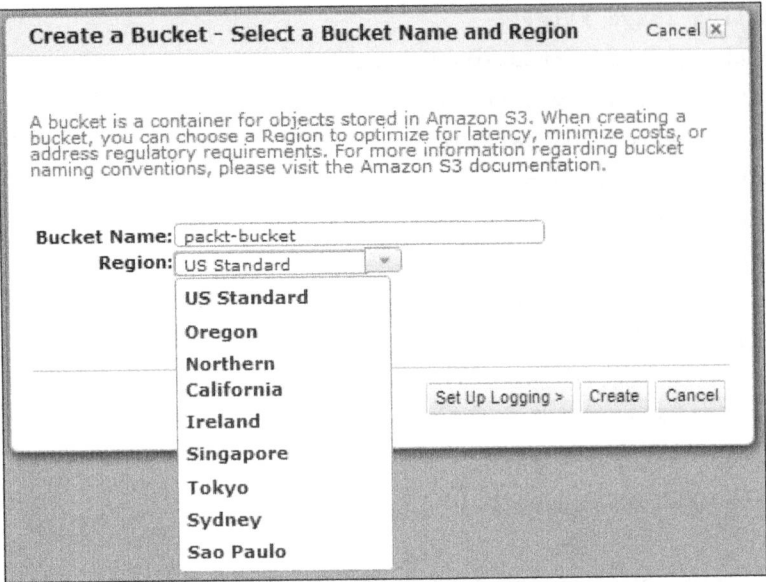

4. Click on the **Create Bucket** button and the bucket will be successfully created as shown in the following screenshot:

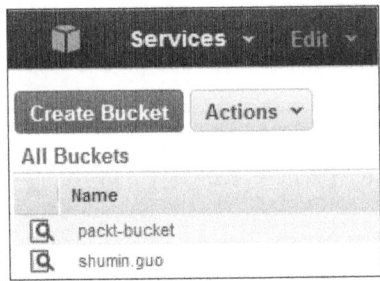

5. Upload the bundled file into S3 using the following command:

```
ec2-upload-bundle -b packt-bucket -m /tmp/centos.img.manifest.xml
-a AKIAJ7GAQT52MZKJA4WQ -s QDHHZO/Mj5pDYFWKpqEzXhwjqM1UB+cqjGQQ613S
```

This command will upload the bundled image parts to the specified bucket (`packt-bucket` in this case), which is specified with the `-b` option. The option `-m` specifies the location of the manifest file, the option `-a` specifies the access key, and `-s` specifies the secret key. Note that for security purposes, the manifest file will be encrypted with the public key before being uploaded.

The command will give output similar to the following:

```
Uploading bundled image parts to the S3 bucket packt-bucket ...
Uploaded centos.img.part.00
Uploaded centos.img.part.01
Uploaded centos.img.part.02
Uploaded centos.img.part.03
Uploaded centos.img.part.04
Uploaded centos.img.part.05
Uploaded centos.img.part.06
Uploaded centos.img.part.07
Uploaded centos.img.part.08
Uploaded centos.img.part.09
Uploaded centos.img.part.10
...
Uploading manifest ...
Uploaded manifest.
Bundle upload completed.
```

6. When the upload completes, we can check the content of the bucket by clicking on the bucket name. The bucket should now contain all the image parts as well as the manifest file as shown in the following screenshot:

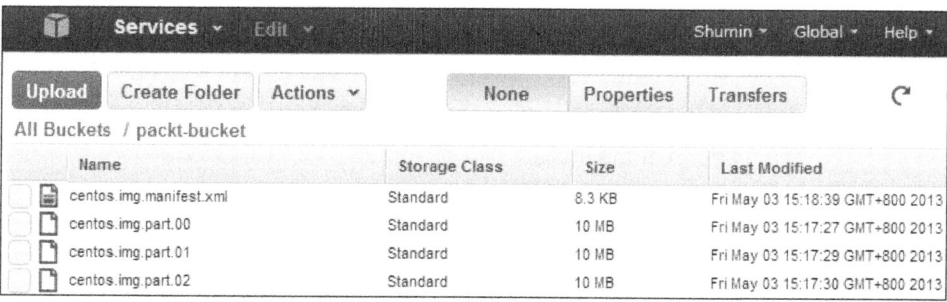

7. Register the AMI using the following command:

```
ec2-register packt-bucket/image.manifest.xml -n packt-centos-
6.4-x64 -O AKIAJ7GAQT52MZKJA4WQ -W QDHHZO/Mj5pDYFWKpqEzXhwjqM1UB+c
qjGQQ613S
```

The command will give us an ID for the newly registered AMI similar to the following:

```
IMAGE    ami-9f422ff6
```

The AMI registration step is required in order for EC2 to find the AMI and run instances with it. Note that once changes are made on the image part files stored on S3, re-registration is required in order for the changes to take effect.

8.   We can check the details of the new AMI using the following command:

```
ec2-describe-images ami-9f422ff6
```

The output will be similar to the following:

```
IMAGE    ami-9f422ff6    869345430376/packt-centos-6.4-x64
869345430376    available        private        x86_64    machine
instance-store  paravirtual      xen
```

The meaning of each column is:

   ❑   The IMAGE identifier
   ❑   The ID of the image
   ❑   The source of the image
   ❑   The ID of the image owner
   ❑   The status of the image
   ❑   The visibility of the image (public or private)
   ❑   The product codes, if any, that are attached to the instance
   ❑   The architecture of the image (i386 or x86_64)
   ❑   The image type (machine, kernel, or ramdisk)
   ❑   The ID of the kernel associated with the image (machine images only)
   ❑   The ID of the RAM disk associated with the image (machine images only)
   ❑   The platform of the image
   ❑   The type of root device (ebs or instance-store)
   ❑   The virtualization type (paravirtual or hvm)
   ❑   The Hypervisor type (xen or kvm)

9.   Once the registration is completed, we can start an instance with the new AMI using the following command:

```
ec2-run-instances ami-9f422ff6 -n 1 -k shumin.guo
```

This command specifies to run the instance with our new AMI, option -n specifies the number of instances to start, and option -k specifies the key pair to use for logging into these instances.

The output will be similar to the following:

```
RESERVATION       r-ca8919aa        869345430376    default

INSTANCE          i-0020e06c        ami-9f422ff6    pending shumin.
guo       0                 m1.small            2013-05-03T08:22:09+0000
us-east-1a                            monitoring-disabled
instance-store    paravirtual    xen                sg-7bb47b12
default false
```

The first line of the output is the reservation information, and the meanings of the columns are:

- ❑ The RESERVATION identifier
- ❑ The ID of the reservation
- ❑ The AWS account ID of the instance owner
- ❑ The name of each security group the instance is in

The second line shows the instance information, and the meanings of columns are:

- ❑ The INSTANCE identifier.
- ❑ The ID of the instance.
- ❑ The AMI ID of the image on which the instance is based.
- ❑ The public DNS name associated with the instance. This is only present for instances in the running state.
- ❑ The private DNS name associated with the instance. This is only present for instances in the running state.
- ❑ The state of the instance.
- ❑ The key name. If a key was associated with the instance at launch, its name will appear.
- ❑ The AMI launch index.
- ❑ The product codes associated with the instance.
- ❑ The instance type.
- ❑ The instance launch time.
- ❑ The availability zone.
- ❑ The ID of the kernel.
- ❑ The ID of the RAM disk.
- ❑ The platform (Windows or empty).
- ❑ The monitoring state.
- ❑ The public IP address.

❑ The private IP address.

❑ [EC2-VPC] The ID of the VPC.

❑ [EC2-VPC] The subnet ID.

❑ The type of root device (`ebs` or `instance-store`).

❑ The instance life cycle.

❑ The Spot Instance request ID.

❑ The instance license.

❑ The placement group the cluster instance is in.

❑ The virtualization type (`paravirtual` or `hvm`).

❑ The hypervisor type (`xen` or `kvm`).

❑ The client token.

❑ The ID of each security group the instance is in.

❑ The tenancy of the instance (`default` or `dedicated`).

❑ Whether or not the instance is EBS optimized (`true` or `false`).

❑ The **Amazon Resource Name** (**ARN**) of the **IAM** role.

The output message shows that the ID of the instance is `i-0020e06c`.

10. After waiting for a while, we can check the status of the instance using the following command:

```
ec2-describe-instances i-0020e06c
```

The output will be similar to the following:

```
RESERVATION       r-ca8919aa        869345430376     default

INSTANCE          i-0020e06c        ami-9f422ff6      ec2-54-224-240-
54.compute-1.amazonaws.com       ip-10-34-102-91.ec2.internal
running shumin.guo        0                 m1.small        2013-
05-03T08:22:09+0000       us-east-1a                 monitoring-
disabled      54.224.240.54     10.34.102.91
instance-store                               paravirtual
xen               sg-7bb47b12       default false
```

The instance status tells us that it is in the **running state**.

Alternatively, we can check the status of the instance from the web UI. For example, we can get the status of the instance similar to the following screenshot:

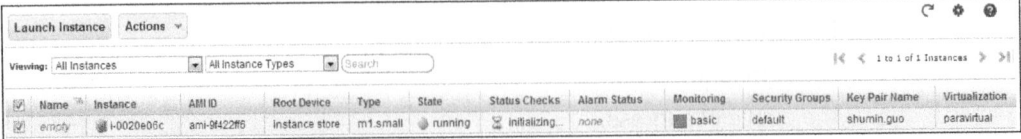

11. Log in to the instance using the following command:

```
ssh -i ~/.ec2/shumin.guo.pem root@ec2-54-224-240-54.compute-1.
amazonaws.com
```

In this command, `-i` specifies the key pair to use for login and `ec2-54-224-240-54.compute-1.amazonaws.com` is the public domain name of the EC2 instance.

There's more...

As we mentioned previously, there are other methods to create AMIs. One method is to create an AMI from an existing AMI. Another method is to create an EBS-backed AMI.

Creating an AMI from an existing AMI

This section lists steps to create an instance store-backed AMI from an existing AMI. We assume that you have registered with AWS and have successfully configured the security credentials in a local machine. We also assume that you have downloaded the key pair and saved it to the proper location.

In this section, we assume the private keys, certificates, and key pairs are all located in the `.ec2` folder.

1. Start an instance from an existing AMI. For example, we can start an instance with the new AMI created in the *Creating an Amazon Machine Image (AMI)* recipe using the following command:

    ```
    ec2-run-instances ami-9f422ff6 -n 1 -k shumin.guo
    ```

    This command will start up one instance from the new AMI. The key pair `shumin.guo` is used to log in to the instance remotely.

2. Copy the private key and X.509 certificate into the instance using the following command:

    ```
    scp -i shumin.guo ~/.ec2/pk-*pem ~/.ec2/cert-*pem root@ec2-58-214-29-104.compute-1.amazonaws.com:~/.ec2/
    ```

3. Log in to the instance using the following command:

    ```
    ssh -i ~/.ec2/shumin.guo.pem root@ec2-58-214-29-104.compute-1.
    amazonaws.com
    ```

4. Configure password-less login with the following command:

    ```
    ssh-keygen
    ```

5. You will be prompted to enter the paraphrase; leave it empty by pressing the *Enter* key.

    ```
    ssh-copy-id localhost
    ```

6. Download and install Java following the steps outlined in the *Installing Java and other tools* recipe of *Chapter 2, Preparing for Hadoop Installation*.

7. Download the latest Hadoop distribution from `http://www.apache.org/dyn/closer.cgi/hadoop/common/`.

8. Use the following command to decompress the Hadoop package and create the symbolic link:

```
tar xvf hadoop-*.tar.gz -C /usr/local/
ln -s /usr/local/hadoop-* /usr/local/hadoop
```

9. Add the following environment variables to file `.bashrc`:

```
export JAVA_HOME=/usr/java/latest
export HADOOP_HOME=/usr/local/hadoop
export PATH=$PATH:$HADOOP_HOME/bin
```

10. Add the following content into the file `$HADOOP_HOME/conf/core-site.xml`:

```
<configuration>
<property>
<name>fs.default.name</name>
<value>hdfs://localhost:54310</value>
</property>
<configuration>
```

11. Add the following content into the file `$HADOOP_HOME/conf/mapred-site.xml`:

```
<configuration>
<property>
<name>dfs.replication</name>
<value>2</value>
</property>

<property>
<name>dfs.data.dir</name>
<value>/hadoop/data/</value>
</property>

<property>
<name>hadoop.tmp.dir</name>
<value>/hadoop/tmp/hadoop-${user.name}/</value>
</property>

</configuration>
```

12. Add the following content into the file `$HAOOP_HOME/conf/hdfs-site.xml`:

```
<configuration>

<property>
<name>mapred.job.tracker</name>
<value>localhost:54311</value>
</property>

<property>
<name>mapred.system.dir</name>
<value>/hadoop/mapred</value>
</property>

</configuration>
```

13. Download and install all other Hadoop ecosystem components by following the steps outlined in the recipes in *Chapter 3, Configuring a Hadoop Cluster.*

14. Install the AMI tools package using the following command:

```
rpm -ivh http://s3.amazonaws.com/ec2-downloads/ec2-ami-tools.
noarch.rpm
```

15. Disable SE Linux using the following command:

```
setenforce 0
```

16. Disable iptables using the following commands:

```
iptables -F
chkconfig iptables off
```

17. Bundle the image using the following command:

```
ec2-bundle-vol -e ~/.ec2 -kpk-*pem -ccert-*.pem -u 123412341234
```

In this command, -k specifies the name of the file that contains the private key, -c specifies the file that contains the X.509 certificate, -u specifies the 12 to 15-digit count ID without dashes of the current user, and -e specifies the location/directory that contains the private key file and the certificate file.

18. Upload the bundled AMI to S3 using the following command:

```
ec2-upload-bundle -b packt-bucket -m /tmp/image.manifest.xml -a
AKIAJ7GAQT52MZKJA4WQ -p QDHHZ0/Mj5pDYFWKpqEzXhwjqM1UB+cqjGQQ613S
```

In this command, -b specifies the name of the bucket on S3, -m specifies the location of the manifest file, -a specifies the access key string, and -p specifies the secret key string.

19. Register the AMI using the following command:

```
ec2-register packt-bucket/image.manifest.xml -n centos-hadoop-1.0
-O AKIAJ7GAQT52MZKJA4WQ-WQDHHZ0/Mj5pDYFWKpqEzXhwjqM1UB+cqjGQQ613S
```

In this command, the first parameter specifies the location of the manifest file in the S3 bucket, the `-n` option specifies the name of the AMI, `-O` specifies the access key string, and `-W` specifies the secret key string.

Creating an EBS-backed AMI

Creating an EBS-backed AMI is straightforward from the **Web Management** console. This section will guide you through the steps to create an EBS-backed AMI from a running EC2 instance. For more information, you can visit Amazon's official document at `http://docs.aws.amazon.com/AWSEC2/latest/UserGuide/creating-an-ami-ebs.html#process_creating-an-ami-ebs`.

Use the following steps to create an EBS-backed AMI:

1. Go to `https://console.aws.amazon.com/ec2/v2/home#Images:` and filter the AMIs with conditions similar to the following screenshot:

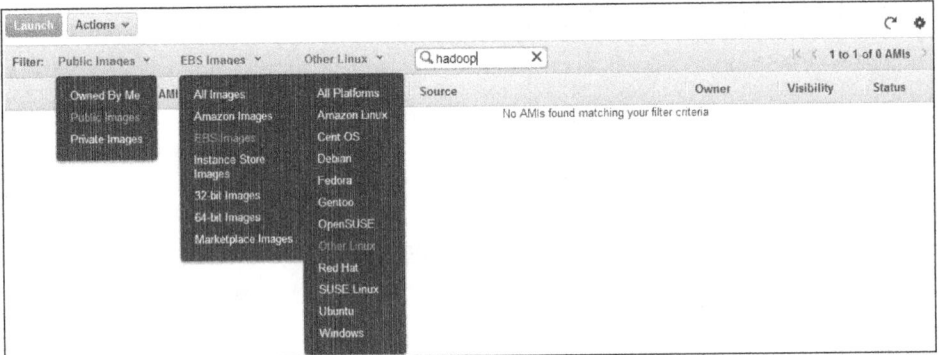

2. Start an instance by right-clicking on one of the AMIs and then click on **Launch** as shown in the following screenshot:

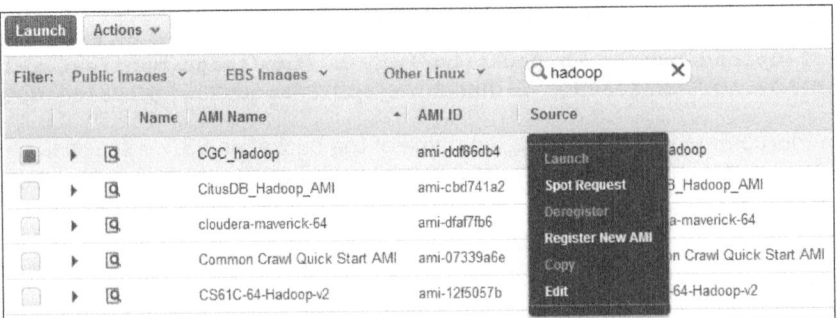

3. When the instance is running, log in to the instance and make changes according to your requirements. Then, from the **Web Management** console, right-click on the running instance and then select **Create Image (EBS AMI)** as shown in the following screenshot:

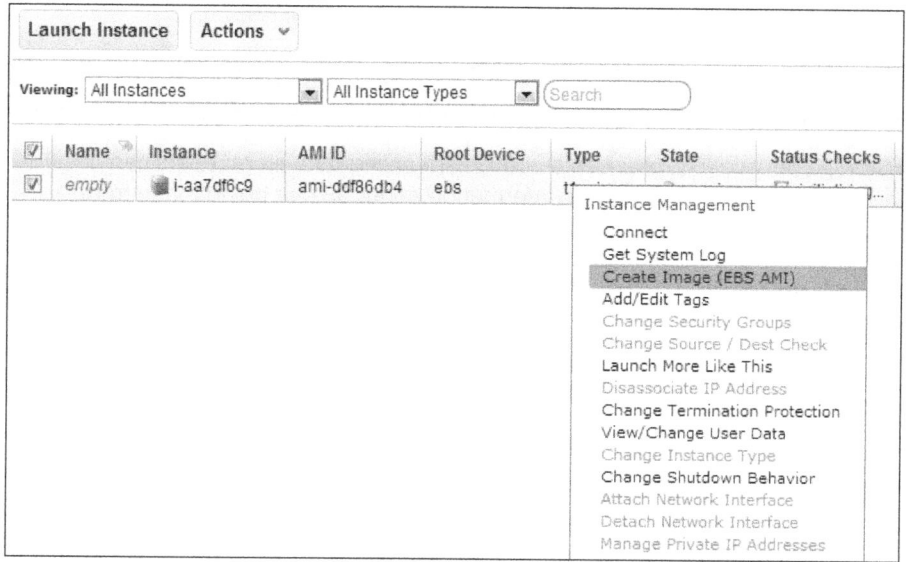

4. Go to the **AMIs** tab of the **AWS web** console and select **Owned By Me**; we will see that EBSAMI is being created as shown in the following screenshot:

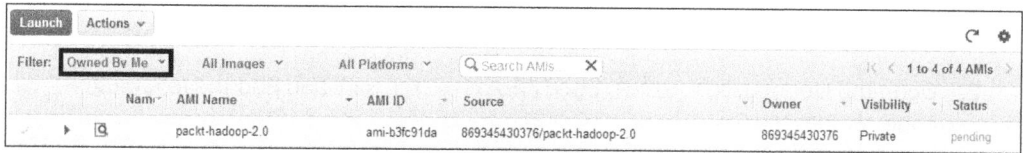

EC2 creates a snapshot for the new AMI. Similar to the image part files stored in S3, the snapshot stores the physical image of the EBS-backed AMI.

See also

▸ The *Installing HBase* recipe of *Chapter 3, Configuring a Hadoop Cluster*

▸ The *Installing Hive* recipe of *Chapter 3, Configuring a Hadoop Cluster*

▸ The *Installing Pig* recipe of *Chapter 3, Configuring a Hadoop Cluster*

▸ The *Installing ZooKeeper* recipe of *Chapter 3, Configuring a Hadoop Cluster*

> ▶ The *Installing Mahout* recipe of *Chapter 3, Configuring a Hadoop Cluster*

> ▶ Refer to http://docs.aws.amazon.com/AWSEC2/latest/UserGuide/
> Tutorial_CreateImage.html

> ▶ Refer to http://docs.aws.amazon.com/AWSEC2/latest/
> CommandLineReference/command-reference.html

Using S3 to host data

Simple Storage Service (S3) provides a convenient online data store. Users can use it to store and retrieve data. More information about S3 can be obtained from http://aws.amazon.com/s3/.

This recipe will outline steps to configure S3 as the distributed data storage system for MapReduce.

Getting ready

Before getting started, we assume that you have successfully registered with AWS and the client machine has been successfully configured to access the AWS.

How to do it...

Use the following steps to configure S3 for data storage:

1. Stop the Hadoop cluster using the following command:

    stop-all.sh

2. Open the file $HADOOP_HOME/conf/core-site.xml and add the following contents into the file:

    ```
    <property>
    <name>fs.default.name</name>
    <!-- value>master:54310</value-->
    <value>s3n://packt-bucket</value>
    </property>
    <property>
    <name>fs.s3n.awsAccessKeyId</name>
    <value>AKIAJ7GAQT52MZKJA4WQ</value>
    </property>

    <property>
    <name>fs.s3n.awsSecretAccessKey</name>
    <value>QDHHZ0/Mj5pDYFWKpqEzXhwjqM1UB+cqjGQQ613S</value>
    </property>
    ```

The first property configures Hadoop to use S3 as a distributed filesystem.

3. Start the cluster using the following command:

```
start-mapred.sh
```

 As we are using S3 instead of HDFS as the data storage filesystem, there is no need to start the HDFS cluster anymore.

4. Check the configuration with S3 using the following command:

```
hadoop fs -ls /
```

We should be able to list all the files in the bucket. For example, we should see the following content:

```
Found 49 items
-rwxrwxrwx   1        8560 2013-05-03 03:18 /centos.img.manifest.
xml
-rwxrwxrwx   1    10485760 2013-05-03 03:17 /centos.img.part.00
-rwxrwxrwx   1    10485760 2013-05-03 03:17 /centos.img.part.01
-rwxrwxrwx   1    10485760 2013-05-03 03:17 /centos.img.part.02
...
```

Configuring a Hadoop cluster with the new AMI

Starting a Hadoop cluster with the new AMI is simple and straightforward. This recipe will list steps to start up a Hadoop cluster with the new AMI.

Getting ready

Before getting started, we assume that you have registered with AWS and have successfully created a new AMI with Hadoop properly configured.

How to do it...

Use the following steps to configure a Hadoop cluster with EC2:

1. Run a number of instances either from the command line or from the web interface.

2. After the instances are all in running state, run the following command to get the internal hostname of these instances:

```
ec2-describe-instances | grep running | egrep -o 'ip.*?internal' |
sed -e 's/.ec2.internal//g' > nodes.txt
```

The `nodes.txt` file will have contents similar to the following:

```
ip-10-190-81-210
ip-10-137-11-196
ip-10-151-11-161
ip-10-137-48-163
ip-10-143-160-5
ip-10-142-132-17
```

We are assuming to use the `ip-10-190-81-210` node as the master node and the public domain name of this node as `ec2-174-129-127-90.compute-1.amazonaws.com`.

3. Copy the `nodes.txt` file to the master node using the following command from the local machine:

```
scp -i ~/.ec2/shumin.guo.pem nodes.txt ec2-user@ec2-174-129-127-
90.compute-1.amazonaws.com:~/
```

4. Log in to the new instance using the following command:

```
ssh -i ~/.ec2/shumin.guo.pem root@ec2-user@ec2-174-129-127-90.
compute-1.amazonaws.com
```

5. Use the following commands to create a `hosts` file:

```
cp nodes.txt nodes.ip.txt
cp nodes.txt slaves
sed -i 's/ip-//g' nodes.ip.txt
sed -i 's/-/./g' nodes.ip.txt
sed -i '1d' slaves
paste nodes.ip.txt nodes.txt > hosts
```

The hosts file should have the following content:

```
10.190.81.210    ip-10-190-81-210
10.137.11.196    ip-10-137-11-196
10.151.11.161    ip-10-151-11-161
10.137.48.163    ip-10-137-48-163
10.143.160.5     ip-10-143-160-5
10.142.132.17    ip-10-142-132-17
```

6. Move the hosts file to `/etc/hosts` using the following command:

```
for hosts in 'cat nodes.txt'; do

   echo 'Configuring /etc/hosts file for host : ' $host

scp hosts $hosts:/etc/hosts

done
```

7. Configure the `slaves` file using the following command:

```
cp slaves $HADOOP_HOME/conf/slaves
```

8. Open the file `$HADOOP_HOME/conf/core-site.xml` using a text editor and change the `fs.default.name` as follows:

```
<property>
<name>fs.default.name</name>
<value>hdfs://ip-10-190-81-210:54310</value>
</property>
```

9. Open the file `$HADOOP_HOME/conf/mapred-site.xml` using a text editor and change the `themapred.job.tracker` property as follows:

```
<property>
<name>mapred.job.tracker</name>
<value>ip-10-190-81-210:54311</value>
</property>
```

10. Copy the configurations to all the slave nodes using the following command:

```
for host in 'cat $HADOOP_HOME/conf/slaves'; do

   echo "Copying Hadoop conifugration files to host: ' $host

   scp $HADOOP_HOME/conf/{core,mapred}-site.xml $host:$HADOOP_HOME/
conf

done
```

11. Start the cluster using the following command:

```
start-dfs.sh
```

```
start-mapred.sh
```

When the cluster is running, we can start to submit jobs to the cluster from the master node.

There's more...

An alternative method of running a MapReduce with the Amazon cloud is to use **Amazon Elastic MapReduce** (**EMR**). Amazon EMR provides an elastic parallel computing platform based on EC2 and S3. Data and results can be stored on S3. EMR computing is handy for ad hoc data processing requirements.

Data processing with Amazon Elastic MapReduce

Before using EMR, we assume that you have registered with AWS. An S3 bucket (for example, `packt-bucket`) has been created using the S3 web console. In the following recipe, we will use the `wordcount` job, which is shipped with the Hadoop examples' JAR package, as an example.

We will use the following steps to use EMR for data processing:

1. Create the input directory (with the name `input`) and Java library directory (with the name `jars`) under the bucket from the S3 **Web Management** console.

2. Upload data into the `input` folder from the web console as shown in the following screenshot:

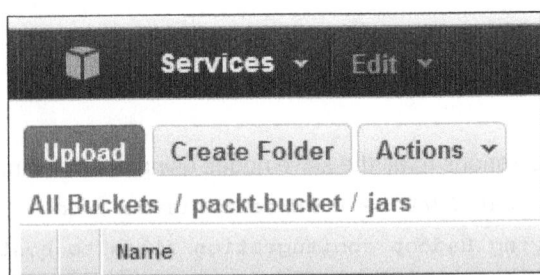

3. Upload the required JAR file (`hadoop-examples-*.jar` in this example) into the `jars` directory.

> If you have configured S3 using the command in the previous recipe, you can also use the following commands to finish the preceding steps:
>
> ```
> hadoop fs -mkdir /jars /input
> hadoop fs -put $HADOOP_HOME/hadoop-examples-*.jar /jars
> hadoop fs -put words.txt /input
> ```

4. `words.txt` contains the input data for the `wordcount` job.

5. Open the URL `https://console.aws.amazon.com/elasticmapreduce`.

6. Click on the **Create New Job Flow** button as shown in the following screenshot:

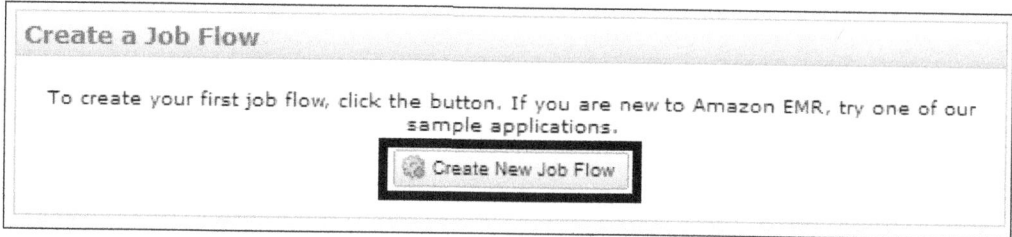

7. Next, enter the **Job Flow Name**, select the **Hadoop Version**, and select the job flow type as shown in the following screenshot:

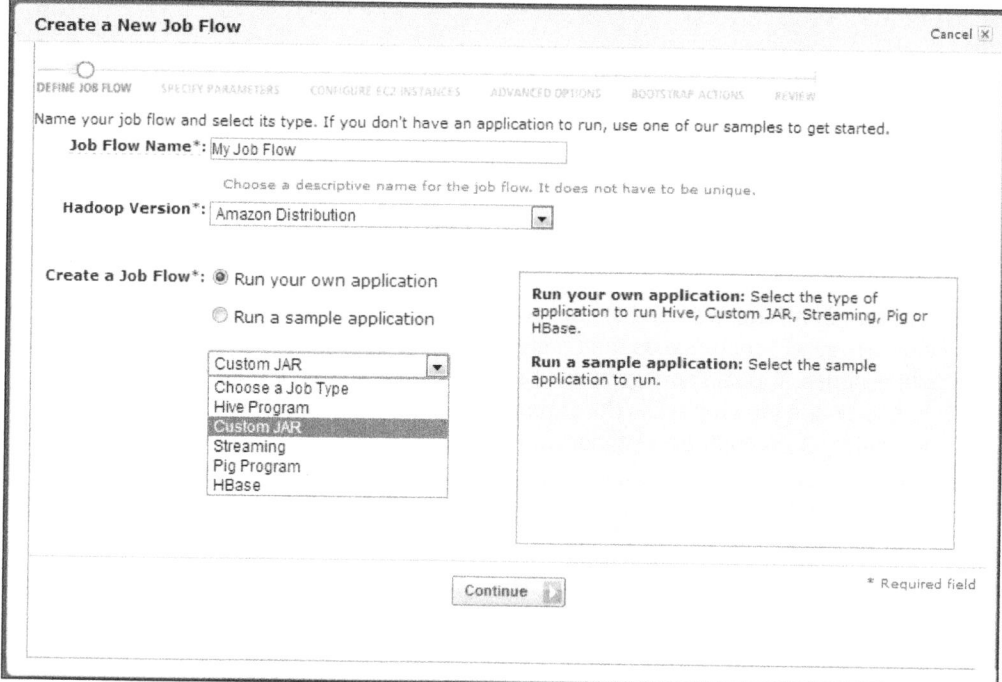

To test a simple job flow, you can choose **Run a sample application** instead.

8. Click on the **Continue** button at the bottom; the next window asks for the location of the JAR file and the parameters for running the Hadoop MapReduce job as shown in the following screenshot:

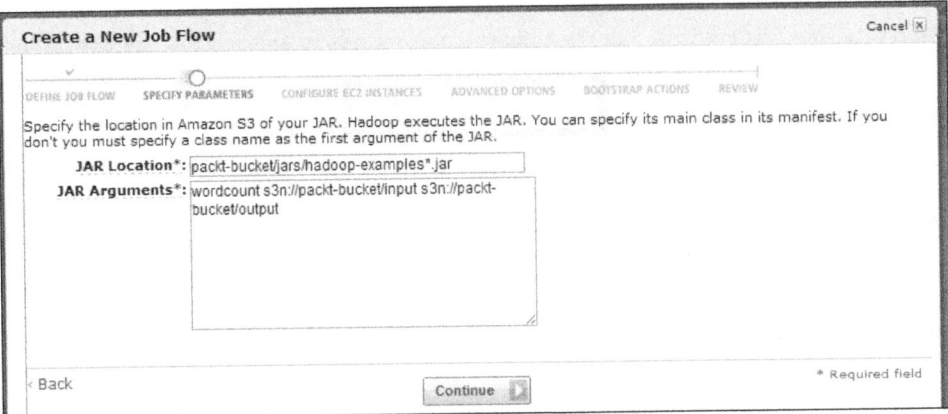

In this step, we need to specify the location of the JAR file and the arguments to run a job. The specifications should be similar to option specifications from the command line with the only difference that all the files should be specified using the S3 scheme.

9. Click on **Continue**; we need to configure EC2 instances. By default, there will be one m1.small instance as the master node and two m1.small instances as the slave nodes. You can configure the instance type and the number of instances based on the job properties (for example, big or small input data size, data intensive, or computation intensive). This step is shown in the following screenshot:

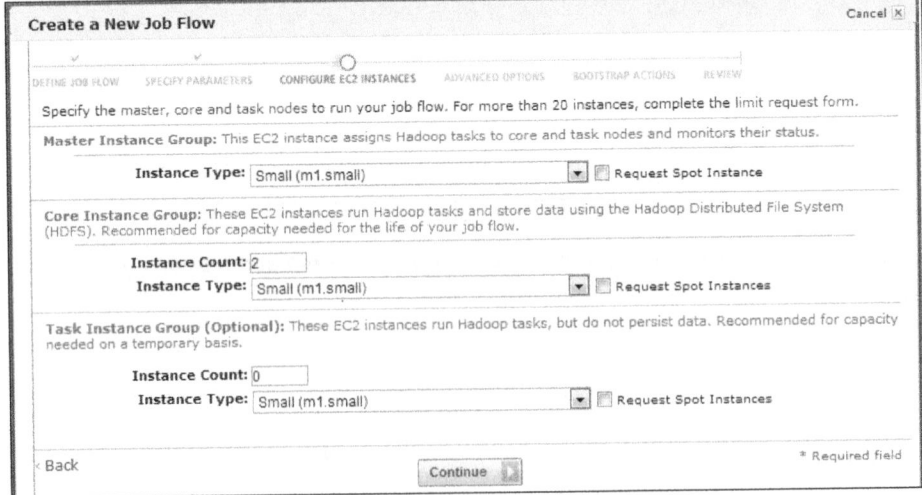

10. Click on the **Continue** button and we will go to the **ADVANCED OPTIONS** window. This window asks for instance boot options such as security key pairs. In this step, we can choose the key pair and use all others as defaults and click on **Continue**.

11. We will go to the **BOOTSTRAP ACTIONS** window. We can simply use the default action in this step and click on Continue.

12. The **REVIEW** window shows the options we have configured; if there is no problem, we can click on the **Create Job Flow** button to create an EMR job flow. This step is shown in the following screenshot:

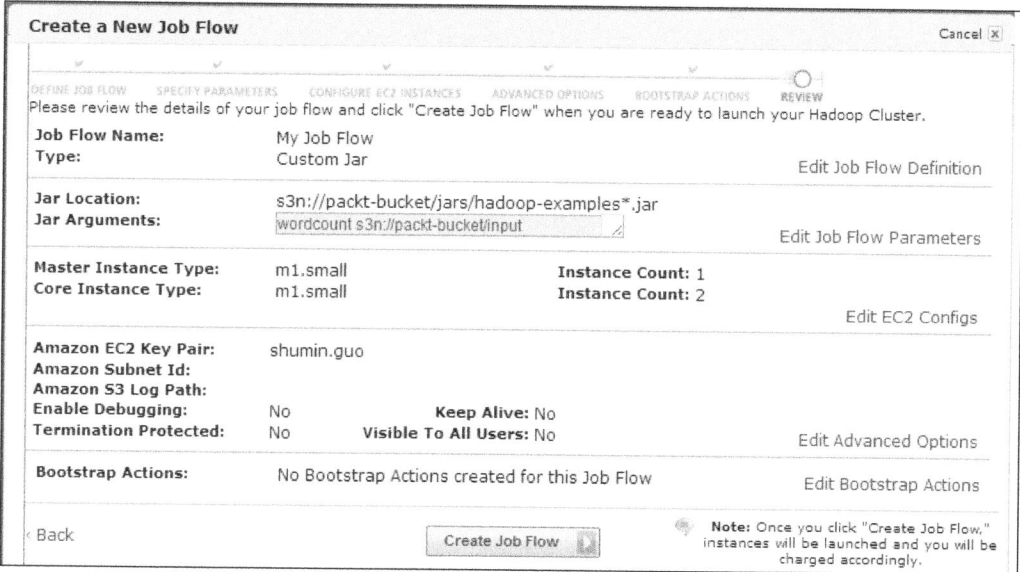

13. The job flow will be started and we can check the output when it completes. We can get its status from the web console as shown in the following screenshot:

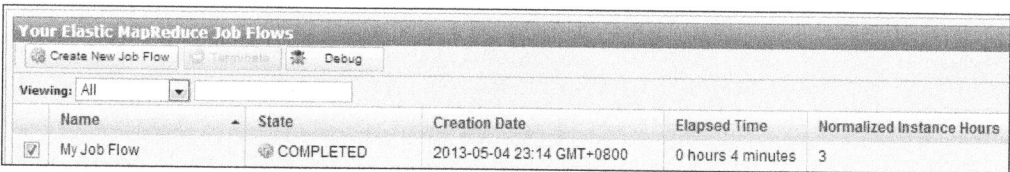

See also

▸ Chapter 3, Configuring a Hadoop Cluster

Index

A

CentOS 6.3 23
check_jmx Nagios plugin 217
Chukwa
    about 200, 235
    configuring, for Hadoop monitoring 237-241
    features 243
    installing 235-237
    URL 235
    working 242
Cloudera
    about 14
    URL 14
cluster administrator machine
    configuring 23-28
cluster attribute 208
cluster network
    designing 21, 22
    working 22
compression 278
configuration files, for pseudo-distributed
        mode
    core-site.xml 58
    hadoop-env.sh 58
    hdfs-site.xml 58
    mapred-site.xml 58
    masters file 58
    slaves file 58
core-site.xml 58
current live threads 205

D

data
    importing, to HDFS 133, 135
data blocks
    balancing, for Hadoop cluster 274-276
Data Delivery subsystem 16
data local 274
DataNode
    about 94
    decommissioning 111, 112
Data Refinery subsystem 16
data skew 274
decompression 278
dfsadmin command 100

dfs.data.dir property 69
dfs.replication property 69
DHCP
    configuring, for network booting 37

E

EBS-backed AMI
    creating 334, 335
EC2 307
EC2 connection
    local machine, preparing 316, 317
Elastic Cloud Computing. *See* EC2
EMR. *See* Amazon EMR
erroneous iptables configuration 46
erroneous SELinux configuration 46
erroneous SSH settings 45

F

Fair Scheduler
    about 146
    configuring 147, 148
    properties 149
files
    manipulating, on HDFS 136-139
folder, Rumen 259
fsck command 100
fs.default.name property 69
fully-distributed mode 60

G

Ganglia
    about 199, 207
    configuring, for monitoring Hadoop cluster
        207-215
    metadata daemon 207
    monitoring daemon 207
    web UI 207
    working 216
GitHub
    URL 242
GNU wget 42
Gold Trace 259
GraphLab
    about 15
    URL 15

Thank you for buying
Hadoop Operations and Cluster Management Cookbook

About Packt Publishing

Packt, pronounced 'packed', published its first book "*Mastering phpMyAdmin for Effective MySQL Management*" in April 2004 and subsequently continued to specialize in publishing highly focused books on specific technologies and solutions.

Our books and publications share the experiences of your fellow IT professionals in adapting and customizing today's systems, applications, and frameworks. Our solution based books give you the knowledge and power to customize the software and technologies you're using to get the job done. Packt books are more specific and less general than the IT books you have seen in the past. Our unique business model allows us to bring you more focused information, giving you more of what you need to know, and less of what you don't.

Packt is a modern, yet unique publishing company, which focuses on producing quality, cutting-edge books for communities of developers, administrators, and newbies alike. For more information, please visit our website: www.packtpub.com.

About Packt Open Source

In 2010, Packt launched two new brands, Packt Open Source and Packt Enterprise, in order to continue its focus on specialization. This book is part of the Packt Open Source brand, home to books published on software built around Open Source licences, and offering information to anybody from advanced developers to budding web designers. The Open Source brand also runs Packt's Open Source Royalty Scheme, by which Packt gives a royalty to each Open Source project about whose software a book is sold.

Writing for Packt

We welcome all inquiries from people who are interested in authoring. Book proposals should be sent to author@packtpub.com. If your book idea is still at an early stage and you would like to discuss it first before writing a formal book proposal, contact us; one of our commissioning editors will get in touch with you.

We're not just looking for published authors; if you have strong technical skills but no writing experience, our experienced editors can help you develop a writing career, or simply get some additional reward for your expertise.

[PACKT] open source*
PUBLISHING
community experience distilled

Hadoop Beginner's Guide

ISBN: 978-1-84951-730-0   Paperback: 398 pages

Learn how to crunch big data to extract meaning from the data avalanche

1. Learn tools and techniques that let you approach big data with relish and not fear

2. Shows how to build a complete infrastructure to handle your needs as your data grows

3. Hands-on examples in each chapter give the big picture while also giving direct experience

Hadoop MapReduce Cookbook

ISBN: 978-1-84951-728-7   Paperback: 300 pages

Recipes for analyzing large and complex datasets with Hadoop MapReduce

1. Learn to process large and complex data sets, starting simply, then diving in deep

2. Solve complex big data problems such as classifications, finding relationships, online marketing and recommendations

3. More than 50 Hadoop MapReduce recipes, presented in a simple and straightforward manner, with step-by-step instructions and real world examples

Please check **www.PacktPub.com** for information on our titles